Our Club Our Rules

FC United of Manchester
For the fans by the fans

Pete Crowther

© Pete Crowther 2006
All rights reserved.

ISBN 978-1-84753-452-1

To everyone involved in FC United
and the North-West Counties Football League
in gratitude for the best season
I've ever spent watching football.

CONTENTS

Introduction   7

Summer 2005: Now is the summer of our discontent   11

August 2005: Should I stay or should I go?   26

September 2005: Playing by different rules   44

October 2005: This is the age of wonder and miracles   57

November 2005: Back to the future?   70

December 2005: Money, money, money   86

January 2006: TV or not TV   101

February 2006: The People's Club   124

March 2006: Till the fat lady sings   137

April 2006: The ties that bind   154

Summer 2006: Summer loving   172

Introduction

Introduction

Why did I write this book? Because nobody else was going to do it. I had in my mind a book that I wanted to read about FC United. It was a book that would celebrate everything that is extraordinary about this club – the people, the principles, the football – and it was a book that would launch a coruscating attack on the greedy and the foolish and the cynical who are ruining the game we love. It would be angry and funny in equal measure. It would be passionate and clear-headed, lyrical and political, optimistic and realistic. It would be a love-letter to FC and a poison-pen letter to the Premiership. Above all it would be an expression of love for this magical game that has delighted and fascinated, frustrated and obsessed me all my life. So, if I wanted to read that book, I decided that I'd have to get off my lazy arse and write it.

If you put twelve FC fans in a room, chances are you'd come out with twelve different visions of FC's future, and that's not just because we are a naturally awkward, opinionated, argumentative lot. It's more to do with the fact that we've all come at FC from a slightly different angle and we have subtly different views about what the club should be and where it should go. To some people it's simply a protest vehicle, United by other means until Glazer goes. To others it's an example of going back to the future, bringing back football that means less expense, less hassle and more fun. To others it's a powerful expression of people power, proof that individuals can use their collective talent and energy to defy the crude forces of big business. While to some people the club is a glorious social experiment, using football to re-build what seems to have been lost in recent years – a sense of community. So FC is what you want it to be. And this book is my attempt to define what I want FC to be. It's a purely personal view written by someone with no relationship to FC apart from that of a fan who loves what this extraordinary club is all about. You won't find any tasty revelations or intimate insights about what goes on behind the scenes at the club – I have no inside knowledge – and the ideas put forward in the book do not represent the official FC view on anything. Just my views which I hope will stimulate and provoke FC fans and football fans in general.

I was still writing this book last spring, when I learnt that I had been beaten to the honour of writing the first FC book by our own Rob Brady and his wonderful Undividable Glow. I deliberately put off reading Rob's book until I had finished mine. It's hard enough organising your own thoughts without having someone else's prose floating round your head. I needn't have worried. There was no likelihood of the books overlapping in their subject matter or their style. In fact, I'm not sure any other book could come close to Rob's unique style. Undividable Glow is a magical mystery tour through the recent history of Manchester, from Manchester United to FC United with extraordinary, humorous, surreal detours via family and friends. Like a Cristiano Ronaldo dribble, you don't always know where he's going but it's fun to watch. Touching too. I defy anyone to read the about the loss of Russell Delaney and Rob's father and not be moved. So I couldn't write Rob's book, because, to borrow one of his phrases, I've been on my own "shaping walk". So I had to write this book instead, and I must say in its defence – there's far more football in it than in Rob's!

The book starts in anger and frustration in a sweaty hall in central Manchester in the summer of 2005 and ends twelve amazing months later in wide-eyed euphoria on the terrace of the Bruno Plache Stadium in Leipzig. It wouldn't have been enough simply to relate what had happened. My ambition stretched beyond that. I had to try and explain why it had happened, why FC United was about much more than Malcolm Glazer, why FC United is trying to redefine what a football club should be, and why it matters. So it's more than a diary. It's a plea to all football fans to wake up to the huge cultural changes taking place within football and to start having a debate about the future of the game that means so much to so many of us. Let's not turn round in ten years time and complain that "this is not what I signed up for". Let's look at where football is going and ask ourselves if that's what we really want.

Don't worry – it's not all fire and brimstone. The arguments are interspersed with match reports that try to record the humour and fun and sheer joy of FC United's first season in the North-West Counties League Division Two. It's a structure that seems appropriate: passionate debate alternating with giddy laughter. It's been the story of our season.

Introduction

Our Club Our Rules

Now is the summer of our discontent

Summer 2005
Now is the summer of our discontent

Where were you when United died? Well, seeing that you've asked, I was padding down Sale High St in my lunch-break. Trying to be good. Trying to resist the temptation of a bar of Thornton's marzipan. Trying not to think about United or Glazer or football. Trying not to think. Trying to let the healing power of the famous Manchester sunshine wash away the worry and despondency that had been growing over the last two weeks. It's only football. Bollocks to it. Whatever happened, life would go on. There'd still be sunshine and pretty girls and cold beer and barbecues and holidays and … well, you get the picture. So, by the time I got back to the office, I was in a state of Zen-like calm, the tawdry shenanigans at Old Trafford completely forgotten. Or they were, until I stepped through the office door and the first thing I heard was "Have you heard the news?" Now, what could be worse for a Red than hearing that his beloved club has been sold to someone who looks like a stranger to humanity, never mind a stranger to football? Well, hearing it from a Liverpool fan. There he was, trying not to smile and desperate to tell me the good news: that Glazer now had seventy-six percent of United's shares – a controlling interest. I wasn't taken in by his attempts at sympathy. He was enjoying it. If the positions had been reversed, would I have revelled in his discomfort in the same way, knowing full well that people like Abramovich and Glazer are destroying the game we all love? Well, what do you think? You bet. Football fans know all about schadenfreude. Well, that's not quite true. Most think he was the German left back in 1966.

And it's a silly question, when you think about it. Did United die the day that a reclusive American billionaire took control of the club? Well, there's still a Manchester United listed in the Premiership table. There's still a glass and steel monument to wealth and success in M16. And there are still eleven lads in red shirts running out each Saturday or Sunday or Monday giving a passable impression of the team we used to love.

So did anything die on that day in May? Nothing much, nothing earth-shattering, nothing that made the six-o-clock news. Just a small part of me.

Our Club Our Rules

That small part of me that had spent the last fifteen years performing the schizophrenic feat of loving the shirts while despising the suits. Whatever reservations I had felt about developments off the field, they had always paled into insignificance when set against the dazzling exploits of the team on it. It had been a simple case of filtering out the bad stuff. And there was plenty of bad stuff to filter out, as Martin Edwards and company took a leading role in a series of initiatives that made the heart of a simple football romantic groan time and again in the nineties. There was the decision to float the club on the stock exchange in 1991. If I'm honest, this barely registered on my radar at the time. The word flotation has the same impact on me as the words pension plan, insurance policy and tax return – my eyes glaze over and my brain shuts down. I suppose I'm like most football fans – the money side of the game leaves me cold. I'd like to say that I clearly understood that this was the first step down the slippery slope that leads to Malcolm Glazer, but I'd be lying. I didn't pay much attention to it at the time and I certainly had no money to buy shares. And I wouldn't have bought them if I could. Call it romantic, call it irrational, call it whatever you like, but the idea of having a financial stake in United would have tainted my relationship to the team. United for me was a purely emotional investment, not a financial one.

Other developments followed. Like the decision in 1992 by the country's top clubs to cut adrift seventy league clubs and set up their cosy little Premiership cartel. Not all the blame can be laid at United's door, of course, but they were a prominent player in the deal. There was the decision to remove the words 'football club' from the badge as part of a plan to widen the appeal of the United brand. What did that tell you about the changing culture of the club? There was the decision to allow teams to keep all the takings from their home games, a concession granted by the football authorities after intense lobbying by the major clubs. What a significant step that was in creating the football world we see today in which a small group of elite clubs dominate an ever more predictable and uncompetitive league. There was the increasingly aggressive commercial activity as more and more junk mail began to drop through the letterbox advertising United credit cards and United insurance. Of course, no one made you buy this stuff and it soon found its way into the dustbin, but each time something arrived you couldn't help feeling that United was becoming a little less football club and a little more money-making machine. So I chose to block all this out, to live in denial, and, you know what, it wasn't that difficult.

Let's be honest here and admit that we all found it easy to ignore any misgivings that we felt about the direction the club was taking. This was the most successful era in United's history, a period of undreamt-of success made all the sweeter by the lean years of the 70s and 80s. And that was all we cared about. We're football fans. We're simple creatures. Or more precisely, we accept complexity in other parts of our life – relationships, work, DIY – but we expect football to be an escape from all that. We love

Now is the summer of our discontent

kicking a ball and we love seeing a ball kicked. The spectacle of the game is so all-consuming that we rarely look beyond that glorious rectangle of green. This was especially the case in the 90s when Robson, Cantona and Keane were leading United to triumph after triumph with football that was all dash and swagger, pace and skill. Who cared that Edwards was trying to engineer a European super league, when we were swamping Forest 5-0 to secure the Prem or storming back from two down to overwhelm Juve in the Champions League? How could we be expected to focus on the depressing commercial drift of the club when the majestic Eric was radiating such hypnotic brilliance that everything else was reduced to invisibility by his dazzling aura? We gorged on the best football we'd ever seen and we gorged on success, as an endless parade of trophies came our way. It seemed churlish to complain, and by and large we didn't.

Talk about love makes you blind. It should be tattooed on the head of every football fan. Your devotion to your team makes you suspend all those critical faculties – scepticism, cycnicism, demand for proof, respect for facts – that you routinely apply to other aspects of your life. We're romantics and like all romantics we indulge in make-believe. How else can I explain the little pretence I used to practise on myself when it came to the people running my football club? That part of my brain where logic lives had no illusions about Edwards and Watkins and Kenyon and Gill, but it was always being undermined by that other part that lives on dreams and that wanted to take the rosiest view of all things United. Even the blindest football fan knows that the people running his football club are a different breed to the people who support it. They never love football the way we do. They never love football for its own sake. They love what football brings them: money, power and kudos. It's a vehicle for their ambitions, and as vehicles go, you could certainly do worse. Certainly beats working for Boots or Natwest. They might actually like football. In their position what's not to like? But if there was no money in it, would they be in it? So one part of me had no illusions. Unfortunately, the other part preferred a comforting, self-serving little fantasy that allowed me to believe that, whatever else Edwards and company were, they were United fans in their own way. I was able to tell myself that they were Mancunians of a sort. Okay, they had sprawling stacks in leafy Cheshire rather than a little semi in Moston but they still lived within Manchester's orbit. Edwards and Watkins come from established Manchester families: Louis Edwards was a long-time friend of Matt Busby and Watkins was simply following in his father's footsteps when he became a solicitor in the city centre. Even smarmy Kenyon came from Stalybridge. Sure, there was now a social world of difference between them and most United fans, but they were products of the same geography and culture and I liked to believe that at some impossibly deep, subconscious level that they were impregnated with the spirit of Manchester. They were one of us. Sort of.

Our Club Our Rules

That's why 12th May 2005 hurt so badly. Never mind the 500 million pounds worth of debt. Never mind the hideous vision of future United teams running out at the Budweiser Soccerdome to fireworks and rock music down an avenue of pompommed cheerleaders. That was hard to take but it wasn't what hurt most. What hurt most was the sense of violation: our holy place had been invaded by people who were clearly and indisputably "not us". They were strangers: strangers to our history, strangers to our culture, strangers to our spirit. I would never again be able to look at the people running the club and make-believe that beneath the layers of bullshit and phoniness there was a stubborn residue of Mancunian spirit. The aliens had landed. I felt as if I'd come home from work and found strangers living in my house. That couldn't happen, of course, with your own house. Nobody can buy it if you don't want to sell. But that was our whole problem. All we had and all we'd ever had when it came to United was some vague thing called 'emotional' ownership. Try arguing that one in a court of law. The indisputable, unpalatable, crushing truth was that we owned a big fat nothing. As an American might say, we owned jack-shit.

And an important line had been crossed. Throughout the nineties it was obvious that United as a football club was becoming increasingly obsessed with making money. Nonetheless, it was still possible to convince yourself that the commercial activity was there to serve the team – to pay higher wages, retain your top stars, attract world-class players. Yes, a dividend had to be paid to shareholders but that was often a relatively modest amount. You felt that football was still the most important thing. That changed the day the Glazers took over. The club was now in the hands of private individuals who, despite making the obligatory noises about being genuine "soccer" fans, clearly saw the club as a financial speculation. To them United was simply the greatest franchise in sport and its primary purpose was no longer to play great football but to make huge profits. Football at United was now a means to an end. Of course, playing great football helps - they'll need a successful football team if they're going to generate profit - but do you think the Glazers would care if United were mid-table every season as long as they were getting 76,000 bums on seats? The Glazer takeover marked an epoch – it was the moment when money became more important than football at Manchester United. And it hurt.

We've been here before

You can't say that we hadn't been warned about the threat of United falling into the wrong hands. In 1998 Rupert Murdoch decided that the latest must-have accessory for any self-respecting media tycoon was the world's greatest football club. He was only the latest in a growing line of pantomime villains such as Robert Maxwell and Michael Knighton that had tried to buy the club. In the past, however, these chancers had had more ego than cash-flow and

Now is the summer of our discontent

the dismal scenario of a club loved by millions becoming one man's ego-trip had never materialised. Murdoch was different. He had the money to go with the ego. I think we understood quite clearly the threat posed by Murdoch. Being a PLC sat uneasily with many of us, but at least the owners were faceless financial institutions that had no desire to involve themselves in the running of the club and were satisfied to receive an acceptable return on their investments. They were happy to leave the club in the safe hands of ... er ... Martin Edwards.

Our instincts told us that Murdoch had to be resisted. Could you sit by and do nothing while your club was handed over to a man with no roots in your community, an ignorance of your past and a total indifference to the game you love? Once he was in control, why would he have any scruples about making changes that would betray the tradition of the club and trample over the sensibilities of the fans? What might he do? My fevered imagination came up with a few possibilities. Use his vast wealth to buy up every half-decent player on the market and make an already dominant United into a team that strolled to the Premiership title every season. There was already talk of Shearer joining United at the time. Only the dimmest fan thought that an even less competitive Premiership would be good for football. He might lobby to have United games played at ridiculous times of the day to suit the needs of that lucrative south-east Asian market. He might promote the idea of a European super league – entry by invitation only – that would provide a steady diet of big-name matches. Never mind the fact that the prospect of a derby against City excited fans more than a match against Real Madrid. But perhaps the worst prospect, the one that made me stare at the ceiling in a cold sweat at four in the morning, was the prospect of Sky TV and the Sun newspaper becoming the official mouthpiece of Manchester United. If you were Murdoch, wouldn't you use your media muscle to brainwash the masses into even greater brand loyalty? Obviously, my thoughts were running away with me. I mean, a television channel devoted to spinning the official line on Manchester United? Could never happen, could it?

And Murdoch was successfully resisted. In no small way due to the efforts of the Independent Manchester United Supporters Association (IMUSA) and influential friends in the media and the government. The DTI rejected the bid because ownership of Sky and ownership of Manchester United would have given Rupert Murdoch an unhealthy monopoly over English football. So that was that. No other bored billionaire would try that again. And I went back to watching the glorious football on the pitch and stuck my complacent head up my complacent backside.

First protest meeting: Central Methodist Hall

So what do you do when presented with a fait accompli? Roll over and die? Grumble for a while, then shrug and get on with it? This is exactly what the realists of the football establishment – pundits, ex-players, journalists – urged us to do. Ok, you've had your little protest, marched round Old Trafford, waved your "Not for sale" banners and sung "Die, Glazer, die". Now do as you're told, renew those season tickets, turn up next season, applaud politely, and, most importantly, keep buying the merchandise. Remember, just thirty pounds a week can keep a millionaire footballer in the fatuous lifestyle he's become accustomed to. You can make a difference. And in return, he'll win a few football games for you. If you're lucky.

The cynicism of the people who run the game and their contempt for the 'punters' is breathtaking. Years of treating fans with an indifference verging on disdain and yet seeing them continue to turn up in their thousands has bred this contemptuous view of the average fan. Fans, eh, they'll stand for anything: commercial exploitation, snouts in troughs, anti-social kick-off times, soulless all-seater stadiums, inflation-busting price rises, celebrity footballers and Russian oligarchs with mysterious origins. So, United belong to an American carpet-bagger who knows nothing about them and cares even less, and prefers his football with an oval ball and shoulder-pads. So what? What's your problem? Well, the fact that one of the world's greatest sporting institutions has gone from being debt-free to having £500 million of debt perhaps. Relax, say the football realists, no self-made billionaire spends 800 million on a club without having a cunning master plan. And they know everything, don't they? Well, they certainly know everything about not biting the hand that feeds them.

So two days before the FA Cup final I find myself with other 'punters' in the Central Methodist Hall in Manchester attending a hastily arranged protest meeting. I'm there with my better half Shelagh and mate and fellow-Red Mark. Was this the first step in a journey or a last gesture of defiance? How many people would turn up? Had thirteen years of Sky TV and the Premiership anaesthetised us into submission or were there still people left who cared enough to fight the machine and maintain Manchester's proud tradition of protest and bolshieness? It seemed fitting that a movement that stubbornly rejected the new 'reality' and that wanted to challenge a smug, self-serving establishment should meet for the first time in a Methodist hall.

The hall was laid out with rows of chairs below a raised stage. A balcony overlooked the hall at the back of the room and would be available to take the overflow if needed. On the stage the top table had about a dozen people sat behind it and behind them a huge banner stretched across the back wall proclaiming: Hasta la victoria siempre - a well-known Manchester expression. "I see the bloody Tories got back in, Tommy", "Bugger 'em, Simmo, hasta la victoria siempre". I might be lying. It's actually a slogan from the Spanish Civil War, and means "Ever onward to victory". Mark recognised some of the faces on the top table. They were Reds who were active in organisations such as IMUSA (Independent Manchester United

Now is the summer of our discontent

Supporters Association) or in fanzines such as Red Issue. Some of them had played an active role in defeating Murdoch in 98.

But despite an array of respected Red activists on stage and a hall that was filling rapidly with an encouraging number of fans, this could yet prove to be all sound and fury signifying nothing. Did we have a leader to articulate our anger and organise our protest? We certainly did and his name was Andy Walsh. Andy conducted the meeting, imposed order and stopped it degenerating into a simple outpouring of anger. He made the opening speech. His speech pressed the right buttons. He explained how United was a family tradition, how it united the generations, how he went to games with his father and his kids, and how he had assumed that nothing would bring that tradition to an end. Until Glazer. Until the final straw. Until it had become impossible to close his eyes to the fact that the club he had loved all his life now viewed football and the fans as secondary to the pursuit of its primary aim: profit. He articulated our anger at Glazer, this foreigner that had treated us and our cultural heritage with absolute contempt. We could punish the arrogance of this man by doing everything conceivable to sabotage his business plan. In Andy's ringing phrase, we could "make United toxic".

It was hotting up in the hall and it was nothing to do with the early summer weather and the lack of ventilation. When Andy threw the floor open to everyone, you could almost hear the impatience of people who normally shrink from the limelight, but who had things to say that they could not suppress. There were many tough-looking, time-served Reds in the hall and they didn't look like the type of people that had honed their public speaking skills in the debating societies of Oxford and Cambridge. But the truth will out. And it did – angrily. And surprisingly forcefully and articulately. Everyone found different ways to say that United would not get a single penny while Glazer was there. One lad entertained the room by suggesting that fans should flash-mob shops owned by Vodafone (United's shirt sponsor) and drop stink bombs. Others suggested more conventional means of resistance. We could give up season tickets, stay away from games, refuse to buy merchandise, boycott the products of the club's official sponsors. Those that could not bring themselves to give up their season ticket could lead the fight from within. They could boycott the megastore and the catering outlets, orchestrate anti-Glazer chants, invade the pitch. There was a grim determination to sabotage Glazer's debt-laden business plan and to make him rue the day he had ever dared to buy our club. But no one seemed prepared to tackle one particular question. How could we cripple Glazer financially without crippling the club we loved?

There was an answer, of course, but it wouldn't have found favour at this stage with the majority of those in the hall. It was a step that most hesitated to take. It was easier and more pleasurable to simply get up and vent. I was disappointed that most speakers failed to mention the one measure that would represent the ultimate response to Glazer: to walk away and set up a breakaway club. It had been mentioned in passing in the days before the meeting. It had been referred to in passing early in the meeting. But it had sunk beneath the welter of anti-Glazer rhetoric. I even overcame my usual self-consciousness to take the mic and appeal to people to channel their anger into the positive course of starting a new club, reminding them that a successful new club would be the best riposte to Glazer. I even finished with a little rhetorical flourish that I'd been polishing for the last half hour. That "evil prospered when good people do nothing". In bad taste perhaps, when you consider that the original phrase was used in relation to Nazi atrocities in the thirties, but I was simply being carried away by the current of anger and passion that was palpable in the hall.

It was clear during the meeting that the stock of certain United greats was being re-valued both upwards and downwards. The Ferguson stock was looking decidedly dodgy. I'm not sure what we had hoped to see from him in response to the Glazer takeover. A high-profile resignation? Was it realistic or even fair to expect him to walk away from a club whose current pre-eminent status was largely his own achievement? For many people the problem with Ferguson was two-fold. For a start, he'd always enjoyed this populist image of the shop steward from Govan with impeccable working-class credentials who identified readily the ordinary fan. Secondly, he'd already nailed his colours to the mast in relation to the takeover a few weeks before by declaring that he "did not want the club in anyone else's hands". Inevitably, his silence following the takeover felt like a betrayal. To many people, when push came to shove, he had simply chosen self-interest over principle.

In contrast, the Solskjaer stock was rising and rising. Always a much-loved Red, Ole had now achieved quasi-divine status among the fans following his recent decision to accept a role as patron of Shareholders United, the fans' group dedicated to resisting the Glazer takeover. A footballer going out on a limb for a principle? It'll never catch on, will it? Let's hope his new employers don't bear a grudge. At one stage the mention of his name brought the whole room spontaneously to its feet to sing: "You are my Solskjaer". Funny how it took a lad from Norway to sympathise with the concerns of the ordinary fans and to ask legitimate questions about the future of Manchester United. Are you listening, Keano, Giggsy, Scholesy, Neville?

Towards the end professional Red Pete Boyle took the mic. Boylie is a well-known face among United fans. He pens United lyrics to well-known tunes and orchestrates the singing in his part of the ground. He's even sold them on CD. He told people that he hated Glazer but that he simply could not give up his season ticket or walk away from United. It's not what I wanted to hear, and I challenged him to set an example and give up his ticket. But it was my challenge that was challenged by others in the hall, not his position. And that summed up the mood of the meeting. Most people wanted to fight for United rather than walk away from it. They had listed all the things that had been wrong with the club for years. They had admitted that the club was a cynical mockery of what it had once been. They acknowledged that the Glazer takeover was merely the last straw. They wondered if the club was beyond saving. Yet they found it hard to contemplate the terrible step of walking away and starting again from scratch. It's funny to be one of a crowd of seven hundred people all suffering from incipient schizophrenia.

The meeting ended with a thunderous rendition of "Keep the red flag flying high, coz Man United will never die".

Cup final day

There have been plenty of big games in the past where I've wanted both teams to lose. I mean, when it's Liverpool versus Arsenal, what do you do? I never thought I'd feel this way about any game involving United, but hell hath no fury like a fan scorned. I spent the Friday before the cup final telling anyone who would listen and anyone who wouldn't that a) I wouldn't be watching the final, and b) if I did happen to watch it, I'd be supporting Arsenal.

At two-forty on the Saturday I was firm in my resolve not to watch that bunch of apathetic, self-serving, pampered prima donnas play Arsenal. At two-forty-five I was ringing round everyone I knew to recant my sins – of course I was watching the final, of course I was pulling for the lads. And I did watch. I watched United play with the mixture of spirit and skill that only they can produce. They out-played Arsenal in the most one-sided cup final since 1974. And lost. It was such a travesty that you wondered how the Arsenal players had the cheek to celebrate at the end. But that's what makes football an extraordinary game, isn't it – that the best team can lose. Is there any other game in which you can be superior to your opponents in every aspect of the game but one and not win? By the end of the game it didn't matter. They'd lost the final, but they'd achieved their real aim. We'd been threatening to walk away, but they had reeled us back in. They'd shown us their best face, displayed their most irresistible swagger, and made us realise that you don't walk away from this club. By five-thirty on cup final day I was back onside. Or so I thought.

Second protest meeting: Apollo Theatre

The first meeting had ended with a decision to hold a protest rally at a bigger venue. It took place at the Apollo Theatre on Bank Holiday Monday nine days after the cup final. I didn't want to go, and nearly didn't. The bastards had reeled me in, just when I'd convinced myself that I'd never watch them again.

There was a horrible feeling about the day. It was a brilliantly sunny bank holiday. We should have been having barbecues, lying on a beach, visiting

Our Club Our Rules

Alton Towers. Instead we dragged ourselves down to a dark, cavernous Apollo Theatre in lovely Ardwick. It was hot, and everything felt slow and lethargic. It was summer and nothing was conducive to thinking about football. But a thousand or more of us turned up anyway.

The top table had been reinforced since the last meeting. Local MP Tony Lloyd was there. So was writer and City fan David Conn. And Kris Stewart from AFC Wimbledon had given up his bank holiday to come and tell us about the difficulties and rewards of setting up a fans' club. Andy Walsh took charge of the meeting once again.

The philosopher Thoreau said that most men live lives of quiet desperation. He must have attended a few meetings like this. We seemed to be stuck. Nothing had moved on. It wasn't clear what the purpose of this meeting was. Was it to discuss the formation of a new club? Was it to agree on ways to sabotage Glazer's plans? Was it just to allow people a forum in which to vent their anger? With every person that came down to the stage to say their piece into the mic, I sank deeper into my seat. There seemed to be no consensus on the way forward. The idea of forming a breakaway club barely warranted a mention. Of the invited speakers I can only recall Wimbledon's Kris Stewart actively promoting the idea of starting a new club.

I remember standing on the pavement outside the theatre afterwards. There's something depressing about five o'clock on a sunny afternoon - a sort of accumulated weariness after a day's relentless sunshine. Maybe that added to my despondency. I told Mark that it wouldn't happen – not enough people ready to move on. There had even been a ludicrous suggestion that we should wait and see before taking the drastic step of forming a new club. Wait for what? For all the impetus to drain out of our protest? For the recently organised protest groups to disintegrate? Twelve months from now we could probably hold this meeting in a phone box. People would give up and drift away. It was now or never. It looked like never. So I drove home wondering what I'd be doing on Saturday afternoons next season.

Out of the blue

After the protest meeting at the Apollo I'd had enough of the whole messy Glazer-United-protest-new-team fiasco. It was early summer and the sun was shining and I was tired of being angry, so I just put it out of my mind. There was more to life than football and more to football than Manchester United. Or so I told myself. I reminded myself of how often it had been a chore rather than a pleasure to trek down to Old Trafford last season. I encouraged myself by thinking of all the money I would be saving by not going. To be honest, the simple truth is that I blanked out all thoughts of next season. I'd walked away from United forever and I was convinced that the idea of a new club would never happen, so next season was just a huge footballing void.

Now is the summer of our discontent

So that was my state of mind one Saturday lunchtime in June when I was reading the paper and polishing off a sausage butty, while occasionally glancing up absent-mindedly at Sky Sports News. I suddenly noticed the yellow 'Breaking News' banner scrolling across the bottom of the screen. Now, this is something that I've learnt not to get too excited about over the years. When you have a 24-hour sports channel to fill, news quickly becomes a debased currency. This breaking news could be something as newsworthy as: "Becks exclusive: he tells Sky that Brazil are quite good". Or it might be something along the lines of "Michael Owen seen reading book with no pictures in". Actually, that would be news. But this time it was a piece of breaking news so welcome and so unexpected that I let it scroll past me about ten times before I allowed myself to believe it. And it was just a bald little sentence to the effect that "FC United of Manchester has been accepted into the North-West Counties League". That's us. It's happened! It's amazing how quickly feelings of lethargy and indifference can be swept away by the galvanising force of fresh hope. God knows who played in the NWCL, but who cared. I'd have a team to follow and football to watch.

Birth of a football club

What a difference a month makes. Same place, different vibe. On 5th July 2005 the Central Methodist Hall hosted the first EGM of FC United of Manchester. The same crowd turned up to pack the little hall once more but this time the angry snarls had been replaced by childlike grins. They said it wouldn't happen. I said it wouldn't happen. It's a good job the anti-Glazer co-ordinating committee had had more faith. But only just. I was told that they too had had doubts about the strength of support behind the idea of a new club, but they had had no time to deliberate longer. Under the pressure of deadlines they had decided to take a chance and go for it. In interviews in the coming months Andy Walsh and Jules Spencer would tell reporters that they had seriously considered the worst-case scenario of a new team with no fans playing on a local park pitch in front of one man and his dog. They needn't have worried. One look at this room from the top table would have told them that this was an idea that had found its time.

Mark and I were there again. We had work to do – along with every other founding member of the new club. A founding member was anyone that had donated money to the new club over the last few weeks regardless of the amount. Many people had decided to pledge some or all of the money they would have spent on renewing their season ticket at Old Trafford. Others just gave what they could. It didn't matter. Any contribution entitled you to be at this meeting and to use your vote to influence the first steps of your new football club.

First up was the announcement of the result of the online vote on the name of the new club. There had been three options and I'd hated them all: FC

Our Club Our Rules

United of Manchester, AFC Manchester 1878 and FC Manchester Central. FC United of Manchester? A bit of a mouthful and just Manchester United FC re-jigged. AFC Manchester 1878? But this was 2005. FC Manchester Central? It sounded like a railway station. I'd felt moved enough to contact the club and offer them my own suggestions: Fans United and Real United. Thank God no one listens to me. How embarrassing would they have been. I told myself that I would never under-estimate the sound instincts of my fellow fans ever again, as FC United of Manchester was announced as the overwhelming winner. Looking back now, how could it ever have been anything else?

The next task was to elect the eleven board members. Every member had been given the chance to stand for the board, and about two dozen people ambled reluctantly to the front of the hall in varying degrees of embarrassment. We had ballot papers for this one, so it wasn't quite like picking sides at school. The result of the vote would not be known until the following day.

Then we chose the club badge. The graphic designers among the club's supporters had mocked up three designs for our consideration. We ended up choosing a badge that seemed to be a cunning amalgam of the United and City badges. It took its colours from United and its design from City: a shield with diagonal bars of red and yellow topped by a sailing ship to symbolise the Manchester ship canal, all encircled by the proud motto – Football Club United of Manchester.

It was at this meeting that we first heard the words Independent Provident Society. No, it wasn't an insurance company touting for our business. It was what we were, apparently. It was our official legal status, once the vote had been carried unanimously. In simple terms it meant that we had been constituted as a not-for-profit, democratic organisation just like AFC Wimbledon, AFC Telford and other fan-owned clubs.

Perhaps the highlight of the night came when our recently appointed management team of Karl Marginson, Phil Power and Darren Lyons turned up straight from training. Brilliant, the word training implied that we had some players. In fact, a week before FC United had held its first trials. A staggering nine hundred lads had applied and Karl and his team had invited two hundred down for trials. So we had a board, a manager, assistants, players, we even had a kit – now all we needed was somewhere to play. The club told us at the meeting that sensitive negotiations were on-going and that it could not make an announcement just yet. There was a paranoid suspicion that United might use their clout to persuade clubs in the area to have nothing to do with FC United. It turned out to be nonsense. Our difficulties were more to do with uncooperative local authorities. The name on everyone's lips was the Butcher's Arms, home of Droylsden United, but the local Tameside council eventually put paid to this idea. As it later turned out, they did us a favour. It would have been too small.

Now is the summer of our discontent

It was immediately clear that the board had unearthed a gem in Karl Marginson. They had taken advice among the non-league fraternity and gone for a young unknown with a wealth of experience as a player at this level. Karl had had a long career in the lower leagues with clubs such as Rotherham United, Macclesfield Town and Radcliffe Borough, and he was starting a career in management after being forced to retire through injury. He wasn't a 'name', a gimmick or a publicity stunt. He was a serious manager for a serious team. The real stroke of genius was in appointing a manager whose personality and demeanour chimed so perfectly with the preferences of the fans. He was modest, un-flashy, straightforward, a Red, a Mancunian with vowels so flat that he scarcely had to open his mouth to get them out. It's called serendipity – finding gold by accident.

I walked out of that hall floating. Bring on Leigh RMI. FC United's first ever game in ten days time. If this is a dream, don't wake me up.

We were there

I'm not sure how many enterprises of great pith and moment have taken their first faltering steps in the modest surroundings of little Leigh, but it seemed as good a place as any, as the town-centre shopping precinct bathed in glorious sunshine that felt like the physical embodiment of optimism. I was sporting the t-shirt I had specially ordered from Germany over the internet. Talk about living in the age of wonder and miracles. I had found this web site offering a bespoke t-shirt design service and created my own limited edition FC United top. Red seemed to be the obvious colour to go for – it would match my eyes when I've had a drink - and I chose what I thought was a resonant little motto to go on the back and front: Our club Our Game. I did feel a tad self-conscious walking through the pub as people peered at me trying to work out what it said or possibly trying to work out why I'd bought a t-shirt two sizes too small. T-shirt sizes, eh? The old 'one size fits no-one' approach.

I'd managed to recruit my son-in-law Dave, a staunch Red who'd often used my season ticket when I had been unable to get to games. It was only a couple of months since he'd looked on turning gradually paler as I had ceremonially cut up my season ticket renewal letter. Well, he was here today for FC 's first ever game, so he obviously didn't hold it against me. He was an example of many Reds that I would meet during the season – not ready to turn their back on United but curious and well-disposed towards the concept of FC. We were meeting Mark and Jason in Leigh, so, if no one else turned up, at least there'd be four of us to usher in the start of a new era. Or should that be 'error'? That was the weird thing. How many people would make the trek to Leigh in the middle of summer to watch a friendly played by a team full of lads that none of us had ever heard of? In my heart I was hoping for a show of strength. I was hoping to see Hilton Park packed to the rafters with ten thousand Reds sending out a defiant message to Glazer and the Vichy regime at Old Trafford. Obviously I've been watching too many films.

Whatever the final attendance proved to be, there were certainly enough fans in Leigh town centre to draw puzzled looks from the bemused passers-by. They probably thought Man United were in town and were wondering why there'd been no mention in the local paper. After an hour of drinking cold lager in hot sunshine and standing around feeling slightly weird, we strolled off to find Hilton Park. I'd been to Hilton Park once before about fifteen years ago, but that was to watch Leigh play Wigan at rugby league, and my abiding memory was of a crumbling ground wedged in between rows of terraced houses. Fifteen years on it hadn't changed, but it's amazing what you can do with a lick of sunshine. By kick-off time it was clear that my packed stadium fantasy hadn't quite materialised, but nonetheless the terrace behind the goal that FC were attacking was a solid mass of noisy fans, enjoying the long-forgotten pleasure of standing shoulder to shoulder with mates on an open terrace. The tone was set for the season when in a moment of surreal lunacy an inflatable dinghy appeared and started bobbing back and forth over the heads of the fans. Now call me boring, but I've never had the impulse to take an inflatable dinghy to a football match. It was just the first sign that FC United were about to create a fan culture that would be a little different from the sedate atmosphere of the Premiership.

What about the match? What could you expect from a bunch of lads thrown together a few days before playing on a bone-hard pitch beneath a baking sun? Very little. And that's what we got – in football terms. But in terms of heart and spirit and a willingness to chase every ball however lost and to contest every tackle a hundred percent, we got every single thing we had hoped for. We did not have a clue who any of these guys were. We were simply cheering every pass and tackle and shot from a lad in a red shirt. Lads like Mitten, Torpey and Orr who in the space of a few months would become as familiar as Becks, Giggs and Scholesy. Leigh were a bit better than us, to be honest, as you would expect from a side about five divisions above us in the football pyramid, and only a string of magnificent saves from our keeper kept us in it and earned us a nil-nil draw.

The sense of weirdness that attended the whole day increased at half-time, when we were able to change ends. I'd not done this since the sixties as a kid watching Bury. It got weirder still in the second half when one FC fan decided to top up his tan by stripping naked and running onto the field, followed by his two unlovely assistants. Now call me boring, but …It was in truth about the only entertaining moment in the second half. Of course, the football came a long way behind the occasion. At the final whistle fans flooded the pitch to mob these strangers in red shirts that we loved already on principle. Centre-forward Joz Mitten – I only learnt his name afterwards – was suddenly being carried along on the shoulders of jubilant fans as the strains of "We'll keep the red flag flying high" rang out across Hilton Park.

Now is the summer of our discontent

Who knew what the future held for FC United? An impressive 2,551 fans had turned up to register their defiance of the new regime at Old Trafford, but who could predict how many would be there when the football season started again and there was an alternative attraction down the road at M16? But those thoughts were for another day. Today was about the noisy and colourful celebration of a new arrival: FC United was born.

As we wandered through the back streets of Leigh trying to remember where we'd left the car, we bumped into a group of Leigh fans. They had a question that had been puzzling them all afternoon: "So who do you support then - Man United or FC United?" Not a bad question, eh? It was a question that most of us were going to spend the next nine months trying to answer.

Our Club Our Rules

August 2005
Should I stay or should I go?

Average. Unless you're a statistician, it's a word to avoid. It leads us into making more crass statements than any other word. How often have you heard someone say "the average football fan only cares about what's happening on the pitch" or "the average football fan doesn't care who owns the club"? As though the phrase 'average football fan' actually has some meaning instead of being lazy journalistic shorthand. You can talk about people on average income or people of average height, but there's no such thing as an average person. In forty years of watching football I've never met an average football fan, just football fans in all shapes and sizes. I've met the thoughtful, reasonable, fair-minded fan who's philosophical when things go badly and impervious to the hype when things go well. I've met the loud, shamelessly biased fan that sees the game through red-tinted spectacles and explains every defeat in terms of bent referees and dirty opponents. And for every compliant and apathetic fan with a boundless tolerance for whatever greed-inspired nonsense that those running football devise, there is the thoughtful and opinionated fan who swapped the propaganda of the club programme for the in-your-face honesty of the fanzines years ago. You can under-estimate football fans. Clubs usually do.

So is it impossible to generalise about football fans? Probably, but that's not going to stop me. Because in addition to the obvious passion for the game itself, there is one quality shared by all football fans. There is one quality that football fans claim for themselves and wear as a badge of honour. That quality is loyalty. Every football fan is a one-club man. You can swap jobs, move houses, change wives, but you never change your football team. Your original football allegiance may be an accident of birth, but you are stuck with it. Which is great if you happen to be born in Manchester, not so good if you emerge from the womb kicking and screaming in Rochdale. Like many things in life it's a postcode lottery. However, the long-suffering Rochdale fan that stays loyal to his club through thin and thin deserves our respect. He's a true fan. He travels to Torquay on a Tuesday night fully expecting a

Should I stay or should I go?

heavy defeat, knowing that he'll get to bed at four in the morning for three hours kip before getting up for work. You have to respect that level of commitment, the endless depths of his optimism. Of course, you have to question his sanity, but you can only be impressed by his loyalty. Loyalty, that quality that makes football fans love their team beyond the vagaries of success and failure, beyond doubt, beyond reason.

People think that it's easy for United fans to stay loyal. How hard is it to be loyal to a team that wins trophies every season? Since 1990 all United have done is amass FA Cups and Premiership titles, even a Champions League. And they're right. The test will come when the success dries up. But some of us are old enough to have sat this test before. Some of us are old enough to remember the dark days of the early seventies when the team of Charlton, Law and Best was replaced by a side of jobbing journeymen that served up some of the ugliest football ever seen at Old Trafford. Some of us can remember the turgid pointlessness of the Sexton era in the late seventies and the flattering-to-deceive period under Big Ron in the early eighties. So we feel that we've earned our stripes and proved our loyalty. Attendances have rarely been affected by the quality of the football. Maybe fluctuated by a few thousand at the most. Since when was having a terrible team a reason to renounce your loyalty? It's not - it's another chance to re-affirm it.

Leek CSOB, A, 13/08/05

Part-time supporter! That's what I felt like by the time FC's first ever competitive game came around. I'd just had the mostly badly timed summer holiday of my life. Talk about home thoughts from abroad - two weeks of sitting at pavement cafes staring into the middle distance and thinking "O to be in England, now that FC's there." That's when I wasn't ducking into the nearest internet café to get details of the latest friendly at Wimbledon, Stalybridge or Flixton. Ah, the magic of those names when set aside the names of nondescript conurbations like Barcelona, Perpignan and Montpellier. What does it profit a town to have constant sunshine, swish avenues and beautiful girls, if it hasn't got FC?

Never mind, I'd told myself, I'd be back home for the first meaningful game: the first match of our inaugural season in the North-West Counties League Division Two. It was away at Leek. Not Leek Town who I'd vaguely heard of, but Leek CSOB. Even the name had an exotic Roy of the Rovers quaintness to the ears of a jaded Premiership watcher. It seemed so much more interesting than playing a City or a United. I hoped it stood for "Celebrated Society of Outstanding Ball-players", though it probably didn't. I'd find out what it really meant when I went, or I would have done, if I'd been able to go. Work, that scourge of the leisured classes, meant that while FC United was making its historic debut in league football, I had to be within cursing distance of my laptop poised to apply digital first aid to the company's ailing computer systems. So that was the reason I wasn't at Leek, not the merciless downpour that threatened to dampen the high spirits of 2500 FC fans. Honest.

I had to rely on frequent phone calls from Mark who rang me every time a goal went in. There were seven goals, so he was on the phone quite a lot. Every time he rang, it was like trying to pick out the odd intelligible sound against a background of defeaning radio interference as the roar of the crowd smothered his words and his voice broke through in fragments. After twenty minutes he rang to say it was one-nil. Oh yes, come on the lads, our first ever competitive goal. Except it wasn't. It had gone to Leek. Oh dear, no one had mentioned this possibility in the flurry of excited postings on the forum leading up to the game. In fact, most people seemed to have forgotten that there would be another team playing. Was our debut going to be a damp squib in keeping with the monsoon conditions? Thank god, after ten fruitless minutes trying to be grown-up and philosophical and endlessly telling myself that the result was incidental to the significance of the occasion, Mark rang back to tell me we'd equalised. By half-time two further calls had left the score tied at two-all. How many years had it been since I'd hung on a result with the same anxiety?

After half-time I spent what seemed like an eternity staring at the phone and willing it to ring. Was he holding back the bad news? Did I actually want it to ring or would I settle for a draw? I needed a brew. I tried the time-honoured method of placating the gods: if I could successfully throw this tea-bag into the cup from here, FC would definitely win. It was just too much pressure, and I missed by a mile. So when Mark rang next, it was obvious what the news would be: 3-2 … to FC! And 3-2 became 4-2 and then 5-2. The great adventure had started with a handsome win, and in years to come I could tell my grandchildren … that I wasn't there.

Leek CSOB 2 FC United 5 (att 2590)
Scorers: Spencer(2), Mitten, Torpey, Orr

So loyalty is the defining characteristic of a true football fan. It's a strength, but it's also a weakness. Especially when it becomes blind loyalty. Blind loyalty is writing a blank cheque to a bully. It leads inevitably to an abusive, one-sided relationship. They can do what they want when they want, smug in the knowledge that your basic neediness will have you running back when they snap their fingers. Isn't this how football clubs treat their supporters? We know they treat us like doormats, yet we keep coming back for more. There's no drug like football and we're all addicted. And it is about addiction. It's not about stupidity. I'm an intelligent person – don't listen to my enemies – and yet I've allowed Manchester United to take me for granted for forty years, and paid handsomely for the privilege. Yet in real life I despair when I see people act like doormats. I find myself shouting at the screen "Leave him, you daft sod" when some put-upon woman complains about her slob of a partner. You know the routine: "he slept with my best

Should I stay or should I go?

friend while I was having our fifth child (she's only twenty), spends all the housekeeping on booze, and he gives me a slap if I turn on the hoover while he's watching the football. I keep saying I'll leave, but, you know, he's lovely when he's not drinking or on drugs, and... I still love him" But when I think of it, that's us. We're doormats, and that's what our football club is: an abusive charmer.

To announce that football clubs take supporters for granted is on a par with announcing that David Beckham uses male grooming products. It's not breaking news, is it?. Twas ever thus. Historically, football clubs have always treated fans with an arrogant disregard. For nearly a hundred years they were happy to see fans penned in like livestock on dangerous terraces. The events at Hillsborough and Heysel were tragic, but they were not surprising. In both cases the fans were not blameless, but how much more culpable were the club chairmen and football officials who persisted in dismissing fans as the great unwashed. And after the Taylor report into Hillsborough came out, did we see a public display of penitential breast-beating from Messrs Edwards and Bates? Did we see a public apology for the years of neglect and an invitation to fans from chastened chairmen to take part in consultations about the way forward for football? Er, I don't think so. Or maybe I was on holiday when it happened. The clubs simply used the Taylor report as an opportunity to remove terracing and its troublesome working-class culture and replace it with all-seater stadia and a better class of supporters. A double whammy – price out the riff-raff and increase your revenue. The people's game – you're 'avin' a laugh.

Have things improved since? I think they have, slightly, because they had to. While it's stretching a point to call our top clubs fan-friendly, it's probably fair to call them more customer-focused. They have to be. We live in a prosperous society and there's more competition for our money. But as hopeless addicts, we know that nothing compares to the thrilling, colourful, beautiful spectacle that football provides. Unless you watch Villa, of course. So the game continues to hypnotise us and we refuse to look beyond the touchline. And the people who run our clubs take football in whatever direction they want to take it, knowing that the vast majority of fans won't care as long as they see a winning team on the pitch.

Martin Edwards didn't consult the fans when he made the most momentous decision in United's history. He simply presented United's floatation on the stock market as a fait accompli. He didn't consult the fans about the proposed sale of the club to Rupert Murdoch. And when the fans organised and mobilised and thwarted the takeover, he probably had another reason to despise them. The club chairmen didn't consult the fans when they cooked up that brazen monument to greed known as the Premiership. They never ask the fans about the things that matter. The only clubs with any fan representation in the boardroom are those clubs that have come back from the brink of extinction, clubs that only the fans cared enough about to save.

Our Club Our Rules

Never mind "nil satis nisi optimum' or "superbia in proelia', the motto of the top clubs should be "Turn up stump up, sing up, and bugger off". I'd love to see that on the shirts. But they can do what they want because we let them. We hold all the power, but we don't use it.

Our football club is our drug of choice, but there comes a time when enough is enough. Maybe, just maybe, it's time to get clean.

Padiham, H, 20/08/05

"You're just a small town in Burnley, small town in Bu-u-u-rn-ley". No, not a taunt or a jibe, it's a fact. I know, because I was once dragged to Padiham town hall by my better half for an evening of Cajun dancing. Just imagine if, on that sweaty night years ago, some fairy – the traditional type with wings and magic powers – had allowed me to fast-forward ten years and see images of this sunny August morning - me in my FC t-shirt jumping on a bus to Gigg Lane to watch a team called FC United of Manchester run out against Padiham - and told me that this was my team now, my only team, how would I have reacted? With incredulity? Probably. With ridicule? Definitely. The idea would have been so far off the radar, that my only response would have been: "I'll never believe anything a fairy ever tells me again, and I'll have a pint of whatever you're on."

But the future has habit of making fools of us all, and here I was on the bus to Bury, thinking that it doesn't take much to make a man happy: a flawless blue sky, a new football season and the prospect of my first glimpse of the lads who held my football future in their hands. I was discounting the first friendly at Leigh. That had been all about symbolism rather than football. And anyway the side had already changed somewhat since then. I could see from the forum that some of the players had already managed to make the transformation from strangers in red shirts to budding cult figures, but they were just names to me. I didn't realise that by five o'clock they would no longer be strangers but as vivid and real as Keane, Giggs and Rooney.

I knew this was going to be a season of strange sensations when I was standing with Mark in Bury social club having a couple of pre-match pints while Manchester United were playing Aston Villa on the big screen. A year ago I would have been at that match. I found myself wondering who was sat in my seat, and thinking that I would never make that journey through Lower Broughton and Salford again, never park up near the Colgate factory on Ordsall Lane and stroll past the burger vans and merchandise stalls to get to the ground. But not once, not for a single moment, did I regret ripping up my renewal letter and committing my football future to FC United.

I knew this was going to be a season of strange sensations when I saw policemen in the ground leaning against the wall that rings the pitch looking relaxed, smiling and chatting to the fans that were steadily filling up the Manchester Road End. No wonder they were smiling – this is the easiest over-time they'll ever earn. The authorities had insisted on a police presence.

Should I stay or should I go?

You couldn't blame them. Wouldn't you if you thought a few thousand boisterous Mancs were getting together? They had promised to review things after a few games, and that was a powerful incentive to behave. It was rumoured that it was costing five grand a game to have the police there.

How many would turn up for our first home game? At least the 2500 that had made it to Leek last week in a downpour, surely. Mind you, United were at home, and there was a sizeable number of people who had a foot in both camps: they would watch FC when it didn't clash with United. They were 'doing both' – sometimes on the same day. To prove it, about twenty minutes into the game my mate Barry and his son Daniel turned up after a quick dash from Old Trafford to Gigg Lane. Daniel's only eight and has been going to Old Trafford for about four years, so he's not used to noise. It wasn't long before the incessant waves of singing rolling down from the back of the MRE had him turning round with a pained look on his face and his hands over his ears.

The game itself soon dispelled any patronising notions we might have had about football at this level. Padiham were fit and organised and there was not a beer belly in sight. Not on the pitch, anyway. The same was true of FC but we still had the air of a side that was learning to play together. It took a soft penalty decision to put us in front, when two Padiham defenders were harshly judged to have impeded Rory Patterson as he went for an awkward, bouncing ball. Not that Mr. Mystery (we'll come back to that) was about to waste time debating the matter. He knew his moment had come. He placed the ball on the spot, ran up nonchalantly and executed a perfect Panenka. You know what a Panenka is. It's the last word in outrageous penalties made famous by the Czech player Antonin Panenka in the 1976 European Championship final. You don't place it to either side of the keeper. You don't blast it unstoppably straight and true. You gamble on the fact that the keeper will dive to one side or the other and deftly chip the ball into the space that he's just vacated. Of course, if he just stands his ground and casually collects your chipped pass, you do look like a complete prat. No risk, no glory. We lapped it up: it was pure chutzpah, pure theatre, pure Cantona. We were still admiring it when Padiham scored sixty seconds later. Maybe our defence was still admiring it too, as they allowed the Padiham forwards to run through them for an easy equaliser. Surely the sun was too warm, the sky too bright and the smiles too wide for things to go wrong today. Surely Padiham weren't going to rain on our parade. And they didn't, as Mr. Mystery restored the lead before half-time and Adie Orr finally capped a dominant FC second half performance with a third goal. Fair play to Padiham though. They kept playing football and scored the best goal of the game in injury time, as their centre-forward waltzed round Barry George to make the score 3-2.

Ninety minutes of football and I had a new set of football heroes. Names I'd read about on the forum now had a physical substance: Adie Orr, tricky and tenacious, nine stone nothing but brave as a lion; Joz Mitten, angular and willing, an old-fashioned centre-forward; Steve Torpey, nought to sixty in six seconds with dynamite in his left boot; and the one and only Rory Patterson aka Mr. Mystery, endowed with equal amounts of technique and cheek, a swaggering performer that was destined to light up the season with moments of pure theatre. I even discovered the origin of his nickname. Apparently, he had made his FC debut as a sub in one of the friendlies with no number on his back and earned himself the monicker of Mr. Mystery and a song to go with it:

"The man with no name,
the man with no name,
How the f**k's he get a game,
The man with no name."

Post-match it was back to the pub. I didn't really want another drink, to be honest, but I didn't want to go home either. I was on a high, and I wanted to share it, so I was keen to chat to lads who'd been to the game. I was in my one-off limited edition FC t-shirt, so it was clear where I was coming from. I soon realised that it was far from clear where other people were coming from, and unwise to make assumptions. I'd start a conversation assuming that the lad I was talking to was committed to the idea of FC United, but a few exchanges later I'd start to detect a coolness, if not an outright hostility. Clearly, not everyone in the crowd today was behind the idea of FC United. They had simply come down to see what it was all about. You couldn't easily work out their real feelings towards FC. Maybe they couldn't either. It was going to be a season of division and confusion. Confusion among Reds and confusion within Reds, as individuals tried to work out exactly how they felt about FC United.

But nothing could take the edge of this memorable day for me. Of course, everything felt strange, but everything felt right. It wasn't about today vindicating my decision – I had no doubts anyway – it was the buzz of finding out how good the football could be and how much these lads meant to me after just one game.

FC United 3 Padiham 2 (att 2498)
Scorers: Patterson(2), Orr

In the summer of 2005 about a thousand of us reached our tipping point. Glazer and his £500 million pound debt finally tipped us over the edge. He wasn't the reason we left - he was simply the catalyst. While the team had often thrilled us on the pitch, the club had just as often made us squirm in embarrassment. Every time we heard Kenyon or Gill talk about customers, brand loyalty and revenue streams, another little part of us died. In fact, at some games in recent seasons you could have sworn that most of the crowd had died. The loss of the terraces, the dispersal of match-going mates, a

Should I stay or should I go?

change in the make-up of the crowd - older, quieter, more sensible – had contrived to make most matches a low-key, humdrum affair. Away fans would think themselves wonderfully witty with their "Shall we sing a song for you?" Of course, in the return fixture their ground would resemble a library, and it would only be the United away following creating the atmosphere. That's the way football has gone since 1990. The away fans are the hard-core, time-served fans that still think 'to support' is a verb, you know, a doing word. It declines thus: I support, you sing, we participate. Most home fans think 'to support' declines like this: I watch, you moan, he takes pictures of Giggsy on his mobile when he comes over to take a corner.

But the overwhelming majority of Reds did not defect in the summer, and I honestly want to understand their position without resorting to caricature or name-calling. How could I, when so many close friends whose opinions on football I respect have refused to give up on United. The vast majority of fans still going to Old Trafford are not 'muppets' who walk around with plastic bags from the megastore, take snapshots of Fred the Red and think that football was invented by Sky in 1992. The majority of fans at Old Trafford are passionately loyal, knowledgeable Reds who could give you chapter and verse on every United side since the Busby Babes. Many of them travel all over Europe to support the team, sacrificing a limited supply of annual leave and huge amounts of money to follow United. They have made too great an emotional investment over the years to walk away. They have amassed too many United-based friendships and memories to turn their back on the Reds now. For many of these people, the t-shirts on sale around the ground that say "United is life – the rest is mere details" are barely an exaggeration. Outside of their loved ones, United is the most important thing in life. So don't be misled by comments from rival supporters about United fans jumping on bandwagons. Most of the match-going fans at Old Trafford are loyal, clued-up, football supporters who know the game and love their club.

Fans like Alan. He's just a chap that works in my office and someone that I don't really know very well. The only thing I can tell you about Alan - the one thing that everyone knows about Alan - is that he is United-mad. We run into each other a couple of times a week, usually in the kitchen while waiting for the kettle to boil and we pass an agreeable ten minutes or so chatting about football. Actually, that's stretching a point. The word 'football' implies a breadth of outlook that Alan doesn't really have. His one topic of conversation is Manchester United. Which is fine by me. I've always been able to bore with the best of them on the subject of United. I always see Alan as a classic example of a certain type of United fan: Mancunian born and bred, fifty-ish, been going to Old Trafford since the sixties and absolutely unswerving in his devotion to the Reds. No conceivable set of circumstances could persuade Alan that walking away from United was the right thing to do. Being a United fan is such a big part of who he is that, if he walked away from United, he'd have very little personality left. And even less conversation.

Nonetheless, I used to enjoy our little chats. But that was pre-Glazer. That was before the Glazer takeover threw us into opposing camps. He seemed to accept it. I couldn't. I was walking around angry and depressed and ready to let loose an anti-Glazer rant at the mere mention of United, while he seemed to view it all with blithe indifference. He didn't want to talk about it. Not that he was living in denial or that he found it uncomfortable or upsetting – it just didn't interest him. He couldn't understand why I was so upset. I couldn't understand why he wasn't. He'd rather talk about the cup final against Arsenal or possible new signings in the summer. In contrast, the Glazer takeover was all I wanted to talk about. I could hardly restrain myself from saying that cup finals and new signings were inconsequential bollocks compared to what was happening behind the scenes at Old Trafford. I did manage to avoid saying it - just - by avoiding Alan. We had gone from being fellow Reds with largely convergent views on all things United to fans on different sides of a great divide. He was firmly in the camp of the compliant majority, one of the overwhelming mass of fans who refused to see the Glazer takeover as something to get worked up about, while I was so worked up that, well, normal grown-up people who get things like football in perspective were tiring of my rants and starting to avoid me. I couldn't help it – his casual indifference really pissed me off. Faced with such complacency, you start to question the validity of your own position. Was I working myself up into a state of high dudgeon over nothing? What exactly was I furious about and why wasn't he? When I stopped being angry, I realised that Alan represented an opportunity. By running my concerns past him, maybe I could prove to myself that my fears were well-founded and at the same time get an insight into why Alan – my representative, non-protestant Red – hadn't joined the anti-Glazer protests before the takeover and had no intention of joining them now.

I asked him about the idea of United being in the hands of people from a culture that doesn't 'get' football. Didn't it offend his United sensibilities that his beloved club was now owned by a bunch of odd-looking Americans who referred to football as "socca" and talked about United as one of the world's "premeer sports franchises"? He just shrugged it off. Not bothered. It's nothing to do with the team, and that's all he cares about. Someone has to own the club, so why not the Glazers? Was it any worse than being owned by the Edwards family? Was it any worse than being owned by faceless city institutions as a PLC? I tried to argue that being a PLC had been better. The shareholders had simply owned the club. They hadn't sought any involvement in the day-to-day running of the club and they hadn't tried to change its culture. Now the club would be owned and controlled by people ignorant of the club's traditions. God knows what naff American innovations they might bring in. I dreaded the Americanisation of our football culture.

Should I stay or should I go?

How would he fancy a troupe of cheer-leaders welcoming the team on to the pitch, raucous rock music greeting every goal and queuing up to get in to the Kentucky Fried Chicken Theatre of Dreams. The last one, at least, was bound to happen sooner or later, as I saw it. Could you see the cash-strapped Glazers turning down the chance to improve their tricky financial position by selling off the naming rights to Old Trafford? As the Glazers might say, go figure. Alan wouldn't have it. Just shook his head. The Glazers aren't stupid. They won't change much. They know a winning formula when they see one. As for cheer-leaders, what's wrong with young girls in shorts skirts? I think he was joking. But the prospect of seeing a sponsor's name above the stadium's main entrance hardly bothered him at all. Sure, it sounds classier without one, but whatever they call it, it'll still be Old Trafford to the fans. And if it provides money to buy Ronaldinho, who cares?

So much for appealing to his footballing sensibilities. Time to fall back on an issue that even the most hard-headed United fan would surely acknowledge as a major concern: that mind-boggling £500 million debt. The Glazers had reportedly paid a staggering £800 million for the club. They'd had to – those poker-faced Irishmen at Coolmore drive a hard bargain. The worrying thing for many of us was that according to the press only about a third of this was actually their own money. The rest had been borrowed from hedge funds and banks. Analysts were making conservative estimates of annual interest payments of more than £40m. This figure was significant. The Glazers had bought United with the club's financial fortunes on a high. The club had just enjoyed the most successful fifteen years in its history: eight Premierships, three FA Cups and a Champions League. In football terms this was as good as it got, and success on the pitch equates to success at the bank. For the 2004/05 season that culminated in the Glazer takeover United posted profits of £46 million. That sounds like financial rude health, but it doesn't leave much of a surplus once you've subtracted those astronomical interest payments. It was difficult to see how their business plan could work. Never mind the opinions of economically-challenged know-nothings like me, experts on football finance were queuing up to tell us that the figures didn't stack up. How could the Glazers meet the interest payments, invest in the team and make a profit? And this at a time when the club's football and financial fortunes had never been so healthy. The conventional wisdom seemed to be that they were speculating on some future development that would take the commercial activity of the club to another level. Whatever form this future windfall might take – individual television contracts instead of the current collective deal, exploitation of internet and 4G phone technology, creation of a European Superleague, the opening up of new markets in China – at the present moment no one could make the figures add up. It was funny looking at the Glazers – they didn't look like irresponsible Las Vegas high-rollers, more like cautious Midwest farmers – but their purchase of United was a speculation and a speculation predicated on the assumption of continual success. Yes, after fifteen years in which the Big Four have tried to take every last element of uncertainty out of the game and transform themselves into a self-perpetuating Champions League elite, maybe people were beginning to assume that success was a given. But it's not. Whisper it quietly – even Manchester United can lose that winning formula. Even the advantage of vast financial resources can be frittered away. What would happen if the team's fortunes took a downward turn? What would happen if a couple of under-performing seasons saw them miss out on their share of the Champions League gravy train? To suggest that United could undergo a Leeds-style melt-down was probably stretching a point, but no one could foresee what the consequences would be. Painful, for sure, and not just for the Glazers – they had already managed to offload a large slice of their debt onto the club itself.

    Surely not even Alan's complacency was immune to the thought that it could all go horribly wrong. It was. His usual response was to dismiss it outright as hypothetical and improbable. It was simply scare-mongering - doomsday scenarios put about by anti-Glazer groups like IMUSA and Shareholders United. The Glazers aren't stupid. You don't get that rich without knowing what you're doing. This defence of Alan's came down to blind faith in Uncle Malcolm, the man with the plan. There were other times when he wasn't quite so dismissive, when he tried to offer some counter-arguments – probably times when he was in no rush to get back to his desk. One morning he sounded as if he'd swallowed the Financial Times for breakfast. Debt is good, a sign of a healthy business. All successful companies carry large debt. It's all about making money work for you, leveraging your assets. You speculate to accumulate. It's like a property developer taking out mortgages to buy property to make profit. I felt like pointing out that there was a huge difference between houses made of bricks and mortar that generally don't fall down and Glazer's house of cards. He wasn't having it. He was too pleased with his own arguments. Whether he believed the nonsense he was talking or even understood it – I'm damn sure I didn't – it didn't matter. Some Glazer apologist had come up with some plausible analysis and that was enough to allow Alan to relegate any doubts he might have to some dark corner of his mind. Alan had one final tactic when it came to fending off my admittedly irritating questions. He'd just throw his hands up, say he was bored to death with off-field money matters and ask me what I thought of that screamer from Rooney at the weekend. And that in a nutshell summed up the attitude of most Reds. They're football fans, not financial analysts. The money side is as dull as ditchwater. Who wants to discuss the viability of the Glazer business plan, when you can drool over a Ronaldo dribble or a Rooney thunderbolt?

    There was only one issue that seemed capable of piercing Alan's complacency: ticket prices. It doesn't take a genius to see that the Glazers will need every penny of revenue they can raise and the one source of

Should I stay or should I go?

revenue that clubs have most immediately under their control is ticket pricing. Ironically, the previous board had done a good job in softening the fans up for future price hikes. Even before the Glazer takeover became a reality, they had announced a large increase in ticket prices for the coming season with some season tickets going up by 24%. It's funny in a darkly humorous sort of way, but the board were doubtless responding to accusations of under-performance from major shareholders such as McManus and Magnier. An aggressive pricing policy might keep them on board and make them less likely to consider a bid from the Glazers. Nice try, chaps. But surely price hikes will become the norm under the Glazers. Imagine it from their point of view. You're sitting five thousand miles away in Florida, owner of the world's most popular sporting franchise, and you're watching your customers pay half the price that fans pay to watch little old Arsenal. It's a no-brainer, isn't it? How long before fans at Old Trafford are paying prices more in line with the prices at the Emirates or Stamford Bridge? Of course, you can argue that the Glazers are more astute than that and that they know full well that the market in the north-west won't stand the kind of prices that you can charge in London, but there are a few other things they could resort to.

Fans of the Tampa Bay Buccaneers could tell Alan a thing or two about the Glazers' talent for generating revenue. Or more precisely, their talent for getting fans to cough up large amounts of money for very little in return. When the Glazers took over the Bucs in 1995 they introduced the fans to the concept of the up-front seat deposit. The fans were obliged to sign contracts committing themselves to buying a season ticket for the next ten years. In addition to this at the start of the contract they were required to pay an up-front deposit roughly equivalent to the cost of their season ticket. This was simply an extra outlay for absolutely no return. To be fair to the Glazers, unlike conventional muggers, they would pay this money back - eventually - at a rate of 5% per annum with the remaining 50% paid in full at the end of the ten-year deal. But woe betide you if your circumstances changed or your enthusiasm waned and you no longer wanted to buy a season ticket before your ten-year deal was up. To quote from the original contract signed by the fans:

If you fail to purchase season tickets for the full 10-year term of your agreement, you will forfeit the deposits previously paid and will not be entitled to any type of refund of your deposit.

And you start to realise how the Glazers got to be so rich. But talk about smooth operators. What a wonderful arrangement from the club's point of view. They get a huge cash windfall and a decade of interest payments on your cash and at the same time they give the fans a powerful inducement to commit themselves financially to the club for the next ten years.

Our Club Our Rules

The Glazers aren't the only NFL owners to pull this kind of stunt. A very similar kind of scheme is in operation at many clubs. It's called the PSL: the permanent seat license. It's a variation on the deposit idea introduced by the Glazers except that, once bought, the PSL is yours as long as you continue to buy a season ticket. Clubs such as the Baltimore Ravens require fans to buy a PSL before they can buy a season ticket. A glance at the Ravens website shows that a PSL for the cheapest seat in the house costs $750 while a PSL for the posh seats will set you back $8000. And what do you get for your money? Very little. It's just a gratuitous extra payment that simply gives you the right to buy a season ticket every year. But people pay it. Willingly. In fact, there is a sizable waiting list for PSLs at the Baltimore Ravens. In fact, this is the best bit - they charge you $50 just to go on the waiting list and then there's a $25 admin charge each year to stay on it. Just how much admin is involved in keeping a name on a list? You have to hand it to the NFL owners - they know their market, and they know that people's devotion to their team is a very lucrative asset. And if you think this kind of money-spinning measure could never be successful here, look at the bond schemes that are already in place at some Premiership clubs.

What does Alan think of all this? He's honest enough to admit, he doesn't know. He doesn't know what his upper limit is, and he probably won't know until he reaches it. He certainly didn't think twice about renewing this year when his ticket went up by 14% at the end of a season in which United won nothing, so you wonder what it would take to make people like Alan decide enough is enough. One thing is certain - the Glazers will undoubtedly give Alan the chance to find out what the upper limit on his loyalty is. They will keep pushing the market until the market bites back. Trouble is, speaking to Alan, I got the impression that that day could be a long way off. Especially if the team's fortunes improve on the field. While United keep winning, he'll keep paying.

Eccleshall, H, 24/08/05

I'd heard of Eccles cakes, but not Eccleshall, but that didn't stop me regaling my bemused colleagues with daft jokes: "It's the biggie tonight. Eccleshall at home. Always a toughie." No one laughed. I just got a few smiles and a shake of the head. Mind you, I had made exactly the same comments about the Padiham game. Maybe I just needed some new material. This kind of nonsense was pouring out of me. I could only put it down to the childlike excitement that had gripped me since the Padiham game.

I went down to the game with mum and dad. They had been to the Padiham game and loved it. They weren't just humouring my latest enthusiasm. They hadn't been brow-beaten into submission by a summer of FC propaganda from me. They were genuine converts. There was something about the back-to-basics ethos of the club that stirred up memories of the fifties and the Busby Babes, days of lost innocence when it was still possible to find

Should I stay or should I go?

yourself in the same cinema queue as Duncan Edwards and Bobby Charlton. They already had new heroes: dad kept banging on about Adie Orr, and mum went all glassy-eyed at the mention of Rory Patterson. What is it about a floppy-haired Irish rogue that exerts such an irresistible charm?

It was a glorious mild evening and I decided to enjoy the game from the sedate surroundings of the main stand. It has its advantages: you can still enjoy the massed choir of the MRE and you get a great view of the action. And there was plenty of action to view, as FC put on a sumptuous display of attacking football. All my worries about the standard of football at this level evaporated in the course of one match as FC played a fluent, technical game that was all about skill and pace and passing to feet. It was neat and intelligent in midfield, and quick and incisive up front. The pick of the first half goals came from a Torpey free-kick that arced over the defensive wall and curled precisely into the angle between the keeper's right-hand post and crossbar. A thing of beauty. Cue a chorus of:

"He plays on the left, he plays on the right,
That boy Torpey makes Beckham look shite.
He's faster than you, he's faster than me,
That boy Torpey scores goals for FC"

By the time sub Ryan Gilligan burst through the Eccleshall defence to finish off the scoring with a wonderful individual goal towards the end, it was 7-1 to FC. A magnificent seven and the best ninety minutes I'd seen from any United team in donkey's years. Ryan Gilligan, by the way, is one of those players that English fans love: fearless and fearsome, a rampaging, shaven-headed presence in midfield who, as commentators euphemistically say, 'likes a tackle'. He must be frightening to play against. He frightened me and I was sitting in the stand.

I spent the rest of the night thinking up songs for my new heroes. FC was bringing out talents that had stayed deservedly hidden until now. Still, I was quite pleased with this one for Rory to the tune of Sweet Sixteen:

"He runs like a dream,
A dribbling machine,
Leaves defenders behind.
He's FC, he's Patterson,
And he's fine."

I still think it's bloody brilliant.
FC United 7 Eccleshall 1 (att 1978)
Scorers: Nugent, Rawlinson(2), Torpey, Orr(2), Gilligan

So if United fans are complacent about the threat of Malcolm Glazer, they're hardly going to get exercised by the more general problems facing top-flight football today. Maybe they're quite happy to see young men earning in a week what they earn in four years. Maybe they're quite happy to pay £600 a year to keep Rio and company in bling. Maybe they're quite happy to see Premiership mediocrities retiring as multi-millionaires after a couple of contracts. Maybe they're not bothered that the game is so morally bankrupt that an unknown Russian billionaire is allowed to take over one of our flagship clubs with no questions asked. Maybe they're philosophical about the fact that he can appear from nowhere and promptly pump millions of his oil-gotten gains into buying the Premiership. Maybe their only regret is that he didn't buy their club and do the same for them. I have actually had one United fan say to me that the real problem with Glazer is that he doesn't have Abramovich's money. Maybe they're happy to see a tiny elite of clubs monopolise the money and the talent, as long as they're in that elite. Since 1995 no team outside the big four of United, Chelsea, Arsenal and Liverpool has won the Premiership or the FA Cup. Just as well the big boys use the Carling Cup as a proving ground for their reserves or every other team could abandon their slim hopes of winning a trophy forever. Maybe they're not offended by the cheating that mars every game – the feigning injury, the diving, the last-minute tactical substitutions – all the dismal antics justified by the realpolitik of modern football that says winning at all costs is the only object. Of course it is, when the financial stakes are so high. When relegation from the Premiership can cost you tens of millions, no wonder the game is dominated by ugly, cynical, paranoid football. No wonder the game has run out of characters and that a smile between footballers is as rare as a piece of Newcastle silverware. Maybe they're unconcerned that in its greed the game has sold itself to television. Maybe they're not worried about football losing its special appeal when saturation coverage of football can lead to half the Premiership programme being shown live over the weekend. Maybe they're right not to worry. Maybe I'm just a worrier.

Winsford, A, 31/08/05

If it's Winsford away, we must be playing in … Northwich. The game at Leek on the opening day of the season had been an exception and we were soon to get used to the idea of games being moved to the nearest stadium capable of accommodating the FC hordes. This obviously works in FC's favour as the opposition lose the advantage of playing at home. They do, of course, enjoy the advantage of earning two season's takings in one match. A Wednesday night game meant a mad dash from work down the A56 into the leafy heart of Cheshire. The Northwich ground was a newly built concrete stadium that was very neat if a little functional and lacking in character. Its setting did it no favours, being situated like most of these new builds on an out-of-town industrial estate.

You can't win 7-1 every game. In fact, you can't win at all some games, and this was one of them. Winsford brought us back down to earth with a jolt. After three wins and fifteen goals, it was perfectly natural that we should

Should I stay or should I go?

roll up with the confident expectation of another victory. Well, confident expectations are one thing, football is another. It was soon apparent that Winsford represented a step up in quality from the sides we'd faced so far. They were quick and skilful and causing us problems. We got to the break level at nil-nil, but then soon fell behind to an excellent finish as the Winsford striker arrived at the far post to despatch a left-wing cross in some style. Hold on a minute, we could lose. It certainly seemed possible – we weren't exactly creating chance after chance. If you're not slicing the opposition defence to ribbons with intricate passing movements, it's always handy to have a player that can lash one in from twenty-five yards. Happily we have just such a player in the shape of Steve Torpey. Another left-footed Torpedo brought us level. I can't remember if we were treated to a flash of the great man's thong. Oh yes, Torpey's thong - maybe I should explain. I don't know if you've ever wondered what your favourite player wears under his shorts - no, neither have I - but, whether you wanted to know it or not, it was soon common knowledge at FC that Torps always played in a thong. This information certainly aroused the prurient interest of the female FC fans and, rather worryingly, of a few male fans too.

Anyway, I've lost my train of thought now. Oh yes, Winsford away. I'd have taken a draw. Until five minutes later when a slick left-wing move ended with Adie Orr tapping home from five yards. Now I was getting greedy. Winsford, however, had other ideas, as they secured a well-deserved draw after another cool finish from the winger who profited from an 'After you, Claude' moment in the FC defence.

The crowd was an encouraging 2220 – not bad for a midweek match in the middle of nowhere. It hardly needs saying that they were loud and unflagging, rolling out an endless medley of chants and songs. The start of the season has seen a glorious flowering of terrace invention – you have to go to every match just to keep up. The funniest chant of the night was in honour of our captain and centre-back Dave Chadwick. Chaddy is that classic English defender, you know, ones for whom the word 'uncompromising' was invented. Think Tony Adams rather than Franco Baresi. If you have a brick wall that needs running through, Chaddy's your man. And if you need some windows fitting, he's your man, your white van man actually. That's his day job. Cue the double-barrelled blast of "Davie Chadwick, he's a Red, he fits windows" followed by "Will you do a job for cash?" Surreal and brilliant. I've heard some rather worrying rumours he's a City fan and, whisper it quietly, has a City tattoo. Hard to believe – he looks like such a happy, well-adjusted lad.

Got all sentimental in the car coming back. A wave of emotion swept over me as I looked at the road ahead and saw a long string of red tail-lights snaking through the dark towards Manchester. It was like an army on the move. We're here, we exist, a community is born.

Our Club Our Rules

Winsford 2 FC United 2 (att 2220)
FC scorers: Torpey, Orr

To renew or not renew? Many shell-shocked United fans had been doing Hamlet impressions over the summer. Talk about the slings and arrows of outrageous takeovers. The thought of paying money into the Glazer coffers was enough to make some people feel physically sick and they chose to give up season tickets they had held for decades. This was my choice. I cut my renewal letter into small pieces and posted it back to Old Trafford. It was not a gesture likely to induce a hasty re-think by the Glazers, but it made me feel better. I couldn't live down to Glazer's expectations. Some made a different choice. No matter how uncomfortable they felt about an outsider invading their game, buying their club and stealing their culture, they had too many reasons not to walk away. Not yet anyway. They would wait and see. And some people promised to fight from within. The fight from within would consist of not attending cup matches, not buying food and drink at the ground, staying away from the megastore and boycotting the products of the club's official sponsors. It was hardly likely to send the panic-stricken Glazers scuttling back to Florida, but at least they planned to do something. At least they understood that there was a battle to fight.

The stark fact is that the vast majority of the sixty-seven thousand that attend Old Trafford every week didn't understand. Or didn't care. They didn't turn up at protest meetings. They didn't wrestle over the issue of whether to renew or not. Osama bin Laden could take over the club, but as long as he delivered success on the pitch, they wouldn't care. And after I stopped being angry, and stopped vilifying them as lazy, apathetic lumpen proletariat, I tried to put myself in their tip-up plastic seats and see things from their point of view. They want to watch a winning team playing entertaining football and lifting silverware. They don't care what happens at Manchester United off the pitch. They don't care what Manchester United does or doesn't do in the wider community. They don't care that Manchester United has ceased to be a club and has become a business. They don't care that anonymous executives and businessmen control the fortunes of their club. They don't care that their involvement is actively discouraged. They are happy to turn up and look on passively, happy to be consumers rather than contributors.

Some of us have a different relationship to our football club. For one thing, some of us want to have a relationship with our football club. Some of us want to see a club that stands proudly at the heart of its community. Some of us want to see a club that gives back to its community – not because of some cynical calculation that this will attract more punters through the turnstiles, but because it sincerely believes that a club that loses its connection with its community loses its soul. Some of us want to see a club that actively draws in its community through the setting-up of youth teams and ladies teams,

Should I stay or should I go?

through educational initiatives and social events. Some of us want to see a club where the first team is made up of local lads earning sensible salaries, lads who are happy to mingle with fans in the pub after a match. We want to see a club where ticket prices are kept low because the club wants to be accessible to every member of its community. We want a club where every member has an equal stake in the club, where every member votes on every aspect of the club – pricing policies, social initiatives, sponsorship, stadium development – so that whatever the club becomes, it is always an expression of its fans. We want a club that scorns passive consumers in favour of passionate participants. And we want a club that loves the game as much we do, a club that will always place sporting principles above the desire for success, a club that will never, in the words of Sir Matt, "set the prize above the game".

Here endeth the lesson.

Our Club Our Rules

September 2005
Playing by different rules

I thought every club had one. A little Latin motto that encapsulates the ethos of the club. A pithy little formula that speaks of noble intentions and a serious purpose. A club motto takes you back to the era of Victorian seriousness when the ideals of the club were heroic and uplifting. They still stir the soul when you see them now. Everton have "Nil satis nisi optimum" meaning "nothing but the best". Probably not the phrase that has sprung most often to an Evertonian's mind over the last twenty years, though they can probably relate to the nil bit. Blackburn Rovers have the motto "Arte et labore" meaning "by art and labour". Now, art is not the word that springs to mind when you see Lucas Neill clattering into opposition players. However, it doesn't matter that the plodding efforts of the current team seem to mock the magnificent idealism of the motto. The club motto is not a statement of what the club is, it is an expression of what the club strives to be.

Only two other Premiership clubs have a Latin motto. Tottenham have "audere est facere" meaning "to dare is to do", Obviously, they've not been very daring since the early sixties. Manchester City have "superbia in proelia" which means nothing to most people but sounds magnificent. 'Superbia' has nothing to do with being superb – we're talking about City, don't forget – and is actually the Latin for pride. The motto means "pride in battle", which will surprise many United fans who thought City's motto was "We are a massive club". Chelsea don't have a motto, though surely they should introduce a few well-turned words in Latin to celebrate the new Roman empire. Maybe they could adapt the ancient "pax romana" to "bucks Romana". It wouldn't express heroic idealism but it would chime nicely with the grubby realism of the Premiership. United have no motto either. Maybe the Glazers could introduce one, and I don't mean "Go Reds, Go". I was thinking more along the lines of: "Volemus vostram pecuniam". Now that has ring to it. It has style. It has class. Never mind that it means "We want your money", the fans will never notice. Even if they do, they might appreciate a dose of honesty.

Playing by different rules

At FC United we have a motto. We've eschewed Latin, too classy for a bunch of Mancs in the twenty-first century. We've gone for an in-your-face, no-nonsense clenched fist of a motto: Our Club, Our Rules. Four simple monosyllables that express perfectly who we are, what we have rejected and what we believe in. It is a statement of pride, defiance and menace. You almost feel that it should be followed by "You got a problem with that?" It is a statement to all those who told us to resign ourselves to Glazer's fait accompli. There's nothing you can do. Yes, there is, and we're doing it. We're breathing life back into the tired old phrase "the people's game". To be honest, I've come to hate that phrase. It's a mockery, a cynical commonplace that those that run the game like to use to flatter the vanity of the fans. Yes, it's the game that fascinates, delights and obsesses billions of people on the planet, and in that respect it is the people's game, but we've always known that it's their game and their rules. There's an old saying: the golden rule in life is that the people with the gold make the rules. That's what's happening in football today. The super-rich clubs are imposing their rules on football. Unfortunately, predictably, depressingly, their rule is that greed is good, and that success at all costs is the only thing that counts. We've come a long way, in the wrong direction, from Victorian idealism.

At FC we are tired of putting up with other people's rules, tired of seeing football dragged in a direction that satisfies the greedy few at the expense of the overwhelming majority of football fans. So at FC we have a new set of rules. In fact it's a single rule from which everything else derives: a football club is owned by its fans. It's an entity created by the fans for the fans. As the club's board often say, FC United will go wherever the fans want it to go. It will be an expression of our apathy, of our idealism, of our fickleness, of our love, of our greed, of our selflessness, of our weakness, of our character. But one thing is certain, it's our club and whatever FC United turns out to be, it will be an expression of who we are. Could football's future be in better hands? Could there be a better guarantee of a club's future than to leave it in the hands of the people who love the game for its own sake, who don't see their club as an ego trip or as an instrument of wealth creation, who don't see football as a source of profit, who have spent their lives pouring money into football because they are in love with its beauty and drama? I believe in people, I believe in FC. Our club, our extraordinary future.

Ashton Town, A, 03/09/05

A strange quirk of the fixture list sent us back to Northwich three days later for the away fixture with Ashton. There are continual reminders that this is a leap into the unknown - I spent the week thinking that we were playing Ashton United from Manchester rather than Ashton Town from Wigan. Still, whichever Ashton it was, I was looking forward to it, as we made a leisurely journey down the A56 on a glorious Saturday morning. I was with Paul this time. He's a Heywood lad too and a United fan of many years, though not quite as many as myself, being a mere slip of a lad. Well, compared to me. Two weeks before we hadn't known each other from Adam but a few posts on the fans' forum later and we already felt like old pals. FC United was creating new friendships. Maybe the forum should be called Reds Re-united. In fact, given the born-again feeling that we all seemed to be enjoying, maybe Reds Re-ignited might be more accurate.

Talk about summertime and the living is easy. We stopped at a country pub along the way to meet up with Mark and have a couple of drinks. The sun beat gently down on the empty beer garden, as we wondered how many fans would turn up today. The weather was glorious, there were no Prem matches due to it being an international weekend and if 2200 turned out in mid-week, surely we'd top that for a Saturday lunchtime kick-off. But football's a funny ol' game, innit?

After the reality check experienced against Winsford in mid-week, I approached the game without preconceptions and full of respect for football at this level. Outnumbering the opposition by a hundred to one in the stands counted for little on the pitch. Success had to be earned. As Terry McDermott once famously said: no-one hands you cups on a plate. And this match proved no exception. Maybe the laid-back late-summer lunchtime feeling had communicated itself to the players as the game ambled along for an hour. This was to become the pattern of many of our games. The opposition started off keen and well-organised, and we had to work hard to match them. Then, with about half an hour to go, FC seemed to go up a gear or maybe the opposition went down one, as fatigue set in. This happens a lot in football: quality can be nullified by hard work. But it's hard to keep it up for ninety minutes. Tiredness kicks in and players drop off just enough to allow that little extra quality space to shine. You certainly can't drop off players like Torpey. Another explosive Torpey blast from the edge of the box opened up the game for FC, and it was plain sailing from there on in. Rory profited from a calamitous mix-up to pinch a second and then youngster Scotty Holt came on to help himself to a couple of goals, bursting through a tiring Ashton defence to apply two excellent finishes. And I got my first glimpse of player-coach Phil 'The Tan' Power. He's reached the veteran stage now, but, never mind – youth is temporary, class is permanent. He's a legend in these parts, and scored a bagful of goals to help Sammy McIlroy's Macclesfield into the football league a few years ago. He's usually on the touchline with Margy listening to chants of "Power, Power, show us your tan", but today he was on the pitch doing what he does best: proving that football is a combination of skill, brains and power. He's supposed to be from Salford but looks like he's just stepped off the beach at St Tropez.

At 4-0 with the game won and the sun still shining, the crowd were in party mood. Not content with going through the usual medley of songs, a group of lads in various shapes and sizes decided the time was right for an impromptu conga. Some people are born with natural rhythm. These lads weren't. The

Playing by different rules

last time that I'd seen that much uncoordinated flesh had been on a rather disgusting email attachment that someone had sent me at work.

We found out later that the crowd had been a disappointing 1424 – especially disappointing in the light of the mid-week turn-out at the same ground. Maybe people were still on British summertime and couldn't be bothered getting up early on a Saturday morning for a lunchtime kick-off. Maybe trips to B&Q and the garden centre still took priority over football. Slightly more depressing was the thought that people had sacrificed the prospect of proper football for the dubious pleasure of watching a limp England side labour to a turgid win over mighty Wales. And they missed the worst bloody conga in the world!

Ashton Town 0 FC United 4 (att 1424)
FC scorers: Torpey, Patterson, Holt(2)

I can't see me ever getting this chant going on the terraces: "We're an independent provident society". But in legal terms that's exactly what FC United is. And FC is not the only club or the first club in the country to be an IPS. Most of the fan-owned clubs are constituted as an IPS, and perhaps the most famous is AFC Wimbledon. In fact, it was Wimbledon's chairman Kris Stewart who sold the idea of new club to us at one of the protest meetings in the summer. I'd never heard of an IPS before, but I liked the sound of it immediately. The "independent" part is clearly reassuring for fans determined that no person or institution should ever be in a position to take their club away from them, but I think it's the "provident society" bit that I love most. It takes you back to the days of wing-collars and whiskery sideboards and women in crinolines. It evokes images of Victorian philanthropists who believed in social progress and who justified their worldly good fortune by employing it for the common good. It suggests mutual self-help societies like the original co-operative movement in which people contribute their time and money for a common goal. It suggests all manner of unfashionable virtues: prudence, good husbandry, solidarity. Could anything be more appropriate for FC United?

Can't see this one working as terrace chant either: "We all agree: an IPS is better than a PLC". Apart from the fact that it doesn't scan, two legal abstractions in one chant doesn't really do it, does it? Add in the fact that probably half the fans on the terraces don't know that we're an IPS. In fact, by three o'clock on a Saturday some of the blokes in the MRE can't remember where they live. But although IPS sounds like just another boring legal acronym, it's something we should all understand and be proud of. An IPS is a democratic, not-for-profit organisation. It is comprised of its members who each have "one share in the capital of the club". One member, one vote, one share. Equality of ownership and equality of voting power. It's a noble concept. Being an IPS does not preclude a wealthy supporter making a large donation to the club as long as he recognises that he will have no greater stake in the club than someone who pays his or her ten-pound annual membership fee. You can give all you want, but there's no return on investment here. Apart from the return that cannot be expressed in monetary terms – being part of a football club that sits proudly at the centre of its community off the field and that plays glorious football on it. Not a bad return when you think about it.

At the very start of its IPS rules the club lays out the objects for which it was formed. The club has set itself five objects, and it is no accident that four of these five objects contain the word "community". The concept of community is at the heart of the FC United ethos. It is not a peripheral concern of the club trailing in a long way behind the need to win matches and generate revenue. It is the principle that will underlie everything we seek to achieve, and it is the yardstick by which we will measure our success or failure. If we cannot create a football club that remains a community in which every single member is accorded equal respect and importance, what will it matter if we race up the football pyramid? If we cannot create a football club that is inextricably linked to its wider community and that enjoys the love and respect of that community, what good will it do us to have a swanky stadium and thousands of fans? FC United was formed because Manchester United cut itself adrift from its communal moorings and sailed off on the seas of global capitalism. As Jesus Christ said: "What does it profit a man if he gain the whole world, but loses his soul?" And he knew his football. FC United is all about soul, and our ambition is nothing less modest than to make the world a better place!

Blackpool Mechanics, H, 10/09/05

Warning: FC United can seriously damage your wealth. This game had already cost me twenty quid before I got there. The forum had been buzzing for days with posts about making the Blackpool game FC United's first 'Euro away' and making a weekend of it. Reds are a well-travelled lot and the fans have become used to mini-breaks in far-flung corners of Europe. Blackpool seemed to satisfy the need to travel to an exotic destination with strange customs and bizarre-looking locals. I needed no persuading. I was straight onto the internet to book two nights bed and breakfast in the entertainment capital of the Fylde coast. It was only then that I noticed that the Blackpool game everyone was talking about was in February, and that this weekend's game was at Gigg Lane. Doh. The hotel didn't accept my reason for cancelling – that I was a gormless, middle-aged bloke that shouldn't be allowed out on his own – and refused to refund my deposit. Told you watching FC would save me money this season.

This was the game where I put into practice the FC principle that this club is about giving rather than taking. I offered my services as a match-day volunteer. It meant no pre-game lubrication and turning up at Gigg Lane at midday. I spent the first hour helping Tony put up our new merchandising

Playing by different rules

stall. It brought back bad memories of Meccano sets I'd had when I was a little lad: all poles and screws and bolts that slotted together in a way that was far from obvious. But we got there in the end and stood back to admire a market stall covered with white canvass. A humble erection but it would do the job – not the first time I've used that line. It would soon be christened the 'Megastall' in a joky dig at the Megastore – or the Megawhore to its critics – at Old Trafford. It was only a month into the season and we didn't have much to sell yet – badges, programmes, scarves – but whatever we had we didn't have for long. Business was brisk.

There were still a couple of hours to kick off and I was eager to help, though no one seemed very keen on my helping. I hung around looking appealing. I was willing to do anything – that's what love does to you. I was hoping for a glamour job like selling programmes but was willing to suppress my finer sensibilities and clean toilets if it helped FC. Finally I was foisted upon an older chap who was on car park duties. At Gigg Lane there are two outdoor five-a-side courts immediately in front of the main stand and they are converted into car parks on match day. It's a fairly tight space and you have to pack them in carefully. It goes without saying that I wasn't deemed competent enough for a responsible job like that. Oh no. I was told to stand outside the main stand and point my arms, rather redundantly I thought, in the direction of the car park entrance as cars approached. In fairness, someone did eventually hand me a yellow tabard and this definitely seemed to give my arm-waving more authority.

At three o'clock that tabard was off and so was I, off into the main stand to watch the match. I half expected Blackpool Mechanics to come out in orange overalls. I was about to witness another enthralling game of football between two sides who had only one ambition: to win a football match. It was a six-goal thriller played in a glorious spirit and featuring three magnificent goals, two of them from the Blackpool number six Thompson. We seemed to be cruising in the first half as we eased into a two-goal lead. The second was one of those long-range blasts that always conjures up memories of Bobby Charlton for Reds of a certain age. The ball came out from a corner and landed at the feet of Steve Spencer twenty-five yards out. He looked up for options, couldn't see any, so simply decided that the safest thing to do was to drill it into the top corner. Beautiful. Stevie Spencer: neat, unfussy, quiet but deadly.

The second half saw a brace of goals from Blackpool's Thompson that can only be described as exquisite. A tall, elegant player, he carressed a couple of magnificent strikes beyond a helpless Barry George. The second was straight out of a Matt Le Tissier master-class, as he made time and space to look up on the edge of the box and see the keeper fractionally off his line, before dinking an inch-perfect chip over him and just under the bar. FC fans around me broke into spontaneous applause. We love FC, but we love football too. That brought the score back to a rather nervous 3-2 before Joz Mitten got a brave and well-deserved goal to make the game safe. A score-line of 4-2 made it look more comfortable than it was. It had simply been a fantastically enjoyable game full of great football from both sides. North-West Counties League Division Two, I salute you.

As usual the MRE had been rocking, going through their usual repertoire of songs – Under the Boardwalk, I don't care about Rio, Que sera sera (whatever will be will be, we're going to Timperley) – and tormenting the keeper with the now traditional chant of 'You fat bastard'. The poor lad wasn't fat. Well, he was slimmer than me, which makes him sylph-like in my book. Who's asking you? I just have visions of these lads going home, putting on their kit and asking their girlfriends: does my bum look big in this?

FC United 4 Blackpool Mechanics 2 (att 2266)
FC scorers: Patterson, Spencer, Nugent, Mitten

FC United is a broad church and fans have differing attitudes to the club. For some fans FC United is simply Manchester United by other means. It is an alternative outlet for their Red devotion until the bearded gnome and his ghastly offspring debunk back to Florida. They talk about "when the Glazers go" as though this momentous event will set everything to rights. What do they think will happen when the Glazers leave? That a multi-million pound global corporation will suddenly transform itself into a non-profit-making fans collective? It's a utopian notion at odds with reality – it ain't gonna happen. It will simply be a changing of the guard, and another set of billionaires will come in to replace the Glazers. I want these fans to give up their fixation with Glazer and to buy into the principles of FC United completely. They need to realise that whatever form Manchester United takes in the future, it will never match the extraordinary project that has started at FC.

FC United is not just another football club: it is striving to be another KIND of football club. FC is a reaction to the problems of football at the top level, and FC is an attempt to define what a football club should be. It is offering a radical alternative to the type of football club that is dominating the game today. It is offering fans a principled alternative that will always place sporting values and social responsibility above greed and success at all costs. I want fans at FC and fans who might join us over the coming seasons to "get" what FC is about, because what we are about is creating the kind of football club that fans deserve. If you're disillusioned with millionaire footballers and greedy clubs and looking for an alternative, how do you fancy a club whose five guiding principles promise:

to strengthen the bonds between the club and the community which it serves and to represent the interests of the community in the running of the club to benefit present and future members of the community served by the club by promoting, encouraging and furthering the game of football as a recreational facility, sporting activity and focus for community involvement

to ensure the club takes proper account of the interests of its supporters and of the community it serves in its decisions

to further the development of the game of football nationally and internationally and the upholding of its rules

to promote, develop and respect the rights of members of the community served by the club ... having regard in particular to the need to provide information to members and conduct the affairs of the club in accessible and appropriate ways

I suspect that there's a few words in there that you won't hear very often in the boardroom of your average Premiership club. "Community involvement", "interests of its supporters", "the community it serves", "rights of members"? Madness. What a way a to run a football club. Never work, will it? Watch this space.

Castleton Gabriels, A, 17/09/05

"Can we play you every week?" Cassy Gabs must get sick of hearing that. Only a few weeks into the season and they looked determined to make that bottom spot their own. Leaking goals at the back and lacking goals up front, they seemed to have a few problems. Not the best time to meet a rampant, table-topping FC United then.

The game had been moved, of course. We were playing at Radcliffe Borough's Stainton Park ground. Not a bad venue for the FC fans – on the tram route from Manchester – and a damn sight easier than Northwich. Stainton Park had a capacity of 2500 and it was touch and go whether it would be big enough to accommodate the FC hordes. In the end it managed it with two places to spare as 2498 fans packed the ground.

As usual with FC the game started at three, but the day started much earlier. Well before kick-off the Radcliffe Borough social club was full of raucous fans and ... raucous players. Steve Torpey, Tony Coyne and Scotty Holt were making the most of their injuries to spend the day as FC fans. There they were pints in hand and singing with the rest. The fans even made Torps sing "If you all hate scousers, clap your hands" knowing full well that he was a junior on Liverpool's books and still supports them. He had a big grin on his face, so maybe he's been converted. Can there be a better indicator of a club's health than seeing players and fans enjoying each other's company? It just reminded me of that day when Giggsy and Rio were standing pints for the fans in the Bishop's Blaze at the corner of Matt Busby

Our Club Our Rules

Way. Or am I just making that up? Torps, TC and Scotty then proceeded to spend the whole game wedged in with the fans behind the goal.

The game proved to be not quite the turkey shoot that many fans anticipated. Cassy Gabs defended stoutly and the keeper made some blinding saves and was largely responsible for keeping the score to a respectable 3-0. It was a game that FC were always winning but our passing and finishing was distinctly careless and it was a slightly off-key performance. The only incident on the pitch that sticks out for me is the moment in the second half when Chaddy sent their centre-forward crashing into the concrete wall lining the pitch. Ouch. I felt it from fifty yards away. In the Prem this would have triggered a mass brawl, press outrage and threats of legal action from pampered superstar's agent. In this game the lad just picked himself up gingerly, dusted himself down and carried on. Makes you wonder how we lost the empire.

If the lads on the pitch were misfiring, the lunatics in the stand were not. There was a packed terrace behind one goal open to the elements while along the length of the pitch ran a shed-like little stand that looked like an elongated bus shelter. That's where I was. It was a modest little stand but at least we were under cover. That's all it took to start off some friendly banter between the stands. As the sky clouded over, a chant sprang up around me aimed at all those on the uncovered terrace: "It's gonna rain in a minute" followed immediately by "Let's all do a rain dance". And that was it. We were off. For the rest of the game we were Indians to their cowboys. Cue chants of "We are the Indians" and "You can stick your John Wayne up your arse" and the sound of lads putting their hands to their mouth to make Indian whooping noises. The final surreal act was to adapt the usual "Margy, Margy, give us a wave" chant to "Margy, Margy, give us a 'How'". This lot are bonkers.

So the game was over, but the evening was just about to begin. The Last Orders pub in Radcliffe was about to take one year's takings in one night, as the FC players joined the fans for a post-match drink or six. The players stood smiling in the middle of the pub, not quite knowing how to react, as they were surrounded by fans singing their praises. In fairness, they were still sober and most of the fans had been drinking since mid-morning. It was very funny to see some of the players singing songs about themselves. I believe the evening went on and on and was memorable for the charming Voxra from Norway singing a karaoke version of "What's it all about, Margy" to the FC manager. Trust me to miss the best bit.

Castleton Gabriels 0 FC United 3 (att 2498)
FC scorers: Patterson, Gilligan, Nugent

I never thought I'd own a football club. I always picture a club owner as a fleshy middle-aged bloke with a cashmere overcoat and a big cigar. Nothing like me. Well, I don't smoke cigars or own a cashmere overcoat. But there I am, owner of FC United. Well, me and a few thousand others. Several thousand joint owners each with an identical stake in the club. A stakeholder football club. Very New Labour. But that's what we are. And what a stake to hold. It's not the kind of stake that some FC fans would like to hold over the prostrate figure of Malcolm Glazer, but it's a stake that fundamentally changes the relationship of the fans to their football club. On one level the ownership of FC United by the fans is a simple but important legal fact enshrined in the IPS, but it is the feeling of ownership that the fans are experiencing for the first time that is carrying us along on a tide of giddy excitement. Because FC is our club, everything to do with FC is important to us. What FC fans feel towards the club is protective and responsible. It's like a child having several thousand legal guardians. The fans' forum reflects this. Any reports of unacceptable behaviour – the rare instances of pitch invasions, drinking on the terraces, abuse of stewards – meet with a chorus of condemnation and an appeal to self-policing. The fact that two to three thousand high-spirited, loud-singing, hard-drinking fans have descended on sleepy Lancastrian towns this season and come away with the fulsome praise of landlords and police ringing in their ears is surely eloquent proof that the fans care passionately about the image and good reputation of the club.

In legal terms the key element of the fan ownership of FC United is that no member of the club can own more of the club than anyone else. I could have owned a stake in Manchester United, but what was the point of owning a microscopic percentage of the club when Coolmore and Glazer owned a controlling stake? The significant thing at United is not that individual shareholders had no power. It was that one or two had too much. Manchester United was always teetering on the brink of a takeover. It only required Coolmore or Glazer to sell out to the other for them to take control of the club. So the fate of Manchester United – a club with millions of supporters and tens of thousands of shareholders – was ultimately determined by the whim of two Irish businessmen. This will never happen at FC United. Those fans that were ridiculed for singing "United, United, not for sale" at the end of last season meant what they said. That's why they're at FC United now, and why they created a legal framework for the club that ensures the club remains the collective property of each and every one of its members.

Norton United, H, 24/09/05

How spooky is this? I'd never heard of a place called Norton before we played them, but on the Friday before the game I was travelling to work and spotted two lorries that both hailed from there. I was wondering whether this was a good omen. Were lorries like magpies: one for sorrow, two for joy? Well, I was about to find out. This was also the day that a BBC film crew from the Inside Out program had chosen to come down to Gigg Lane, so that was another portent of ill fortune. We were bound to fall flat on our face in front of national television cameras. The omens were building up and, to make thing worse, I was working that day and couldn't get to Gigg Lane until half-time, so FC couldn't rely on the sheer force of my presence to ward off evil spirits. I was worried, although anxiety seemed inappropriate as I drove down to Gigg on the prettiest afternoon of the year.

I got to the ground to find out that all my fears had been in vain. FC were 1-0 up and clearly on course for another win. We'd even been able to afford the luxury of a missed penalty. I joined mum and dad in the main stand ready to watch my red-shirted heroes embellish another afternoon with a free-flowing display of attacking football. Or could have watched, if some chap hadn't decided to stand by the barrier blocking the view of half the main stand. I asked him to sit down but the ignorant git just gave me a daft look. So I asked the steward to ask him to sit down, which he did. Now, when I related this little contretemps on the forum afterwards, I was verbally duffed up by all and sundry. Getting people to sit down and, worse, resorting to the help of the stewards doesn't go down well with the FC crowd, well, not the outspoken ones that dominate the forum. In fairness, I was being a bit tactless. This type of incident stirred up painful memories of Old Trafford where thugs in uniforms have been known to throw people out for standing up. I was a little miffed, though. FC is a broad church: surely there's room for a few pews. If you want to stand, get to the MRE or the far end of the main stand and let the more senior or more contemplative FC fans watch the game in peace.

The second half was meandering along pleasantly if unspectacularly, when something happened that no one expected: Norton scored. They swung a cross from the right into a crowded FC penalty area and the ball was headed clear. Danger over. Or was it? No, it suddenly struck me that the referee was not following play back up the field – he was planted on the edge of our box pointing to the penalty spot. To this day I still have no idea what this penalty was given for, and no one has been enable toenlighten me, although I have heard the words 'Joz' and 'punch' and 'Norton striker' being bandied about. Maybe that was the case. Joz can be a little, er, enthusiastic sometimes. So up stepped an eighteen year-old lad from Norton for the biggest moment of his short football life. It might be the biggest moment he ever has in his football life. Well, he didn't fluff his lines, as he buried his shot past Barry George in front of the massed ranks of the MRE. He then wheels away with his arms whirling screaming in triumph at the MRE. Now, it would have been an uplifting moment if the MRE to a man (and a woman) had been able to share this wonderful moment in this kid's life by taking it on the chin and magnanimously smiling and applauding. You know, on the basis that, if you give it, you've got to take it. Yes, but that wouldn't be a proper football crowd, would it? His celebration was met with less than magnanimous two-fingered gestures and some choice words. Maybe the lads in the MRE were just predicting the final score, because a few minutes later the Norton number nine ran through to get the winner. All the omens had proved right. Our first

Playing by different rules

league defeat, and to an unfancied team from the bottom half of the table. Maybe it was nothing to do with omens and more to do with Margy doing a Fergie, taking liberties with the opposition and leaving out several regulars. It was a mistake that he wouldn't repeat.

I knew adversity would bring out the best in the magnificent FC fans. There were ironic chants of "Marginson out", but by the final whistle the ground was reverberating to the strains of "We'll support you ever more" and "We'll keep the Red flag flying high". Come on, lads, you lost, but we still love you. Just don't make a habit of it. As we walked out of the main stand, the crowd was pouring out of the MRE and most people were still smiling broadly. The club's general manager Andy Walsh and board member Scott Fletcher were out selling programmes and the fans couldn't resist a chant of "Sack the board, sack the board". I've never heard it sung by grinning fans before.

In a spooky coincidence, on the same day Manchester United lost 2-1 at home to unfancied opposition from the lower half of the table as well. The truth is out there.

FC United 1 Norton United 2 (att 2435)
FC scorers: Patterson

Ownership, democracy and participation. These are the guiding principles of FC United. Don't ask what your club can do for you, ask what you can do for your club. Plenty of FC fans are already doing it. Supporters' branches have sprung up in England and Europe. There's even a branch in the States, though we're not expecting a Mr. Glazer to start one in Florida. There is a flourishing unofficial website with a vibrant forum. There is an endless stream of initiatives put forward and acted upon by the fans: quiz nights, football tournaments, Christmas parties, charity appeals, themed match days. FC United has opened up unsuspected reserves of energy, enthusiasm and talent. And it's all because FC United belongs to the fans.

If you give democracy to a bunch of bolshie, opiniated, passionate football fans, you'd better have the ear-plugs handy. If you're looking for a calm and tranquil life where we all live in harmony side by side on my keyboard, then why don't you ... find a different football club to support. Democracy in action is noisy and messy and things get said and feelings get bruised, and FC United is perhaps not the place for anyone with tender sensibilities. We're here to argue about everything: ticket pricing, shirt sponsorship, player salaries, player agents, Sky TV, standing up at matches, sitting down at matches, the site of a permanent home, the choice of a temporary home, the suitability of songs, the unsuitability of songs, and whether it's a barm or a muffin. All decisions about the future direction of the club are put to the fans by the board at the club AGM. The board have consistently made clear that the club will be what the fans want it to be. Of course, they are fans too. There is a mid-season AGM coming up in March and the board have made a

Our Club Our Rules

mistake. They've only scheduled it for one night. They should have booked it for a week in a room at a local asylum. It will be noisy, it will be passionate, it will be funny, and decisions will be made, and FC United will take another step along the road of its development. God knows where this road will lead us, but it's going to be fascinating to watch. And whatever happens, it will be all our own work. Our club, our decisions.

October 2005
This is the age of wonder and miracles

I'm sat in a shady bar in shorts and t-shirt while the sun beats down on the empty streets outside. It's siesta time in Gerona. It's late afternoon and, after a day spent padding round aimlessly, the unblinking sun has finally burnt off the last reserves of my energy. So I'm sipping a cold glass of San Miguel as the fans whirr gently above me, and specks of dust drift in the sleepy air. I'm listening to the gentle clink of glasses at the bar, sipping on cold lager and … staring at a computer screen. Talk about a busman's holiday. The bar has two internet points against the back wall and I'm sat at one reading about FC United's pre-season friendly at Stalybridge the night before, while two young Russian girls are sat opposite giggling (in Russian, of course) as they type messages into an internet chat room. Unless they're reading about FC United's pre-season friendly at Stalybridge too. Just a surreal cocktail of impressions that have come together to form a special memory. There are moments when you take a mental step back and drink in the fact that we live in age of wonder and miracles. You suddenly realise that we live amongst technological marvels that we take for granted, but that have transformed our lives and made possible things that were inconceivable a few years ago. Things like FC United and its transition from speculative, nay, madcap notion two months before into a living, breathing, singing football club preparing for its first season in the North-West Counties League Division Two. It was surreal to be sitting in a quiet bar in Gerona reading an FC message board that was bursting with the giddy excitement of people who were still buzzing from a wet night in Stalybridge.

T'internet, eh, unbelievable, destroying our notions of time and space, allowing kindred spirits to communicate instantly and connecting people to events taking place on the other side of the world. Talk about a small world. Still, I wouldn't want to hoover it. A few days later we'd left Gerona behind and I found myself in a cyber café in Perpignan ordering my first FC United season ticket and feeling slightly sorry for the strangers around me who were oblivious to the momentous stirrings in Greater Manchester. The poor souls didn't know what they were missing. They had to content themselves with the sun-drenched terraces of the pavement cafes instead of the rain-soaked terraces of Stalybridge Celtic. Who said life was fair.

Over the next few months the internet would play a pivotal role in driving the breathless development of FC United. Ignored by the established media, television and the newspapers, FC would thrive thanks to the people's medium, the inexpensive, democratic, empowering medium of the internet. Give us the tools, and we will do the job – ourselves. No wonder the established media are so sniffy about popular movements like FC United. It brings home to them how the world is moving on, how their monopoly of information is disappearing, how they are becoming increasingly marginalised by the development of technology that is giving power to the people. Sisters – and brothers – are doing it for themselves. Freedom for Tooting!

Oldham Town, H, 05/10/05

What do you do when FC United have no game? Well, I'll tell you what I do. I wander around like a lost soul feeling bereft. That was the case the Saturday after the Norton game - just when we most wanted to get out on the pitch and put that reverse behind us. We had to wait ten days until the home game against Oldham Town for a chance to redeem ourselves. It would be interesting to see if the Norton setback chipped a few off the FC support. It was a mid-week game too, so it was unrealistic to expect a great turn-out. Of course, I hadn't bargained for the impact of the Inside Out programme on BBC2. It had been a ringing endorsement of FC United. There had been interviews with fans on both sides of the debate and even interviews with players like Ryan Giggs and yet there had hardly been an adverse comment on FC. Now, you can't beat positive exposure on national TV, and it certainly appeared to make some converts. The game against Oldham proved to be a milestone in the season: we broke the 3000 barrier for the first time. A frisson of excitement went round the ground in the second half when the ballboys walked round the pitch with number boards announcing a crowd of 3110. In fact, there was a little perverse disappointment among some fans that the crowd had not been slightly less. They would have preferred the legendary figure of 3007 – legendary because this was the size of the crowd at Maine Road when a then Third Division Manchester City played Mansfield in the Auto-Windscreens Shield in 1998. Some things should never be forgotten.

I had abandoned the cosy environs of the main stand for this match and was watching from the MRE with Mark and a couple of young ladies that he'd brought along. How's this for FC United reaching the fans that other teams can't reach. One of the girls was a South African working over here and the other was an Arsenal fan. Neither went to football matches as a rule but they had jumped at the chance to sample the already legendary atmosphere of an

This is the age of wonder and miracles

FC game. By full-time they were not disappointed. They had been bowled over by the non-stop singing of the crowd packed in around them. And we were good that night, inspired no doubt by a magnificent and gripping game of football on the field. By now we had dozens of different FC songs, but the one that caught my ear tonight was to the tune of John Brown's body:
"My eyes have seen the glory and my heart has felt the pain.
While Glazer's at Old Trafford I will never go again.
We've taken all the passion and we're singing at Gigg Lane,
As the Reds go marching on, on, on."

The game was superb. The Oldham team were young and quick and tough as old boots. They all looked like amateur boxers, but they played like professional footballers. They hammered us in the first half and only heroics from Barry George kept the score goal-less at half-time. Oh dear, consecutive defeats looked a real possibility. I couldn't see how we could stem the flow of Oldham attacks. But that's why I'm on the terraces watching and Margy is in the dressing-room running the team. FC came out a different team and we had the classic game of two halves. Suddenly Oldham were being pegged back, even though they still carried plenty of threat on the break. Mid-way through the second half full-back Kevin Elvin crossed from the right and Simon Carden hung in the air before hooking an exquisite volley across the keeper and into the far corner. The tension in the MRE suddenly broke like a wave crashing on the shore, as we leapt around like demented idiots. The relief was palpable. To get your nose in front in a game as tight as this felt like an unhoped-for bonus. Now we just had to keep that slender lead.

FC kept coming forward and, if another goal was going to come, it was more likely to come our way than Oldham's. But they refused to lie down. It was nail-biting, stomach-churning anxiety. At least we got some light relief when Rory tangled with their bull mastiff of a number eight. He seemed to have Rory hemmed in by the goal line, nicked the ball and was about to clear, then dallied and mis-kicked it for a corner under pressure from winder-upper-in-chief Mr. Patterson. The MRE jeers him, he gestures back to the crowd and Rory stands behind him urging the crowd to give him some more. Someone is going to lamp Rory one of these days. Probably Joz, actually, after waiting in the box for the umpteenth time for the pass that never comes.

Anyway, we held on. Some three points are worth more than others, because some games take more winning than others and force you to find hidden reserves of determination and character. Yes, I'd enjoyed the champagne performances against Eccleshall and Blackpool Mechanics, but this had been the best so far. To come out on top by the narrowest of margins after a wonderful contest against worthy opponents felt indescribably sweet. I wasn't the only one buzzing. A group of kids about thirteen or fourteen stopped me on the way out and asked me when the next home game was. Maybe we're winning that battle for hearts and minds.

Our Club Our Rules

FC United 1 Oldham Town 0 (att 3110)
FC scorers: Carden

The boy Lenin was a Red, and he seemed to have some success organising the disenfranchised masses. You have to say that the boy done well, but what could he have achieved with some modern-day weapons in his armoury. I'm not talking about automatic rifles or stealth bombs, I'm talking about that irresistible, apathy-piercing, informational missile known as the internet. With the internet he could have brought about a working-class utopia within five years of seizing power, or at least have offered the toiling masses penis enlargements and pyramid-selling schemes. Yes, the internet, like money, is neutral, a means to an end. It's what you do with it that counts, and the summer of 2005 proved that in the right hands, it's an extraordinary tool.

For many of us the events at Old Trafford in May 2005 unfolded on the internet. Checking the BBC website for the latest developments became the first task of the working day. The internet provided us with the first images of the attractive, charismatic figure that was trying to buy United. The less attractive figure was the percentage of shares that Glazer was hoovering up as he moved towards ownership of the club. So the internet was the harbinger of bad news. However, it was also the means of organising an immediate response. No sooner had the Glazer coup become fact than popular Red websites such as Shareholders United, Red Issue and United We Stand began to organise the resistance. Details of a mass protest meeting soon appeared on the websites, and organisations like Shareholders United were able to email the thousands of fans held on their database. The upshot was that a week after the Glazer coup, the Central Methodist Hall in Manchester was packed to the rafters with angry but informed United fans. Of course, seeds can fall on stony ground, and if an idea finds no echo in the wider population, then popular feeling cannot be mobilised in its favour. This proved the opposite. The fury of the fans was palpable, but it was a volatile, combustible mixture. Anger alone is just energy. It might fuel your weapons of protest but it won't target them accurately. It needs the guidance system of a controlling intelligence. The internet allowed the leaders of the protest to harness the explosive mix, to direct it towards the most effective methods of anti-Glazer protest. And in the end it allowed them to get the idea of FC United off the ground.

Daisy Hill, H, 08/10/05

'United United Day' has a nice ring to it. It was the name given by a group of people at FC to the idea of bringing divided United fans together. It was designed to heal the rift between those fans that had rejected the idea of FC United and stayed at Old Trafford and those who had walked away to form the new club. The match against Daisy Hill was chosen because Manchester United had no game. It was another international weekend and Sven's boys

This is the age of wonder and miracles

were doing what they do best – boring for England. And at Old Trafford, funnily enough, which was more than enough reason for most Reds to give the place a wide berth. The organisers had sent out the message to fans at Old Trafford that FC had not been set up in opposition to United, was not anti-United and was for many fans United by other means. They were inviting Reds of whatever shade of feeling to come down to Gigg Lane and enjoy football like it used to be, before the corporate types got hold of it and turned it into another plastic theme park. It's fair to say that not everyone at FC was equally enthusiastic about this initiative. Some people, myself included, felt that choices had been made and that any glance backward at Old Trafford was a glance wasted. But perhaps the others were right - maybe that stance was too confrontational.

It always promised to be a great day for me. Shelagh was coming to her first FC game, and so was my daughter Jenny. You can never object to the civilising presence of women at football, as long as they don't go on about the 'cute one with the nice bum'. And Jenny's bloke David was coming for his first taste of FC since the friendly at Leigh. Even the wet, clammy weather could not put a dampener on the day. First surprise of the day came when we arrived at Gigg Lane to find ourselves locked out of the MRE. Blimey, what's going on here? We were directed to the main stand, and I was reconciling myself to a more restrained afternoon than anticipated, when I noticed that the far end of the main stand closest to the MRE was full of people standing up and singing. Was this the day that saw the birth of the Main Stand Ultras as rivals to the singers in the MRE? Certainly, ever since that day a debate has raged on the forum about the relative merits of the two sets of fans. The Main-standers see themselves as a cultured, discerning lot with a dry sense of humour, as comfortable discussing post-modern de-constructionist theory as much as the merits of zonal marking, while in their eyes the MRE are just callow young tyros more notable for noise and energy than subtlety. A gross misrepresentation, of course, by a self-appointed intellectual elite. While as far as the MRE are concerned "The Main Stand's full of homosexuals."

You only had to look round to see that the United United Day had worked, not only in terms of numbers but also in terms of the absolutely electric atmosphere that it had generated. The numbers were impressive, though. It was our second record attendance in three days: 3808 had packed into Gigg Lane and they made the place jump. There seemed to be an implicit consensus not to sing songs that could be seen as divisive, so the usual Rio and Fergie songs were less prominent than usual and the shared United songs that we had brought with us from Old Trafford and had continued to sing at Gigg Lane were heard the most. The strains of "You are my Solskjaer" and "Yes, I have a friend in Jesus, and his name is Cantona" echoed round the stadium.

Our Club Our Rules

Poor Daisy Hill – love that name - they probably felt like a rabbit in the car headlights. They were simply blown away as FC romped to a 6-0 win. The slick surface did them no favours as our precision passing cut them open time and again. We saved the best till last, as Adie Orr curled a beauty into the top corner from the edge of the box for the sixth and final goal.

After the game the pub was the only place to go. We were making a day of it and the day was far from finished. We ended up in the Waterloo – a real football pub close to the ground. The England game was on the big screen looking very pallid and insipid after what we'd just seen. When the game ended, the crowd thinned and the pub was left to happy FC fans, and what a magical couple of hours we spent in that pub wedged between the Salford and Middleton supporters, as each group competed for the singing honours. When the Middy lads finished, the Salford crowd started up. It was like a lesson in Manchester United history. They sang songs I hadn't heard since the seventies, songs I'd never heard in full and songs that I'd simply never heard full stop. They were amazing in their variety and richness. I could only listen and join in when I knew the words. There were FC songs too, of course. At one stage we were treated to the spectacle of Dr. Robert Swinefingers sticking his fingers in his lapels and doing a Cockney walk while singing:

"Consider yourself FC,
Consider yourself one of the family.
We won't be going back to see
The Yank or his hybrid family"

In fact, that might be the clean version. Gor blimey, guv, that's was a knees-up an' no mistake.
FC United 6 Daisy Hill 0 (att 3808)
Scorers: Lyons, Carden, Mitten, Patterson, Orr(2)

Twelve months on it feels as if our feet haven't yet touched the ground, and the internet is still central to the development of our fledgling club. Within weeks there were two FC United web sites: the official club site at **www.fc-utd.co.uk** and the unofficial fans site at **www.fcunitedofmanchester.co.uk**. The official site started life as handful of dull web pages earnestly weighed down with essential information: the club's manifesto, the IPS rules, details of fixtures, ticket information etc. It wasn't a visual treat, more the internet equivalent of Aston Villa. Apparently the people at FC United had more important things to do than designing a sexy website, like appointing a manager, assembling a squad, obtaining a kit and finding us somewhere to play. You know, maybe they had a point. After a slow start the official web site began to hit its stride. The content grew slowly and included player profiles once we had a squad. That's if the player's name and a list of his previous clubs plus an unflattering mug shot can be called a profile. There

This is the age of wonder and miracles

was a tentative attempt to create some interactive content. For example, you could make an online booking for a seat on one of the coaches that the club organised for away games. But what really transformed the site and provided a compelling reason to visit was the introduction of an online club shop selling FC United merchandise. The replica home shirts, bar scarves and woolly hats were soon flying off those virtual shelves. The site continues to develop. The FCUM gallery now offers a large selection of FC-related photographs taken by Brolly, who along with lads like Toast and Kipax and AndyB1126 have provided a comprehensive visual record of FC United's historic first season – just a few more members of this team of all the talents. Finally, eight months after its debut, the site has got that long-promised makeover, and now we have a handsome, well-organised, professional web site with a fully-functioning online shop. There are some clever buggers at this club.

If the official club site is the steady, sensible, middle-aged dad, then the unofficial fans site is the excitable, hyper-active teenager with a neurotic streak. In the spirit of FC United, the fans did it for themselves. It was the spontaneous creation of web-savvy FC fans and is completely independent of the official club site. As you'd expect from a style-conscious teenager, the fans site is more visually attractive than the official site. The home page is always dominated by photographs of the latest FC event. This is usually a picture from the last FC match, but is just as likely to be a picture from the FC United Supporters Group 5-a-side competition or a snap of fans enjoying themselves at the latest FC United quiz night. The unofficial site is the nervous system of the club and is visited on a daily basis by hundreds of FC fans. If something FC-related is happening, then you can find it advertised, described, analysed and criticised on the unofficial site. Of course, there is that neurotic streak that I mentioned. Message boards, eh? You're either forum or against 'em. Love or hate them, this is the feature that makes the unofficial fans site a daily, nay hourly stopping-off point. There are several forums – fora? – on the unofficial site and most of them are calm, polite, civilised places to visit – forums that cover the doings of the supporters branches, give details of travel to away grounds, host video and audio files created and uploaded by the more technically-minded FC fans. You can visit these forums and come away with your peace of mind intact. But if you want to be challenged, provoked and exhilarated, then put on your tin helmet and visit the main FC United forum.

Cheadle Town, A, 15/10/05

When I ripped up that renewal letter in May, I thought I was saying goodbye to hastily re-arranged fixtures being moved to inconvenient nights of the week, and here it was happening again. We'd all been looking forward to a Saturday afternoon out in Cheadle when a last-minute decision by the local safety officer had forced a postponement: Cheadle's Park Road ground was not up to accommodating an FC invasion. So here I was on a Monday night straight from work pulling off junction 23 of the M60 and looking for signs for the Tameside stadium. It had recently been completed at public expense and was being used for home games by Curzon Ashton. Nice to see council facilities being provided for cash-strapped local sides like Curzon ... and Manchester City.

This was a milestone night for FC United: our first cup game. The North-West Counties League Cup might not have the same ring to it as the FA Cup, but at least more than four teams have a realistic chance of winning it. And it offered the prospect of testing ourselves against teams from a higher division. Not tonight, though – Cheadle are a Div Two side like ourselves. That test lay ahead – we could fall off that bridge when we came to it. Still, every match at this stage was a journey into uncharted territory against unknown quantities, so there was always that buzz of anticipation. It was a great crowd for a Monday night too, to judge by the wholly unscientific measure of how long it took me to queue up for food before kick-off. And when I got to the front, all they had left were bloody mince and onion pasties. What, no stuffed aubergines? I'm going back to the Prem. But the crowd was clearly a healthy one – if you could ever call an FC crowd healthy - and people were still filing in as the game kicked off. By then Mark and myself had burrowed our way into the midst of the main bulk of the fans on the large terrace facing the main stand.

I told you our games were settling down into a tried and tested pattern: an hour of equally contested play followed by a final third of FC dominance. To be honest, we might have changed this pattern in the first minute, if the referee had not reacted to a scything challenge on Rory by waving his arms in a gesture that said "I'm not falling for that one." Looked a stonewall pen to me seen through a forest of heads from a hundred yards away. As I said to Mark, I'd like to see that one again later on Sky. No, maintaining the time-honoured United tradition of making life hard for themselves, FC fell behind, though in fairness it was to the best goal of the night. The Cheadle left-winger tip-toed his way through a couple of less than convincing challenges, drove in on goal and calmly slotted past Barry George. Oh dear, maybe this wasn't destined to be one of our longer cup runs – not that we'd had any others yet. It's always hilarious to watch the crowd when the match deviates from the script and a goal goes in against us. For a split second there is a hush of surprise and disappointment – the time it takes the brain to absorb what has happened – and then there comes a deafening roar of defiance: "We told you not to score, we told you not to score". One day this chant is going to rebound on us but, fortunately for us, this wasn't the day.

It was a relief, though, when Adie Orr poked home an equaliser just before the break, but, judging by the ebb and flow of the first half, this game was still up for grabs. The next goal was going to be decisive. Happily, it went to us. Player-coach Darren Lyons curled over a cross and the merest touch of

This is the age of wonder and miracles

Rory's head guided it past the keeper. That seemed to break Cheadle's resistance, and goals started to go in at regular intervals. Adie Orr made the night memorable by becoming the first FC player to score a hat –trick. It was well-deserved too, after he chased a lost cause towards the corner flag before lobbing the ball over the advancing Cheadle keeper to get his third. My dad loves Adie, his pace and skill, and his eye for goal, but most of all his appetite for terrorising defenders twice his size. After being released by City he had drifted out of football - until FC came along. Or maybe the drift started when he joined City.

The game finished 5-1, but the score-line was harsh on Cheadle, and made it look like the romp it never was. Still, it did allow the fans to indulge in a little harmless gloating towards the end as we sang "Are you City in disguise?" You have to remember that Cheadle is a suburb of the glittering metropolis of Stockport and, as everyone knows, Stockport is blue. Well, apart from my mate Rob, of course. And not forgetting his mate, Pete, who's a huge Red. And … this could get very boring. There was more goading for the Cheadle lads, when one of their players threw the ball away in a little fit of petulance. Cue the chant of "Just because you're losing". His team-mate was stood a few yards behind him and I swear he was laughing his head off.

And that was that, and we were on our way to … Wembley? … Cardiff? … Timperley? I had no idea, and didn't care. I was just looking forward to the next game. The road was packed with cars leaving the stadium and I was amused to find out afterwards that the official attendance was bang on 2200 despite the game being pay-on-the-gate – conveniently enough, the exact number that Tameside council had granted a safety certificate for. I'd demand a recount.

Cheadle Town 1 FC United 5 (att 2200)
FC scorers: Orr(3), Carden, Patterson

Within six months of the new club's existence the FC United forum had over three thousand registered users. Three thousand FC fans can't be wrong, can they? No, but they can be bolshie, opiniated, passionate, witty, surreal, aggressive and downright insulting. So I always think that when you access this forum, you should get a little popup box that says: "This forum contains strong language and scenes of a violent nature". Or simply "Abandon hope all ye who enter here". Well, abandon any notions of sensitivity. And plunge into the invigorating democratic free-for-all that is FC United. The threads on the forum range from the gloriously silly and surreal – is it a muffin or a barm? – to the passionately serious – should a sponsor's name ever sully the pristine FC shirt? – but every thread is a showcase for the wit and wisdom of the FC family. Get on the forum, get it off your chest, get abused, and get that priceless sense of being alive.

A wise man once said that you should never discuss politics and religion. Can I add something else to the list? On the FC forum never start a thread

Our Club Our Rules

with the title "Never going back" or "FC better than MUFC". As for "All those that stayed at OT to pay the Glazer shilling are unprincipled, spineless bastards. Discuss", don't even go there. This is one area that brings unresolved conflicts to the surface. I don't mean conflicts between fans. I mean conflicts within fans. The wounds are still open. It's too sensitive a topic. And there is still too much anger, bitterness and confusion around our attitude to Big United for us to be able to discuss this issue calmly. The truth is that the feelings of FC fans towards Big United is a continuum ranging from complete renunciation to temporary suspension of devotion to be resumed when the ginger troll leaves. Feelings run high and the debate often descends into abuse. The abuse and aggression is encouraged by the fact that the forum allows us all to hide behind the anonymity of our user names. It's amazing how the prospect of a fistful of knuckles on the nose moderates your opinions when discussing things face to face. On the forum people can abuse each other in perfect safety. Should we welcome the anonymity of the message board as an aid to honesty? I'm not sure. Sometimes it's just an inducement to irresponsibility. Thank god for that irrepressible FC humour. There's always some aging hippie to calm the troubled waters by urging the warring parties to go and hug a tree. He knows who he is.

How many clubs in the world can boast a message board that is visited by the players? Can't imagine Rio logging onto the Red Issue forum and responding to suggestions from irate United fans that he is a money – grabbing, over-rated, fanny merchant who goes missing when the going gets tough. Can't imagine Rio being able to turn the bloody thing on, to be honest. So how astonishing is it for fans to find that among their fellow forumistas are the very lads that wear the FC shirt? Our captain Chaddy comes on as Whitevanman, centre-forward Joz Mitten comes on as Muff and right winger Scotty Holt comes on as Number7, to name just the ones I know about. Always worth bearing this in mind when you're about to slag the team off after a shock defeat at home to Nelson.

The forum is the like the wild west – unregulated, not for the faint-hearted. It is the perfect expression of what FC United is all about. At times all it seems to do is highlight the divisions among us, but these times are few and far between. What it really does is reflect the life of a vital, chatty, close community. Not all FC fans log onto the forum, and you should be wary of assuming that the forum is a reliable reflection of the feelings of the FC community at large. But I can't think of anywhere better if you want to take its pulse. I take its pulse several times a day and, believe me, it's throbbing.

Nelson, H, 22/10/05

How's this for a weird coincidence? It's the Friday before we are due to play Nelson and all I can hear on breakfast TV is Nelson this and Nelson that. No, we've not suddenly become the darlings of the national media. It just so happens that this weekend is the 200th anniversary of the Battle of

This is the age of wonder and miracles

Trafalgar. Now, after the Norton game, this kind of coincidence makes me nervous. Was it going to be the portent of another defeat? Were we going to go the way of the French fleet at Trafalgar? I was so desperate for reassurance that I even consulted my horoscope in the morning paper. "Beware strange men from the north coming south and united under the name of a famous English naval commander." Oh dear, that didn't sound promising. And there were other bad omens. Nelson had been one of the original founding members of the football league, had a proud history, and in fact had beaten Manchester United in the 1920s. Thankfully, nobody from that side was in the present team, but it still augured badly for a paranoid football fan like me.

It was another weekend complicated by work commitments, so it meant another dash down to Gigg Lane for the second half. We were 1-0 up. Does this sound uncannily like Norton all over again? Even the names are almost interchangeable: Nelson, Norton. I decided to distract myself by listening to the surreal chants coming from the wits in the MRE. This 200th anniversary thing had clearly inspired them, as they sang "You only win at Trafalgar" and, in a reference to the one-armed naval hero: "If you all come from Nelson, clap your hand." Glorious.

I sat back waiting for the inevitable, when all of a sudden, it didn't happen. When the fifth FC goal went in, it was all I could do not to turn to the bloke next to me and say "Kiss me, Hardy". FC played gloriously and swept Nelson away. We seem to have the habit of saving the best till last and Simon Carden's goal was a gem, as he chipped the ball nonchalantly over the stranded keeper. Yes, he might have been two yards offside, when he received the ball, but let's not quibble over details. The poor Nelson keeper was having a nightmare. He must have had Teflon-coated gloves, because nothing stuck. He dropped every cross and fumbled every shot. Not really what you want in front of the massed ranks of the MRE. The lad looked like he couldn't wait to get off. Some keepers love it and return the banter. They know that the fans shout "You fat bastard" every time they take a goal kick, so they run up to the ball, shape to kick it, but stop and turn to the crowd with a big grin on their face. Class. Not this poor lad, though.

I got chatting to the chap on the end of our row. He turns out to be a Bury fan who loves watching FC, when Bury are away. Why not, when it's only a fiver for a pensioner? He's not abandoned Bury, though, and he sat there with an ear-piece in listening to scores from Bury's game at Chester. He loves watching our games, but is he typical of Bury fans in general? How many Bury fans must have mixed feelings about the ground-sharing arrangement with FC? You have to sympathise with them. They have a long and proud history. They won the FA Cup twice in 1900 and 1903, but nowadays they live in the shadow of the Manchester giants. Old Trafford and Eastlands are within ten miles of Gigg Lane, and they struggle to pull in decent crowds. That's not surprising, is it, when their precarious financial position forces them to charge fans sixteen quid to watch a team struggling at the foot of the second division and in real danger of going out of the football league. How many football league clubs live beyond their means and are forced to charge ridiculous prices for sub-standard fare?

FC United 5 Nelson 0 (att 3093)
FC scorers: Mitten(Paul), Spencer, Carden, Orr(2)

   One year on it's difficult to look back on what has been achieved without shaking your head in disbelief and the internet has played a decisive role in making it possible. It has allowed us to communicate and organise in a way that was simply not possible even a decade ago. While Manchester might have been the epicentre of the anti-Glazer storm, there were United fans scattered across the world who believed in the principle of walking away from Old Trafford and forming a new club. Ten years ago they would have been voices in the wilderness, isolated and powerless. Now the internet allows them to be part of a community of kindred spirits. The unofficial fans site has a message board for every FC United supporters branch. There are currently twenty-four different branches including branches from Holland, Germany, Norway, Switzerland, Australia, Poland and the United States. This is for a team that didn't even exist a year ago. The unofficial site also contains links to web sites belonging to the official Supporters Group and the Junior Supporters Group. The pace at which new groupings, new initiatives and new web sites appear is head-spinning. The description of FC United as a club "of the fans for the fans by the fans" is not just an empty slogan. It's a truth that FC fans are proving every single day. They have always had the energy, the talent and the passion, and now they have the tools. T'internet, eh? They'll be putting men on t'moon next.

   What would have happened if FC United had been formed in 1995 instead of 2005? Ten years ago surf was just waves hitting a beach, a net was for catching fish, and webs were, well, … of no interest to anyone but spiders. In the space of ten years the internet has changed our lives and given us the chance to create new communities based on shared interests, shared passions and shared ideals. The people's medium is driving the breathless development of the people's club.

By the way ………

This is the age of wonder and miracles

………… it's a muffin.

Our Club Our Rules

November 2005
Back to the future?

Have you been watching that BBC series in which a detective from 2005 wakes up to find himself in 1973? Well, there's about three thousand FC United fans having the same experience every match day. Every Saturday it feels as if some good fairy has transported us back to a pre-Premiership golden age when football meant less hassle, less expense and more fun. Ask any fan over a certain age what it's like at FC and the chances are his eyes will mist over and he'll babble on about the good old days. Of course, nostalgia is a one-eyed business and memory always filters out the bad stuff, but I know what he means. Let's be honest, the seventies was a mixed bag of a decade, with lots of things that were grey, grim and downright ugly. There was football hooliganism, social unrest, industrial action and bugger all to do on a Sunday. Not to mention the tank tops, the platform shoes and the feather cuts. But in football terms there were many things to make romantic football fans, ie. all of us, look back nostalgically.

It was cheap. You didn't need to take out a small mortgage to follow your team week in week out, and I can't recall much grumbling about the price of tickets. It was pay on the gate. You didn't have to apply four weeks in advance for a ticket. You could get up Saturday morning, see how you felt and, hangover permitting, turn up at the ground and pay at the turn-style. You could enjoy the match as a bunch of mates. You were not scattered to the four corners of the ground. You could stand with your mates. In fact, you could stand – full stop. You could stand together and share the singing, the jokes, the cheering and the moaning. Nowadays, the closest you get to a feeling of togetherness is ringing your mate in the opposite stand at half-time on your mobile. And what about the football itself? You might get the impression from watching Sky that football didn't exist before 1990. Well, it did, and, though it came with rougher edges, it was the same colourful, enthralling spectacle that football always is. And it was more competitive and less predictable. And it was a home-grown affair with hardly a foreign player in sight. And, believe it or not, skill and finesse did not did not enter the

Back to the future?

English game with the introduction of Eric Cantona. Even amidst the full-bloodied thud and blunder of English football in 20 BC (Before Cantona) the artists always rose above the artisans – the George Bests, the Eddie Grays, the Alan Hudsons, the Tony Curries, the Frank Worthingtons, to name but a few. How many artists can you name today among the Premiership's unsmiling automatons? And even though English football in the seventies might have lacked a certain continental polish, it was also thankfully free of all the other dubious foreign imports: diving, feigning injury, brandishing imaginary cards. Blimey, I'm getting seventies withdrawal symptoms as I write.

So football in the seventies was a football fans' paradise? Er, well, not exactly. Distance lends enchantment to the view and memory is expert at suppressing those things we'd prefer to forget. Pay on the gate often meant a frightening crush around the turn-styles as the pubs emptied at five to three and handy-looking older lads joined everyone else trying to force their way in before kick-off. It meant standing too close to horses whinnying nervously and noisily shifting their fearsome-looking hooves as mounted police forced the fans into orderly lines. The seventies meant piling on to steep terraces where the physical safety of the spectators was an after-thought, if it was a thought at all. Just make sure you were the right side of that crush-barrier when your team scored. You were lifted off your feet, carried ten feet forward, swept back on the tide of bodies, then usually, miraculously, happily, returned to your starting position. How nothing worse than the odd pair of specs got broken, I'll never know. And the seventies meant primitive, stinking toilets, if you could get to them. I've still got the mental scars from being packed on to a terrace at Wembley and feeling a warm liquid down the back of my leg, and it wasn't spilt coffee. But the worst thing about football in the seventies was the aggro: the stupid, ugly, mindless violence. The roaming gangs of hard-looking lads snarling hatred and aggression was a seventies reality. I wasn't a hoolie. I've always been the sensitive, artistic type, more a writer than a fighter – okay, a bit of a wuss – and never really got it. I went for the footie. But you couldn't ignore the frequent outbreaks of aggro: the mass pitch invasion by the Stretford End as they poured past the coppers and ran across the pitch to taunt the Scousers in the Scoreboard End. Or the lunatics from Leeds who smashed windows and set fire to the top deck of the buses that brought them from the station to Old Trafford. Although much of the violence was nothing more than the macho posturing of teenage lads, it cast its harsh and ugly shadow over football in the seventies.

So how could the atmosphere at FC be a re-run of the seventies? We've all moved on, grown up and chilled out. It's the velvet revolution, the summer of love.

Our Club Our Rules

Eccleshall, A, 05/11/05

Bonfire night. We must be guaranteed fireworks then, he-he, especially as we put seven past the same team a couple of months ago at Gigg Lane. But that's just it – it's not the same team. That's one of the features of football at this level: a rapid turnover of players. Teams change all the time, and the team we played at Eccleshall only contained three survivors from the hammering at Gigg. And they had a point to prove, and they were determined to prove it.

This was a genuine away trip – a 75-mile journey down the M6 to Stafford on a gloomy November day. I was travelling down with Paul who was kindly doing the driving honours, which left me free to enjoy the hospitality of Stafford's many fine hostelries. This has been one of the unexpected joys of watching FC this season: having a reason to go to parts of the country that I would never have gone to. Leigh, Northwich, Ashton, Stafford – places redolent of poetry and steeped in history! I had no mental picture of Stafford, but I was favourably impressed as we strolled through the Saturday afternoon shoppers looking for the local Wetherspoons. We found it eventually in a converted cinema. It was quite amusing to watch the good burghers of Stafford popping in for what they thought would be a quiet lunch and being confronted by groups of noisy but good-natured FC fans erupting into a burst of "I don't care about Rio" every few minutes. God knows who they thought we were. They probably saw the red and white scarves, heard those dulcet Mancunian tones and assumed Manchester United were in town for a friendly with Stafford Rangers. "But there was no mention of it in this week's Chronicle, Arthur."

Three or four pints and a fifteen-minute walk later, we were queueing up to get into Stafford Ranger's Marston Road ground. We were struck by the heavy police presence. Not literally, of course. It did seem excessive, but some police forces seem less laid-back than others. There had certainly been no history of trouble at previous FC games. Have you noticed that being a policeman seems to require a very literal mindset? They don't do irony, do they? We were whiling away the time by having some banter with the queue next to us, singing "The left side sings, I don't know why, cos after the match, they're gonna die" and varying this with the old seventies favourite "You're gonna get your f**king head kicked in." It was playful and harmless - you know, post-modern irony – and the daft grins on people's faces might have been a giveaway. Not for the policeman, however, who pulled one of the lads out of the line and cautioned him to behave, or else. Come on, lads, get with the programme.

Some days the football glitters like pure gold, other days it lies there like an oily puddle. Today definitely fell into the latter category, as FC and Eccleshall played out a dreary goal-less draw beneath a lowering grey sky that seemed to suck the colour out of the players' shirts. There were

Back to the future?

mitigating circumstances for the lads. The pitch was heavy, game-breaker Steve Torpey was still missing, and Eccleshall were unrecognisable, literally, from the team that played at Gigg Lane. The keeper was the same, though, and he got his revenge for all the 'fat bastard' chants – and he really was built for comfort rather than speed – by defying our increasingly desperate attempts to steal a winner. A disappointing draw, but not a disappointing day. We'd had a few drinks, we'd sung our songs, and we'd had ninety minutes of endeavour, if not inspiration, from our red-shirted heroes. We were happy enough. Happier than Chaddy who marched off the pitch like a bear with a hangover. And happier than Margy who slated the players afterwards for their off-key performance. He felt they had let down the fans that had travelled a fair distance to support them, but I felt like telling him: Karl, we can take it. We don't expect to win 'em all. You don't swap Old Trafford for Marston Road to watch North-west Counties football if you're just a bunch of spoilt glory-hunters.

Eccleshall 0 FC United 0 (att 2011)
FC scorers: Not if we'd played till Sunday.

Match day at FC is like a seventies revival with all the bad bits left out. There's no hooliganism – that's so last century. There's no mounted police. In fact, there's no police at all. After two home games in which the police had stood arms folded grinning at the antics of the good-natured lunatics in the Manchester Road End, GMP decided that there was nothing to police. We self-police, and even the stewards usually spend two hours looking for gainful employment. There's no crumbling terrace. In fact, there's no terrace at all. Just shiny blue stands with rows of tip-up seats. And that's the beauty of FC United: the tip-up seats remain tipped up while the noisy, swaying, singing FC masses stand beside them. As Kevin Keegan said, you can't sing sitting down unless you're Val Doonican. Okay, he knew nothing about subtle tactical ploys like defending, but Wor Kev was a fan at heart and he saw clearly that all-seater stadia were killing football as theatre and turning the cauldrons of Old Trafford and Anfield into sterile environments. So take yourself down to Gigg Lane when FC are playing and remind yourself of what football used to be and should be. And enjoy the new ingredients we've added in keeping with our ironic, post-modern, chilled-out times: the smiles, the wit, the singing, the colour, the fans as noisy actors rather than silent observers. Football as carnival? In Bury? Surely that's more suited to Rio? Talking of Rio, that brings me on to the songs…

It's what the manager Karl Marginson calls the ninety-ninety effect: ninety percent of the fans singing for ninety percent of the time. And he says this in disbelief. Like the rest of us, he's got used to the deafening silence of echoey Premiership stadiums where the shouts of the players can be heard in the long lulls between the half-hearted chants. At Gigg Lane sometimes you can't even hear your mate who's standing right next to you. No sooner does one song tail off before the next strikes up, and you end up walking out at full-time hoarse of throat and exhausted. That's how football used to be. That's how football should be. It's called atmosphere.

How many times in recent years have you heard this on radio phone-ins. "We've got Jez on the line, he's on the M6 heading away from Old Trafford. What have you got to tell us, Jez?" "Hello, Alan, Just watched Albion get mugged at Old Trafford. The ref gave us nothing, turned down five stonewall pens, all their goals were offside, and it was like sitting in a library. There was only the Albion singing". Well, in fairness to United fans, it's hard to get worked up about West Brom at home. But if Old Trafford is a library, God knows what that makes Anfield or Villa Park – chapels of rest? Twenty years ago the Stretford End was a churning, restless, sea of humanity pumping out a relentless, ear-splitting wall of sound. Now it simmers quietly on a low light like a soft murmur that bursts occasionally into life, usually in response to the "You're supposed to be at home" and the "Shall we sing a song for you?" goading of the away fans.

We've a lot of fans at FC who remember what it used to be like before football supporters turned into theatre crowds. United fans have always had a fantastically rich and varied repertoire of songs. These songs have come with us to Gigg Lane. And in an extraordinary outpouring of musical creativity, we've added a whole new FC songbook in the space of a few months.

Colne, A, 13/11/05
This was something different: a Sunday afternoon kick-off, the second round of the North-West Counties League Cup and a chance to test ourselves against a team from the division above us. I remember Colne from the eighties when a local businessman's money brought in players like ex-Liverpool star Alan Kennedy and propelled them up the non-league football ladder. I think it all fell apart when the local council refused to back his building plans and Colne dropped as quickly as they had risen. But it still felt like a big name in local non-league circles to me.

The game was being played at Accrington Stanley's Interlink Stadium, which explained the switch to Sunday - Accrington had played there the day before. This was the first away game for my mum and dad, and I think it spoilt them for all the others. We were able to park right next to the ground, they got in for a concessionary price of three quid and they were able to spend a very civilised hour in the social club. They took Accrington to heart, which was just as well, as we'd be back this season, and more than once. Today was Remembrance Sunday and a chap had posted references to the Accrington Pals on the forum in the week leading up to the game. I had no idea who these people were until I read the post and discovered that they were a brigade of soldiers from the town and surrounding area that had suffered horrific losses in the First World War. The traditional minute's silence was held while I was queuing up for pie and peas, and the only noise

Back to the future?

you could hear above the impeccably observed silence was the crackle of fat in the burger van.

   The day was beautiful, one of those crisp, dazzling autumn days that has a glass-like perfection. The ground looked beautiful too, nestling beneath the Pennine hills visible beyond the terrace behind the goals. Anyway, maybe that's enough scene-setting. I could feel myself coming over all Thomas Hardy for a minute. The game was hard-fought. In the first half Colne looked like a team that was a league above us. It was evident in little things: more fluency in midfield, more tempo in the passing, and a bit more pace up front. But we hung in there and grew into the game in the second half. With two minutes to go, I couldn't believe that free-scoring FC were going to produce a second consecutive goal-less draw. I didn't even know the rules of the competition. Would we play extra time? Would we have penalties? Would there be a replay at Gigg Lane? I don't think anyone around me knew, and it proved to be academic anyway, as right in front of us a Colne player hit a twenty-yard curler past a flailing Barry George and into the far corner. It was obviously the winner, as there was hardly time to come back. Happily, no one had told our returning superstar Steve Torpey. It was joy unconfined on three sides of the ground, as he fired home a free kick to bring us level a minute later. For what must have been, ooh, all of sixty seconds. A speculative punt up-field found two FC defenders running through quick sand, as the pacy Colne striker raced between them to fire home. Could we retaliate before the clock ran out? Yes, but not in the way that we hoped. The all-action finish had obviously got both sides whipped up into a fever of excitement, which must explain why the normally impeccable Phil Power set about a Colne player intent on time-wasting and sparked off a mass brawl in front of the manager's dug-out. It was like a silent movie, only funnier. We just stood in the stand and laughed as players and officials from both sides indulged in two minutes of vigorous pushing and chest-jutting. Trust Rory to come off the bench and throw a limp punch at a Colne player, not enough to take the skin off a rice pudding but enough subsequently to earn him a 35-day ban. Ouch. They don't mess around at this level. It soon calmed down and by the time the ref blew his whistle a few minutes later, it was all hugs and handshakes. And we stood and clapped Colne off as worthy winners. At least we can now concentrate on the league, ho-ho.

   We headed off home, but plenty of others didn't. Win or lose, on the booze, and they were straight back to the local boozers to carry on the party. At the risk of being accused of disseminating FC propaganda, I have to record the comments of a local landlord who was astonished by the good behaviour of the FC fans. He was quoted afterwards as saying: "If you're like this when you lose, what are you like when you win?" Mind you, he also remarked on the lack of swearing, so that must cast some doubt on his credibility, or maybe his hearing. But what it does do is point up an interesting phenomenon. When people identify with a club and feel a sense of ownership, they behave better. Not simply because they know they can damage the club by their behaviour, but because the process of going to the game is about so much more than the match itself. It's about meeting up with friends, having another party, turning football into the celebration it should be.

Colne 2 FC United 1 (att 2762)
FC scorers: Torpey

If you wanted to answer the question: what's FC United about?, you could do worse than stand in the middle of the MRE and listen to our songs. Yes, our roots are in United, and the strains of "Ooh aah Cantona", "You are my Solskjaer" and "Follow, follow, we are the Busby Boys" echo around Gigg time and again, but there's an equal number of new songs, FC songs. Songs that tell you what we are and what we are not. Songs that tell you what we love and what we hate. Songs that tell you what we've left behind and where we're going. Like an itch that must be scratched, the same themes return again and again: greedy clubs, mercenary players, Sky TV, Malcolm Glazer. Given that FC United is both a protest and a project, it's no surprise that all our songs present this double face – glancing critically back, looking optimistically forward.

You don't need to look any further than the first FC anthem, courtesy of the prolific pen of Redmanc7:
"I don't care about Rio,
He don't care about me,
All I care about
Is watching FC"

It's nothing personal, Rio. You just embody today's hired mercenary, the kind of modern player who can fail to turn up for a drugs test, spend eight months banned on full pay, return to the team for twenty games before promptly demanding a pay increase to a hundred grand a week. Well, it's a short career, isn't it? In fact, I take it back - it's definitely personal. Wouldn't it be ironic if his only claim to fame in fifty years time is this song echoing round a packed FC stadium.

Sky fares little better than Rio, as the fans see Sky money rightly or wrongly as the root cause of many of the game's current evils. Another early FC favourite targets Sky in a gloriously camp version of the Old Drifters song. Get down to Gigg and enjoy the strangely enthusiastic falsetto rendering of "FC-eeeee" from burly middle-aged blokes:
"Under the boardwalk,
Watching FC-eeeeee,
There are no knobheads in jester hats
Or Sky TV"

Back to the future?

Do dessicated old billionaires harbour a suppressed longing to be loved, to hear their name praised in song by grateful fans? If they do, they'd best give Gigg Lane a wide berth. As you'd expect, our favourite Malcolm features prominently in the FC repertoire. First aired at Old Trafford, sadly, this one's now only sung at Gigg Lane:

"Malcolm Glazer's gonna die,
Malcolm Glazer's gonna die.
How we'll kill him, we don't know,
Cut him up from head to toe?
All I know is Glazer's gonna die"

It's not my favourite song. It's too one-dimensional, a simplistic venting of hate. The best songs combine different elements: they celebrate a glorious past, lament a troubled present and point to an exciting future. This song resounds to the tune of John Brown's body:

"My eyes have seen the glory,
And my heart has felt the pain.
While Glazer's at Old Trafford,
I will never go again.
We've taken all the passion
And we're singing at Gigg Lane,
As the Reds go marching on, on, on"

As the season draws to an end, we seem to have adopted a new anthem, one which hits the spot for many FC fans. It gives voice to our defiance of Glazer, our rejection of Sky, our timeless rivalries, our divided loyalties and our invincible spirit. Not bad in four short lines. Take it away, boys (to the tune of Spirit in the Sky):

"Won't pay Glazer, work for Sky,
Still sing City's gonna die,
Two Uniteds but the soul is one,
As the Busby Babes carry on"

But we've added some new rivalries now and adapted the old classic:
"We hate Blackpool Mechanics,
We hate Cheadle Town too (and Flixton),
We hate Manchester City,
But United we love you"

Blackpool Mechs, Cheadle, Flixton and City in the same song. I couldn't imagine that twelve months ago.

Our Club Our Rules

Darwen, A, 19/11/05

The build-up to this game sticks in my mind more than the game itself, which is not surprising, I suppose, given that I wasn't there. It was another of those weekends when I had to subordinate my wish to watch FC to the need to pay the mortgage, another weekend when the closest I got to the game was refreshing the page on the website that was carrying the match updates. So I don't have any vivid memory of the game, but I do remember the build-up.

Who said, children are the future? Not the suits who run the Premiership, obviously. Premiership crowds are aging. I think I read somewhere that the average age of a Premiership season ticket holder is forty-four. Sounds about right based on a survey of Premiership season ticket holders in my house. Ex-Premiership season ticket holders, of course. No wonder the only noise you hear these days is the sound of people sucking on a Werther's original. To be honest, it used to be one of the only things I looked forward to last season: feeling young for an hour. Joking aside, it's a worrying trend. The conviction among FC fans is that Premiership greed has priced most youngsters out of football. That's why one of the principles that we feel most strongly about is making football affordable for young people, and why it costs under18s the princely sum of two quid to get into an FC home game. So when Darwen announced that all tickets would cost six quid and that no concessions would be available, many fans worked themselves up into a lather of indignation on the forum. It really touched a chord with many fans. After years of being fleeced by United, they objected to this display of Premiership tendencies from a non-league club. No one objected to an adult price of six quid, but six quid for kids was abusing our generosity. The club reacted by making a representation to the Darwen directors, but without success. The fans reacted in their usual way by creating a song for the occasion:

"Six quids for kids,
You're having a laugh.
Even Dick Turpin
Wore a mask"

There was talk of fans boycotting the match and some people probably did, though judging by the 1715 crowd, plenty of others needed their FC fix. We were having a mini-wobble by our standards following the draw at Eccleshall and the defeat to Colne in the cup, so it seemed important to bounce back at Darwen. I'd like to give you an authoritative account of the game but I can't. I was relying on the fragments posted on the web site and they didn't amount to much more than score flashes, and there weren't many of those. Fortunately, the one goal that did go in in the first half went to us. Scored by Brown. Who? Had I missed something? How could that be, when I checked both sites, official and unofficial, everyday? Never mind, if he was scoring goals for FC, Mr. Brown would do for me. I found out later that this was

Back to the future?

defender Dave Brown from Heywood, the town I live in. He probably lived three doors down from me.

As well as not granting any concessions, Darwen had the further bad manners to equalise in the second half. Now, a point away from home is not terrible, but there's something flattening about a draw when you've been in front. What was I talking about, a draw? We could lose yet. I started refreshing the screen with my hand over my eyes and then opening my fingers ever so slowly. Yes, a bit pathetic for a man in his forties, but I don't care – it worked. A late Simon Carden goal gave FC a narrow but valuable win. That boy Carden seems to have a happy knack of coming up with goals when you need them.

I later learnt that the board and the team registered their dis-chuffedness with the Darwen stance on concessions by pointedly refusing the offer of post-match refreshments. I know clubs at this level need every penny they can get and I don't want to vilify Darwen, but playing FC has been an undreamed-of bonanza for clubs anyway. FC fans are genuinely happy to be putting money into the grassroots football rather than David Gill's pension plan. But please don't take the piss.

Darwen 1 FC United 2 (att 1715)
FC scorers: Brown, Carden

For a game that's awash with money, where the participants earn seven-figure salaries, smiles are depressingly thin on the ground. The huge sums involved have raised the stakes and suddenly it's all too serious to be fun. Football as fun? Clear off to the North-West Counties League, you fools, and leave top-level football to the grown-ups, ie. the people obsessed with money and riddled with fear. So we did, and we've never had so many laughs in our life.

Take our manager, Karl Marginson. In fact, no, don't take our manager. We love him, we need him, we want to keep him. This guy must survive on four hours sleep a night. In addition to managing FC United, he's up at four every morning to do his day job delivering fruit and vegetables across the north-west. Not too many games had gone by before the FC faithful had christened themselves "Marginson's fruit and veg army". That was daft and endearing enough, but still left scope for one more surreal twist of the tail. Cue the unsurpassable chant of "He sells asparagus, he sells asparagus". This from the pasty-faced patrons of the MRE who look as though they've spent a lifetime picking the lettuce off salad sandwichers.

At the end of September, after starting the season with six wins and a draw, we slumped to a shock defeat at home to Norton. Time for an ironic re-working of some classic chants. How could the fans resist a chant of "Marginson out" followed by a resounding chorus of "Sack the board, Sack the board". It's the first time I've heard it sung by hundreds of fans with grinning faces. This was being sung as fans streamed out of Gigg Lane past board members Andy Walsh and Scott Fletcher who were out selling programmes. They were grinning too.

Do opposition goalkeepers stop eating, lose weight and spend sleepless nights before facing FC in anticipation of the merciless banter they know they are going to get? Some maybe, but most seem to love it. I can't remember the first time that a keeper stepped up to a goal kick accompanied by a steadily rising rumble of "Who-o-o-o-a" that climaxed into "YOU FAT BASTARD" as his foot connected with the ball. This immediately followed by a demented, sense-defying screech of "AAAAARGH!". It's not big and it's not clever, but it's bloody funny. Soon the theme of the fat keeper was pushing the wags at FC to greater efforts. Keepers up and down the North-West Counties League have been treated to chants of "I predict a diet", "Singing pie, pie, chippy, chippy, pie", "Have you ever seen a salad, have you f**k?" and witty little ditties along the lines of:
"The keeper's fat,
We know why,
He doesn't like salads,
He likes meat pies"

And my favourite – which doesn't get the airings it deserves, in my opinion:
"Build a pasty, build a pasty,
Put the gravy on the top,
Put the mince meat in the middle,
And he'll scoff the bloody lot"

This is all the funnier for being sung by less than waif-like middle-aged blokes who think a balanced meal means having a packet of crisps with your pint.

Imagine our horror when the opposition occasionally turn up with a gangly bean pole in nets that no suspension of disbelief can transform into a portly guardian. Snookered, eh, boys? Not for long. In that case it's "Who's the stick between the sticks?" and "Feed the keeper, let him know it's Christmas time".

Like fans at many other clubs we have a player of the month award. So far so normal. However, we have also instituted a jester of the month award presented to the player who has done the most that month to forward the cause of the unintentionally hilarious in football. It might be a Rory Patterson miss from four yards after dancing through the entire opposition defence. It might be Steve Torpey's decision to wear a lovely acrylic cardigan with formal trousers and training shoes. It might be Chaddy proving the old adage that no chance is unmissable. Whatever the football or fashion disaster, a red and yellow jester's hat with silver bells is presented to the sheepish-looking winner before a home match. Priceless. And the manager Karl Marginson has assured the fans that the lucky winner has to wear the hat for every training

Back to the future?

session that month. I don't know how this goes down with the players, but I did notice towards the end of the season that the old jester's hat seemed to have mysteriously disappeared. Bloody touchy prima donnas.

New Mills, H, 23/11/05

As this game approached, I was just hoping that New Mills were about as good as Danny Mills. Actually, one of the guys I work with lives in New Mills, so for the first time this season I could have a bit of banter with an opposition supporter. He assured me that New Mills were well up for it and that the fans were going to turn up in numbers at Gigg Lane. Well, they certainly turned up - in two double-decker buses. Now, after three: "We're all going on a …".

By the time the game arrived, events had cast a shadow over the match and relegated thoughts of the outcome to a secondary consideration. We had lost an important member of our club: Russell Delaney. Russell had made Herculean efforts in the summer to help the club become a reality despite being seriously ill, but had barely lived long enough to see the result of his labours. People who knew him well characterised him as a generous, ever-cheerful guy who was a total stranger to self-pity. I wished I'd been lucky enough to meet him. I kept thinking of that banner at Matt Busby's funeral a few years ago: "Heaven 1 Manchester United 0". Maybe Russell deserved something similar. Lots of people commented that Russell hated solemnity, so it was decided that a minute's applause would be more appropriate than a minute's silence. In the end he got both.

In a strange coincidence another figure dear to many fans had hung up his boots the day before. George Best had heard last orders called for the final time. Whatever your opinion of Best as a bloke – lovable but weak Irish charmer or irresponsible, selfish drunk – you couldn't deny his genius as a footballer, or forget the way he illuminated football for a frustratingly short time in the sixties. What's the secret of George's enduring appeal? Is it that James Dean thing – an iconic figure seemingly hell-bent on self-destruction? Actually, I think it's just the football: the mazy dribbles, the extraordinary goals, the toying with defenders, the skill, the balance, the cheek. Farewell, Georgie. Will we ever see your like again?

I almost forgot to mention it – it was my five minutes of fame. I was presenting the monthly player awards. I handed the player of the month trophy to keeper Barry George who has proved himself a magnificent shot-stopper game in game out, and I presented the jester's hat award to player-coach Daz Lyons. I don't know what piece of footballing farce Daz had earned this for – maybe I'd missed that game – but he didn't seem too impressed. And the curse of the player of the month award struck inside two minutes as New Mills ran down our end and opened the scoring. All I could think of was "Don't lose, lads. I've got to face Simon tomorrow." I knew they wouldn't let me down. Well, I felt a lot more confident that they

Our Club Our Rules

wouldn't let me down, when Chaddy bundled in an equaliser after twenty minutes. After that, the red shirts poured forward like an irresistible lava flow. Only a red one, of course. Goal-machine Simon Carden grabbed himself a hat-trick as FC over-whelmed New Mills 6-1. The pick of the bunch saw Carden beat the keeper with a delicious chip from the edge of area at the end of an intricate passing move. Don't tell me that this is just the North-West Counties League – that goal was pure poetry at any level.

The second half was illuminated by two hilarious moments. The first came when that master of excess Rory Patterson showed that, if you're going to miss, do it properly. He ran at the New Mills defence, beat one defender, then another, then a third, carried on, took the first left at the lights, asked a policeman for directions, doubled back on himself, stepped round the keeper, stopped, steadied himself in front of the unattended net, and … put it wide. A fitting tribute to George himself: sublime genius and embarrassing cock-up – the story of George's life.

The other memorable incident came when a rare attack by the visitors saw the Millers centre-forward turn Chaddy inside out. Now you see me, now you don't, and there he was driving into the FC penalty area. A flailing Chaddy reaches out his right arm, grabs the lad's shirt and spins him like a top. A penalty so nailed on that we just looked at it and laughed – you can do that when you're five up. That's what's so endearing about the football at this level – it's so honest. Even the fouls are artless and obvious. Except to the linesman who was standing five yards away. He must have been fooled by Chaddy's cheeky smile and innocent expression. No penalty! Cue an absolutely shocking outburst from the New Mills manager. Shocking because it did not contain a single swear word. You're a better man than me, my son. Obviously not a graduate of the Peter Reid charm school.

FC United 6 New Mills 1 (att 2297)
FC scorers: Chadwick, Carden(3), Orr, Patterson

Gigg Lane holds over ten thousand, so the main stand and the MRE to its right are usually enough to house the three thousand FC fans. The empty Cemetery End opposite the MRE is set aside for the FC flags. The black, red and white of the flags adds a colourful contrast to the backdrop of blue plastic seats. Just like the singing and the banter, the flags themselves are eloquent expressions of what FC is about. There's the defiance of the huge "Hasta la victoria siempre" banner that was seen at the early protest meetings. There are flags that hint at the quasi-religious fervour that we bring to our football: "The resurrection, the light", "Young Soul Rebels", "Breaking into Heaven", "Heaven's gates won't hold", "There is a light that never fades" or simply "FCUM – it's a love thang". There are echoes of Madchester in the banners that say: "FCUM – Happy Daze" and "24hr Party People" and "FCUM – The In Crowd". There is the sublime slogan of the Junior Supporters Group: "Children of the Revolution". And finally there is the surreal and the simply bonkers: "FC United – by eck, luv, it's gorgeous", "Warning – this club contains nuts", "FC United – punk football", "Salford is pink" (don't ask) and making an important philosophical statement: "It's a FCUM muffin".

It's not just the flags that turn FC games into a riot of colour. FC replica shirts and bar scarves dapple the stands with red and white. Even dedicated followers of the "too cool for school" fraternity who used to cast withering looks at the replica-shirted patrons of the megastore can now be spotted proudly sporting FC scarves, even if a shirt is a fashion concession too far for some. When we score, the MRE explodes into a vivid, twirling mass of red and white bar scarves. And, in accordance with the mysterious and unfathomable logic of football crowds, it has become a ritual to twirl those scarves in time to the singing of "Que sera sera, whatever will be will be, we're going to Timperley, que sera sera".

It goes without saying that all the kids turn out bedecked in hats and scarves and shirts. You only realise how drably middle-aged Premiership crowds have become when you find yourself continually struck by the number of youngsters around you at Gigg Lane, adding their own note of youthful colour to the party.

Cheadle Town, A, 26/11/05

There was only one song today:
"And number one was Georgie Best,
And number two was Georgie Best ..."
All the way to number twelve, to the tune of 'Yellow Submarine" and rounded off with:
"We all live in a Georgie Best world"

An almost boringly simple song, but eloquent testimony to the place he holds in people's hearts and people's memories. In fact, no one under the age of thirty could have seen him play, but they've seen the videos and that's enough to appreciate his genius. Today was the day when he was being buried in Belfast with considerable pomp, but looking at the FC fans that had over-flowed from the pub and into the street and stood singing this song beer in hand, that seemed to me an even more appropriate send-off.

We were across the road from Stockport County's Edgeley Park ground. Sale Shark's Edgeley Park ground, to be precise. The local rugby team had taken advantage of County's cash-strapped situation to buy the ground last year. Imagine how much that must hurt if you're a County fan. Cheadle's decision to move the game to Edgeley Park was obviously a wise one, as the crowd was already building up impressively. It was a handy location for any fans trying to persuade open-minded United fans to sample the FC experience. I'd done just that and prevailed upon Rob to come and see his first FC match. We had been going to Old Trafford together for the last ten

Our Club Our Rules

years. In fact, last season he had bought one of my season tickets off me. Maybe I should have consulted him before ripping up both renewal letters. In truth, Rob hadn't given up on United and still went occasionally, but he's a genuine football lover and he was keen to see the team I'd been banging on about for months. Myself, Rob and Mark had a pint or four before the game outside a pub on Castle Street, Edgeley's main and only shopping street, that seemed thronged with FC fans. One little lad was walking through the crowd selling cans from a 24-pack of Stella. I wonder if the local Somerfields was experiencing more shrinkage than usual that day.

Lengthy queues at the ground meant that the game had started by the time we got in. All the FC fans had been guided towards the huge Robinsons Stand behind one goal. It holds about five thousand and, by the time we arrived, it looked pretty full. It dwarfs the other stands, and when FC scored and the fans bounced up and down, I thought the ground might tip up. FC's goal was a response to the opener from Cheadle. I thought they were a decent side in the cup at Ashton and that 5-1 was a very flattering score-line, and today would prove me right. It was to be a difficult afternoon, despite a trademark Torpey free-kick and a typical piece of Carden goal-sniffery putting us 2-1 up at half time.

Did I mention that it was bloody freezing. Well, it was, and at half time we burrowed into the crowds inside the stand in search of food and warmth. I'd never seen so many people at an FC match, and was convinced we'd broken our record attendance. I was still convinced the following day, when the official figure indicated otherwise. It was a slog getting through the densely packed crowd to get to the food counter, but what a reward awaited us there: sausage and mash. I thought I'd died and gone to football heaven. There was a price to pay for this treat. We lost track of time and by the time we came back out for the second half we'd missed two goals. The scoreboard was now showing 3-2 and I was wondering who'd scored our third goal. I was still wondering fifteen minutes later, when it suddenly dawned on me that it was Cheadle leading 3-2. I couldn't believe it. I'd spent the last quarter of an hour watching the game under the illusion that we were leading. I had to admit this embarrassing gaffe to Rob and Mark, who … said they'd thought exactly the same. What do they put in that mashed potato?

I couldn't believe that I'd brought Rob along to his first FC game and we were going to lose. It looked that way until the referee helped us out with a generous penalty decision. Up stepped Rory in front of an expectant Robinsons Stand and confidently smashed the ball … against the post and out. Rob, you're a jinx, and you're not coming again. Just as I was reconciling myself to a rare defeat, the lads proved they were a side straight out of the classic United mould. It's the last minute and Dave Brown swings over a cross from the left. Up goes Chaddy at the far post to power home a close-range header. Cue pandemonium in the stand as the fans party like it's 1999. To be honest, I wasn't there and I've no idea how good Barcelona was,

Back to the future?

but I can tell you Stockport in 2005 was rocking. It's only a draw and a fair one at that but everyone pours out grinning and still singing "And number one was Georgie Best".

Cheadle Town 3 FC United 3 (att 3373)
FC scorers: Orr, Torpey, Chadwick

    The match day experience at FC is a joyous, noisy, boisterous carnival. Yes, you can sit quietly in the main stand and watch the game, but it's the loud, good-natured hordes behind the goal that give the game its flavour. Even the too young, the slightly older or the simply more reserved drink in the atmosphere that spills over in sustained and noisy waves from the MRE. We didn't realise how tired we'd become of the insipid fare of the Premiership until we sampled the richly seasoned, highly flavoured dish set before us at FC. Too many cooks spoil the broth? Not this broth. It tastes fresh every time you go and you walk away after every match feeling invigorated, restored and glowing. The magnificent fans at FC have added back all the ingredients that have been removed from the bland, one-taste-suits-all Premiership mix: the noise, the movement, the colour. It's like gorging on home-made food after living for years on processed stodge: you'd forgotten how good it tasted.

    As Shakespeare said: "I love, I love, I love, I love an atmosphere" Or was it Russ Abbott? Who cares. If you want to return to football that makes your blood pulse, your heart pump and your throat hoarse, get down to Gigg Lane and become part of the FC United roadshow.

Our Club Our Rules

December 2005
Money, money, money

Money, eh? Who needs it? Well, we all do. Even a football club created as a reaction to the naked greed and rampant commercialism of the Premiership. It does seem, though, that there are some people who have a conception of FC United as some kind of hippie collective that survives on free love and good vibes. Nice work if you can get it. I dare say life would be a lot simpler and easier if we could look down from our Olympian heights and distance ourselves from the sordid business of making money. But FC United is not about making a principled retreat from the world. It's about being in the world and making that world better. Well, the world of football. You can't make bricks without straw, and at FC we have some very ambitious building plans.

"They're just like us on a smaller scale" was the response of Manchester United's commercial director Andy Anson to the news of FC's venture into selling merchandise. Now you can read into that little comment all manner of things. Is he being wilfully ignorant about FC? Is he deliberately misrepresenting our motives? Is he just being sneeringly dismissive? Whatever complexion you want to put on his remark, a question remains that deserves a response: does he have a point? Well, both clubs sell replica kit and scarves and DVDs, so, Q.E.D., we must be the same. Yes? Er … no. The commercial operations of the two clubs are a world apart, and not only in scale, but in nature and intention.

At Old Trafford the commercial operation is driven by financial necessity. They have backed themselves into a financial corner in which they must resort to any means available to maximise revenue. They have to service that huge wage bill. They have to satisfy those hedge funds. They have to deliver profits to those mysterious Glazers. Small wonder, then, they have exercised so little taste and restraint over some of the commercial initiatives they have set up in recent years. Initiatives that have nothing to do with football and everything to do with squeezing the last drops of profit out of the fans. Call me an old romantic, if you like, but I still look back fondly to the days when

Money, money, money

a football club didn't need a financial services department. Not any more. Log on to the United web site and you'll find MU Finance eager to sell you mortgages, credit cards, personal loans and insurance – even off-shore bank accounts. I kid you not. We've come a long way from jumpers for goalposts.

It strikes me that the commercial people at Old Trafford have an unshakeable conviction in their ability to persuade the United faithful to shell out their hard-earned cash on over-priced tat. How else do you explain the latest marketing master-stroke? It's the pompously titled … wait for it … Manchester United Opus. This opus is a book. Yes, you know, sheets of paper bound together with pictures and writing on them. And it retails at a giveaway THREE THOUSAND POUNDS. Now that's what you call brand exploitation. Gross exploitation, more like. Of course, it is a limited edition. If you buy one, you will be the proud owner of a prestige item – along with a select band of 9,999 others. And it is signed by Alex Ferguson and Bobby Charlton. That's alright then, I'll take two. In fact, make it three and then at least we've covered Rio's wages for a whole day. Isn't this a perfect example of rampant commercialism: a transparently cynical marketing ploy with no higher purpose than to line the pockets of already rich individuals? Of course, you can argue that no one is forced to buy them, but that's not the point, is it? What's so depressing is that the club are prepared to sell them.

Let me make one thing clear: generating revenue is not bad in itself. Football clubs cannot survive on fresh air and promises. But there's a world of difference between rampant commercialism and valid commercial activity. It's a question of how you go about it and what you intend to spend that revenue on. At FC United we're touchy about commercial activity. We examine our own motives. We have to be wary of becoming too enthusiastic about flogging merchandise. That type of operation acquires a momentum of its own and can become an end itself. Let's be honest, it's human nature to believe that you can never have enough money. The club must avoid the danger of slipping into this mindset. One way it does this is to allow the merchandising operation to be driven by demands from the fans themselves. And believe me, the demand is there. It's our club – we're all joint owners – and we want to plough our money into it. The hardest task for the club is to find things for us to buy. We're proud of our club and we want to advertise our allegiance. I still remember the satisfaction of walking into the office one morning and plonking my new FC United mug on my desk, especially as it was wittily inscribed with "Our club our rules" on one side and "My cup my drink" on the other. Even the coffee tastes better out of it. A strong white coffee with one sugar and just a hint of self-righteousness – you can't whack it. Since then I've bought a home shirt, an away shirt, a red bar scarf, a black bar scarf, a black executive scarf, three t-shirts, three DVDs and God knows what else. I knew giving up my season ticket at Old Trafford would save me a fortune. But that's the difference. When you believe in the things that the money is being spent on, you want to put money into the club.

Our Club Our Rules

New Mills, A, 03/12/05

If it's New Mills away, it must mean a trip to … somewhere a long way from New Mills. The Millers had switched this cup game to the Moss Rose stadium in Macclesfield, which was a shame really because I'd read that their Church Lane ground nestles among verdant Peak District hills. Maybe it was for the best - the sight of all that greenery might have been too much for a crowd of Mancs. We panic if we're more than a hundred yards from a lamp-post. For some reason people seemed to be expecting a reduced turn-out for this match due to a combination of bad weather and Xmas shopping. And maybe due to a little complacency after the recent hammering we'd inflicted on the Millers at Gigg Lane. But this was a sudden-death cup game – anything could happen.

How can I say this without remembering that I am a worthless, feeble, undeserving sinner. I was nearly one of those people who gave it a miss. I nearly allowed the threatening weather and the beginnings of a cold to keep me away from my beloved FC. Forgive me, Margy, for I have sinned – almost. At one-thirty I was ensconced by the fire with a mug of tea trying to convince myself that I felt worse than I did, when I suddenly jumped up like a scalded cat. Three minutes later I was in the car and Macclesfield-bound. This team grabs you by the heart strings, spins you around and won't let you go. "If the Reds should play in Rome or Mandalay (or Macclesfield), I'll be there".

It's almost three o'clock by the time I've negotiated a busy A6, parked up and started to walk to the ground. The sky is a blanket, livid grey and the red brick houses stand out darkly along the road as the rain sheets down. By 'eck, luv, it's grim up north today. But once I'm in the ground, the floodlights beam out crisply and the grass gleams vivid green and the teams dazzle in a pristine red and white. It's a soul-stirring act of colourful defiance. As the rain slants across the floodlights and the shadowy presence of the hills looms over the opposite stand, it's all just so bloody beautiful. Jeez, life is sweet. And one of my favourite bits of Eric comes back to me: "Even the cops on horseback are beautiful".

The colour is matched by the noise as the FC roadshow rollicks along behind the goal to my right, and it's just bliss to watch the football and listen to the singing that echoes resonantly around the ground. For the next ninety minutes Macclesfield is treated to the full repertoire, as a richly varied wall of sound pours from the stand and prickles the hair on the back of my neck.

And the game? Oh yes, the game. It's another superb display from a rampant FC against a plucky New Mills who never at any stage throw in the towel. We have a new winger now, Josh Howard, He was captain of the United youth team that contained Wes Brown, so he's got pedigree, chum. His accomplished technique thrives on the lush turf of the Moss Rose, and he leads the Millers' left back a merry dance. If that's not enough, Steve Torpey

Money, money, money

is having one of those days when he looks several leagues too good for this division, and he helps himself to a hat-trick. The fifth and final goal is one to remember. Not simply because of Josh's precision set-up play, but because it is scored by player-coach Phil Power. Phil is a legend in these parts, and scored a bucketful of goals when he played here for Macc. His grin lit up the grey afternoon.

Credit to New Mills. They kept at it and continued to play football to the very end. What's more, their manager proves gracious in defeat, and it's nice to think that they've made a few quid out of this game. And to think I almost didn't go. So you've got a hangover, a cold, you're clinically depressed. Whatever ails you, FC is the cure.

New Mills 0 FC United 5 (att 1473)
FC scorers: Carden, Torpey(3), Power

Next time you hear the chief executive of one of our top clubs being grilled on the radio about ticket prices, see how long it is before he wheels out the following argument: going to a football match is not really that expensive if you compare it to the cost of going to a pop concert or making a trip to the theatre. Now, that might be true, but I call that a pretty selective comparison and a pretty flawed argument. For a start, I don't go to a pop concert 19 times a season. Maybe I'm just middle-aged. I probably won't go to the theatre 19 times in my life. Maybe I'm just a philistine. So, we're not comparing like for like. A pop concert is a one-off special event. We're lucky to see Madonna re-inventing herself once a year. Did I say lucky? Anyway, you get the point. Why doesn't the chief executive compare going to the match with a more obviously equivalent leisure activity: a night at your local multiplex? Well, that comparison clearly doesn't suit his purpose, not when it costs thirty quid for ninety minutes at your local football ground and a mere six quid chez Warner Bros. Someone might be tempted to add too that you get free parking, a choice of entertainment, comfy padded seats and enough leg room for a normal sized human being. He would tell you, of course, that Warner Bros don't have to pay Rio Ferdinand and company a hundred grand a week. To which I would respond: neither do you, mate. Stop it right now, let the money-addled mercenaries clear off and get some sanity back into our game.

Manchester United have never been the worst offenders when it comes to ticket prices. That honour has always gone to the London clubs. That's one table in which the fans have been pleased to see United enjoying mid-table mediocrity. But even at United there has been an inexorable annual increase in ticket prices at a rate comfortably above inflation. I first managed to secure a season ticket at Old Trafford in 1996, when the huge North Stand went up. I was 'dead chuffed' as we say round here. These were my lettres de noblesse – my promotion into the ranks of Manc aristocracy. I was sure that these two season tickets would become treasured family heirlooms, especially as I

Our Club Our Rules

knew that if I ever gave them up, there were three million people waiting to take my place. And I didn't really resent the fact that as sure as night follows day every season saw an increase of £1 per game. But by the start of the 2005-2006 season they were starting to get cheeky. My season ticket shot up from £513 to £570 – that's an increase of 11% - and for the first time I seriously considered not renewing. Of course, Malcolm Glazer came along and rendered those considerations academic. But it's significant that, even before the Glazers arrived, I was already balancing the ever-increasing cost of going to Old Trafford against the reality of too many dull matches in an almost silent stadium. If I had stayed at Old Trafford, my season ticket this year would have gone up by 16% to £665 or £35 a game, meaning that the cost of my seat has all but doubled in the space of ten years.

How do clubs justify the annual increase in ticket prices? They don't. They don't have to. They are businesses and the market tells them whether their prices are justified or not. Their only intention is to get the best price the market will stand. They will point to full stadiums and tell you that the price is right. There certainly seems to be no shortage of people willing to come on down. Ok, your average crowd is getting older as fewer and fewer youngsters can afford the tickets – no wonder the atmosphere is dying on its feet. Ok, a large section of the community has been priced out of football – it's hard to justify the expense even when you can afford it. Ok, there are growing signs that demand is not unlimited – notice the swathes of empty seats at many domestic cup games. Nevertheless, by any measure you care to apply – attendance figures, total gate receipts, season ticket sales – business is booming. So why would a business accept a lower price for its product than people are willing to pay? It would be business madness and a dereliction of duty in regard to its shareholders. Maybe in regard to its customers, the fans, too. I've heard plenty of fans say that they're happy to keep stumping up as long as the money is going back into the team. Manchester United operates no differently to Marks and Spencer: they offer a top-of-the-range product at top-of-the-range prices. If you can't afford to shop at M&S, there's always Netto down the road. Football's role in fostering social inclusion? Making the people's game accessible to everyone? A football club as a community asset? Nope, we've tried running these ideas through our accounting software and it just won't compute. Just throws up a little box saying: "Are you 'avin a laugh?"

Could a club like United freeze or even reduce ticket prices? Leaving to one side the fact that turning money down is business heresy, could they actually do it if they wanted to? Well, they could use the ever-increasing television bonanza to subsidise ticket prices for the match-going fans. They could, but they never will. In today's football you can never have enough money. You can always find a good use for it – like paying rich young men even more money to kick a ball. And that's the problem. Winning is everything. Once upon a time clubs could accept the cyclical nature of

Money, money, money

success. You had a few good seasons, a few bad seasons and an awful lot of mediocre ones. Now and again you were lucky enough to win a trophy. But it was a bonus, and tasted all the sweeter because it wasn't the norm. In the brave new world of the Premiership that's all changed. The top clubs have a business model predicated on success. They have a new breed of fan who is forking out big money and who expects to see a winning team. When the going gets tough, they'll be the first to get going. That brings it own pressures. Clubs like United have to be in it to win it, and they have to pay what it takes. And what it takes is paying players a hundred grand a week, because if they won't pay it, their rivals will. Even the clubs admit that the situation is unhealthy, and it's not unusual to hear an exasperated chairman talking about ridiculous wage demands. So you'd think that they would welcome an eminently sensible proposal like a salary cap. You're joking. Create a level playing field and give the fans exciting, competitive football? Risk the big four suddenly becoming a big twelve and make it even harder to pick up that vital silverware? You're confusing sport with business. Business hates competition – sport is nothing without it. So the big clubs will keep upping salaries in an attempt to secure an advantage over their rivals and ticket prices will have to keep going up to pay for it.

At FC United we're not a business, just a not-for-profit football club, so we can do things that a business can't. Ironically, we can actually contemplate luxuries that the big clubs cannot afford. We can allow non-business considerations to influence decisions on matters such as ticket pricing. That's not the same as saying we can be financially irresponsible. Every club needs to cover its costs or it won't be around for long, and, with an average home gate of three thousand, FC has costs that other clubs at the same level don't have to face. It costs the club five grand to hire Gigg Lane for a match. Add to that a weekly wage bill of three thousand pounds, and you can see that even a club with good intentions has to be serious about money.

Nevertheless, there is one principle that we choose to apply when setting ticket prices that has nothing to do with prudent housekeeping or business logic. It's the principle of making football accessible to every member of our community: the low-waged, the no-waged, pensioners, students and kids. That's why the club set ticket prices at £7 for adults, £5 for OAPs and students and £2 for under-18s. That's £2 for under-18s when it's not one of those matches where the club lets kids in for free. And where can a family of four get an afternoon's entertainment for less than £20? And there's a gently irony in keeping prices low out of a genuine commitment to principle: it might prove to be good business, as more and more fans are attracted to a club that sees itself as a community asset rather than a private wealth-creation scheme.

Principles cost money, and FC fans know that, and turning down potential sources of income has consequences. All the money that we spend on other things - keeping ticket prices low, involving the community in sporting and educational projects and employing people to run them, setting up youth teams and women's teams, building club facilities – is money that could have been spent on the team instead. But that's the kind of football club that we want to build. So we have to accept the consequences: the team will progress more slowly and we will settle at a level that is consistent with our means and our principles. Of course, a hundred thousand FC fans paying £7 a time should allow us to go an awful long way. The fans have already had a chance to show that they will not sacrifice principle in the pursuit of money and success. At the club's first AGM in March we voted to freeze ticket prices for the coming season. In fact, the club board actually went further than this and decided to reduce the cost of season tickets for under-18s to £1 a match. We also voted not to bring out a new home shirt – it brought back too many memories of what we're trying to get away from. Perhaps the most costly decision was the overwhelming vote in favour of keeping the FC United shirt free of a sponsor's name. Taken together these decisions probably cost us sixty or seventy thousand pounds, but it's a price we're willing to pay. It's not that money doesn't matter. It's that some things matter more. I hope we continue to make decisions that cost us money if that's what it takes to preserve our principles. These decisions might impact on the team, but we have to believe that the definition of success for FC will always go beyond what happens on the football field.

Castleton Gabriels, H, 10/12/05
"We often score six but we seldom score ten". I didn't expect this to be anything more than humorous exaggeration, even against the lesser teams of the NWC Division Two. And they certainly don't come any lesser than Cassy Gabs. Bottom of the table with –3 points. They had managed a single draw so far this season but then had 4 points deducted for fielding an ineligible player. They don't go in for half measures in this league. I suppose Cassy Gabs could have threatened to drag the league committee through the High Court to get the points restored – though being guilty probably weakens their case. Mind you, it didn't stop Alan Sugar forcing a back-down from the FA some years ago. No, Cassy Gabs have taken it on the chin and can now set themselves the target of reaching a positive points tally by the end of the season. Having seen them defend on Saturday, I wouldn't bet your money on them achieving it.

Talking of fining clubs for fielding ineligible players, shouldn't this apply to any Premiership club that picks Robbie Savage? Surely he's ineligible by dint of his complete lack of technical ability, his preoccupation with goading every player more skilful than himself, ie. every player, and his delusion that he deserves to earn millions of pounds playing football, not to mention that bloody hair and that expression of wild-eyed vacancy that always makes me think that there's a village somewhere missing an idiot.

Last home game before Xmas. What would the crowd be? Good-natured

Money, money, money

and tipsy, obviously. No, I mean the size of the crowd. Would we be hit by Xmas shopping duties? Would we be boosted by Big United's traumatic exit from Europe? Plus the fact that United don't play until tomorrow. In the end we got an excellent turnout of 3154. Our home crowd is settling into a figure of 3000 plus, especially for Saturday games.

Drove mum and dad down to the game but we parted company at the ground. Felt like a jig and a sing, so I joined Mark in the MRE and left mum and dad to the more sedate pleasures of the main stand. MRE was full by kick-off and in full festive voice from the off.

Whatever the Cassy Gabs game plan, it probably didn't include conceding after 45 seconds, as the ghost of Scholes past Simon Carden strolled through to fire into the corner. As 1-0 became 6-1 before half-time, I didn't know whether to be pleased or embarrassed. How can you not enjoy a half in which you score 6 goals, some of which (Adie's nonchalant lob, Carden's extravagant scissor-kick, Torpey's mazy dribble) were things of beauty? But there's a part of you that thinks that a proper football match shouldn't have a 6-1 score-line at half-time. At least Cassy Gabs managed a good goal and an even better goal celebration. The scorer ran across the pitch towards the empty South stand, jumped over the hoarding, sat down on a front-row seat and applauded himself. Absolutely brilliant and the MRE showed its appreciation in the only way it knows how by taking the piss: "What the f**king hell was that?"

Cassy Gabs improved in the second half. Well, they only conceded four. The portly Cassy keeper was right in front of the MRE who were at their merciless best. But fair play to him - he kept his sense of humour thru all the chants of "Have you ever seen a salad?" and "fat boy, fat boy, what's the score?" He showed even more class towards the end when Simon Carden went in late and two-footed – a bit unnecessary, I thought, when you're 10-2 up and you've already scored five. Imagine if this had been Wayne Rooney on Jens Lehmann. We'd have had twenty-two players squaring up to each other, two one-eyed managers defending their guilty players, Tarquin from Virginia Water on 606 talking about role models, the Sunday papers loud with outraged indignation and four days of Sky Sports showing the challenge every few minutes while pretending to deplore it. Thank god for non-league football. Never mind over-reaction - the Cassy keeper hardly bothered with any reaction at all. He left that to the number 7 and FC's number 9 Joz Mitten. After a few seconds of vigorous chest-thrusting, both players got sent off. And that was that. The whistle went a few minutes later and everyone walked off pals.

The MRE was even gracious enough to pass on its festive wishes to Cassy Gabs:

Our Club Our Rules

"We wish you a Merry Xmas,
We wish you a Merry Xmas,
We wish you a Merry Xmas,
We're sorry you're shite".

FC United 10 Castleton Gabriels 2 (att 3154)
FC Scorers: Howard, Carden(5), Mitten(2), Torpey, Orr

The words "rampant commercialism" are not the first words that spring to mind when you see Geoff and Dave behind the counter of the FC United megastall outside Gigg Lane on match days. We're not talking five thousand square foot of prime retail space: we're talking twenty square foot of white tarpaulin stretched over a slightly unsteady metal frame. Let's be honest, it's a tent with a counter. But the fans love it judging by the patient, good-natured scrum of people that surround it before and after the match. I remember its first appearance, mainly because I helped to erect it. It was at the Blackpool Mechanics game in September, and originally it only sold scarves, badges, programmes and baseball caps. It was another three months before you could buy a replica home shirt, The range has gradually increased since then and you can now get away shirts, executive scarves, t-shirts and DVDs, Still a modest selection of items and all football-related.

Merchandising at FC is driven by the fans. They request something and our over-worked merchandising team tries to satisfy that request. Occasionally the team will use the fans' forum to canvass interest in a new piece of merchandise. At Christmas they mooted the idea of a mid-season highlights DVD, and got trampled in the rush. Sometimes the suggestions come from the fans themselves. The FC supporters' branches approached the club about producing a range of polo shirts in different colours with each colour representing a particular branch. This gave those rough lads from Salford the chance to show their mastery of post-modern irony by choosing pink: "Salford lads, we are here. We wear pink, but we're not queer" as they've sung ever since.

Of course, the megastall acts like a magnet for all the kids that come to FC. It's hard to find a youngster at FC who's not swaddled in a bar scarf and kitted out in an FC shirt. But the real surprise is the number of grown men that you see in bar scarves and replica tops. Exactly the same guys who treated the megastore at Old Trafford like the Chernobyl exclusion zone. Funny what love does to people.

Xmas Party

I had no idea what this would be like. And how do you dress for it? Smart? Smart casual? FC-fan-been-on-the-booze-since-lunchtime dishevelled? God knows. Erred on the side of dapper. I had persuaded my better half Shelagh and mum and dad to be a part of this historic first FC Xmas party and at a fiver a ticket, you couldn't really lose. So it was down to the Barnes Wallis restaurant at Umist in central Manchester that we trekked, not knowing what to expect.

Big room with rows of largely empty tables when we first arrived with most people hanging round by the bar – very FC. If the crowd numbered in dozens at first, it had swollen to hundreds within an hour as people arrived in a steady flow, many clearly having come straight from the game via a few pubs. The 'do' soon resembled a slightly disorganised wedding reception as young kids in FC shirts ran about the room. I kept looking towards the entrance like a star-struck kid as I waited for the players to arrive. Is this strange behaviour in a supposedly intelligent and mature (ho-ho) man of 46? Mum tells people that I'll never grow up. Not sure she means this as a compliment, but that's the way I take it. Players do arrive and there's a buzz of excitement as I hear that Torpey is in da house. That buzz might only be in my ears, but I don't care. Eventually other players can be seen mingling at the bar: Simon Carden, Darren Lyons, Joz Mitten, Tony Coyne, Paul Mitten, Rob Nugent. And not a minder in sight. Manager Karl Marginson and Mr FC Andy Walsh have been here from the start.

Andy decides to impose a bit of shape on proceedings by leading Karl and the players to a raised dais in the middle of the room for a question and answer session. It would have been the highlight of the evening ... if the microphones had worked. A player would get two words into an answer before the mic cut out. Cue spontaneous shouts of "Sack the board" from the crowd. To everyone's disappointment, the exercise had to be abandoned after twenty minutes when attempts to fix the mic and efforts to speak loudly without one proved unsuccessful. There was still time for the following exchange:

Q: Where do you hope FC will be in five years' time?
Margy: Five leagues higher.
Q: Yeah, but where do you think we'll be in five years' time?
Margy: Five leagues higher.

Deadpan delivery. Goes down a storm. I love Margy's lack of dreamy impracticality. The hard-headed, not-carried-away shrewdness. I just have a slight concern that the expectation of continual success could turn us into the thing we're fighting against. Can't the problems with the Premiership be put down to an unhealthy emphasis on success to the detriment of sporting values? I'm going to have to take these feelings away and think them thru. But at the Xmas party I just decide to go to the bar for more drinks.

What's wrong with sponsorship? Absolutely nothing. Can you think of a better way to redistribute the surplus funds of private enterprise than by investing them in a community asset such as a football club? Isn't it better to have that money working for FC United rather than sitting in a company's bank account? I have no problem with sponsorship and neither does the club.

Our Club Our Rules

On the right terms. And NEVER on the club shirt.

Each sponsorship opportunity must be judged on its own merits. If the price of that sponsorship is too high, we must be prepared to turn it down. In years to come I don't want to see FC running out at the FC United Carphone Warehouse Stadium. Stadium naming rights seem to be the latest commercial asset exploited by various clubs – think of the Cellnet Stadium, the Reebok Stadium or, the best yet, the indescribably ugly Friends Provident St Mary's Stadium. These sponsorship agreements make perfect financial sense – new stadiums cost money – but they grate on our football sensibilities. It may be a cliché – though it's no less true for that – but for many fans football is religion and the stadium is a solemn place of worship. We don't want a sponsor's name defining where we play. Would church-goers like to attend the Burger King Westminster Abbey? We can stick to this principle if we are prepared to accept the consequences: we might have to wait longer and build smaller.

It's not a case of political correctness gone mad to pursue an ethical policy on sponsorship. It's simply consistent with the ideals that lay behind the creation of the club. We walked away from Manchester United because we could no longer stomach the money madness that has taken over top-level football, so we cannot now allow money to become our master. We can and must be fussy about where our money comes from. We have to be principled in our choice of sponsors. Multinationals with sweatshops in the third world need not apply. There is absolutely no reason why a choice of sponsorship should not be an added source of pride for a club. It's no accident that FC United's main sponsor in its first season has been the Bhopal Medical Appeal that seeks justice and compensation for thousands of Indians poisoned by the Union Carbide chemical disaster over twenty years ago. Powerless individuals being screwed over by American big business? Sound familiar?

The sponsorship mix at FC United reflects a desire to maintain the club's freedom of action and to avoid dependence on a single major sponsor. The club has a number of small sponsors. This is a sensible basis on which to proceed, as the club will not be plunged into a financial crisis, if a sponsor withdraws. As befits a community club, most of the sponsors are local businesses: software houses, solicitors, engineering companies. The solicitors are actually named Glaiysers – thank God the spelling is different. They are all members of the cryptically named 127 Club. This figure is not a reference to the number of years until Manchester City next win a trophy, but the number of years between the formation of Newton Heath in 1878 and the formation of FC United in 2005.

So the right kind of sponsorship is to be welcomed, and the club is happy to see it – in the programme, on the web site, even on pitchside hoardings when we get a stadium of our own. But never ever on that pristine shirt.

Money, money, money

Holker Old Boys, A, 17/12/05

Another game with a team plucked from the pages of the Victor. How colourless the names of teams higher up the league sound in comparison. I could see the headlines now if we lost: FC roasted on the HOB. Just a pity I couldn't see the match. It was that one Saturday in four when work commitments prevent me from going to the game. Nothing to do with the fact that this was our longest away trip of the season – 85 miles into the heart of darkest Cumberland. In fact, I fancied a trip off the beaten track to a mysterious backwater. Never mind. I'd have to wait for Flixton on Boxing day.

The game was played at Craven Park, home of the Barrow rugby league team, and the rugby posts were left in place and loomed over the newly-installed football nets. You don't see that on Sky. It appears that it was a tough game that we edged in the second half with goals from the prolific Simon Carden and one from Adie Orr. Heading into the tough winter months and no sign of the wheels coming off the FC bandwagon. No sign either of the fans beginning to flag, as over a thousand made the long trip to Barrow and were commended for their behaviour by the local police chief. Talk about the age of wonder and miracles.

Holker Old Boys 0 FC United 2 (att 2303)
FC Scorers: Carden, Orr

It's going to be a quiz question in years to come: what do Barcelona and FC United have in common? Ronaldinho played for both? Both are fans' clubs with over a hundred thousand members? No, the right answer will be: neither club has permitted a sponsor's name to appear on their shirt. Neither club succumbed to the temptation to trade on their iconic status and sully their pristine shirts with a garish logo.

What's so terrible about shirt sponsorship? Nothing at all. It is an entirely valid and sensible way to generate income for a team. In fact, it's the only lucrative way of generating income for most teams. For most teams the shirt they play in is the only valuable advertising space they have. Even at the lowliest level shirt sponsorship is the norm. Nip down to your local park this weekend and you'll see "Taylor's Skip Hire" emblazoned across the chest of Cedar Hill Under-11s. So why did the fans of FC United formally vote at the club's AGM to reject shirt sponsorship? Was it just a gimmick to attract publicity and secure the moral high ground? Was it just an example of gesture politics and points-scoring at the expense of the Premiership fat cats who seem to believe that everything is for sale? Was it just us in an act of bloody-minded Manc perversity cutting off our nose to spite our face just to make a point? It was none of these things. It was a clear-headed and conscious decision to use the issue of shirt sponsorship to make a very public statement of FC's guiding principle: some things matter more than money. The club is using the highly visible symbolism of a sponsor-free shirt to send out the message that commercial considerations will never over-ride the duty that FC United owes to football, its fans and its community. We know that taking this stance will cost us money, but it's a price we're willing to pay. The intention is to allow a vote on the issue of shirt sponsorship at every AGM, so in theory the policy could change. But I have every confidence that fans will continue to believe that this is a principle worth paying for. But what if in the future we find ourselves in desperate need of cash? The short answer is – we won't. This club will live within its means and within its principles, and we have to have enough character to accept the consequences of that: slower progress up the leagues. For FC United there will always be more to success than just winning football matches.

Flixton, A, 26/12/05
   Talk about Bleak House. Try Valley Road, Flixton, in the grim mid-winter, if you want to sample football at its unloveliest. I've been reading Bleak House for about a month now – it's a big book and I'm a slow reader – and I half expected to find Krook, trooper George and little Jo stood next to me under the bus-stop at Flixton. The bus-stop is the quaint shed-like stand about 8 feet deep that runs along one side of the pitch. It earned its name when FC played there in a pre-season friendly. This being a traditional grey English Xmas, the pitch was wet and spongy and tricky under foot, but predominantly green and free of frost. For me there's something about football that is forever tied to the idea of defiance in the face of grim reality – an assertion of energy and colour and skill, a celebration of the human spirit, in spite of drab surroundings and dismal weather. And that's we got at Flixton. Apart from the skill.
   After a couple of pints in the Greyhound, we set off into the drizzle in search of the ground. There were four of us today: myself, Paul, Mark and his father-in-law Derek, attending his first FC game. Valley Road is tucked away at the back of a housing estate and, as you approach the ground, you find yourself funnelled towards a single turn-style. So we stood under a grey sky queuing to get in, happy to stand in line with our fellow FC fans. This is FC, one member one vote, everyone together and everyone equal in importance. Unless your mate Paul knows one of the bouncers who's stood on the clubhouse balcony above you guarding the entrance to the hospitality suite. I didn't want to do it, but before I knew it, we're nipping up the clubhouse steps and into the hospitality suite, past a number of tables packed with guests and straight to the bar for another pint before the match. Funny how that pint had a bitter taste of prawns. I offer no excuses and promise to say 10 Hail Margy's as a penance. In our defence we turned down the offer to watch the match from the balcony – best view in the house and access to the bar at half-time – and piled downstairs to join the great unwashed under the bus-stop.
   Maybe we should have stayed in the bar. The game was an ugly affair and

Money, money, money

perhaps the conditions prevented either side from playing fluent football. FC were lucky to go in at half-time 1-0 up thanks to an Adie Orr swivel and shot on the quarter hour. I kept telling myself that you have to have grey days in Flixton in December to earn the right to sun-kissed Saturdays at Gigg Lane in April. Didn't I say that at Stafford? Watch out for that phrase – you might hear it again. There was more entertainment off the pitch. The bus-stop stand backs on to a row of houses and some poor lady was spotted at three-thirty in the afternoon shutting the curtains in her dressing-gown. Well, it is Boxing Day. Cue shouts of "We can see you in your jimjams". This was one of very few songs from the bus-stop boys on the day in one of our weaker singing performances. Blame it on the lack of acoustics, blame it on Xmas, blame it on the game, blame it on the boogie. Who knows.

The second half saw Flixton take control and deservedly equalise, though the scorer was apparently yards offside. You never get decisions at Flixton! But they hit the post and spurned other chances to win, so we came away with a fortunate point. They're a good side and obviously high in the table on merit. Not many sides will come to Flixton and take a point, I told the guys, delving into the Encyclopaedia of Football Cliche that I'd just received for Xmas.

Flixton 1 FC United 1 (att 2050)
FC Scorers: Orr

I know we all quote the bible to our own ends. I just wish we'd get it right, when we do. The bible doesn't say: "Money is the root of all evil". It doesn't say it, because that would be plain stupid. There was nothing evil about the millions of pounds donated to help the victims of the tsunami, was there? Money is morally neutral. It's like intelligence or energy or imagination. It's what you do with it that counts. What the bible actually says is: "Love of money is the root of all evil". The love of money, an obsession with money, the elevation of money and its accumulation above all other things. Remind anyone of top-level football? What else other than an obsession with money makes multi-millionaire footballers insist on a three hundred grand fee for the honour of representing their country in the World Cup?

Love of money will never be the guiding principle at FC United. There are too many other things that we love more: the game, the friendship, the craic. As forum regular and unofficial FC philosopher Herbert-Prefabs puts it: FC is about "making friends not millionaires". Yes, we're prepared to sell merchandise and we're prepared to accept sponsorship, but we're also prepared to say no. No to any commercial propositions that undermine our principles. Mind you, I've just had a belter. What about a range of Steve Torpey thongs? All signed by the thongmeister himself. All very tasteful, of course, and in a range of different styles. Something plain and inexpensive for everyday wear, and something a little fancier for those two weeks spent soaking up the sun lying on the beach in Fuengirola – a sort of thong for Europe! I think it's a winner.

TV or not TV

January 2006
TV or not TV

You can learn a lot about football fans by just listening to the songs they sing, especially when the lyrical content of those songs dates back all of twelve months. You can learn a lot about FC fans by standing in the Manchester Road End and listening to the ever-growing repertoire of freshly-penned ditties that roll off the FC production line. You'd learn about our general qualities: that FC are inventive, ingenious, cruel, funny, self-mocking and plain barmy. You'd also learn about our specific hatreds: City, Rio, Glazer and, last but far from least, Sky. By listening to the songs, you'd learn that we "won't pay Glazer" or "work for Sky", that we look forward to a future in which "there'll be no jester hats or Sky TV" and in which the team we support runs out at three o'clock on a Saturday "because we don't work for Sky Sports any more". What's more, if we had our way, it would be a future in which we'd "destroy Glazer and Sky". Can you see a pattern developing? That looks to me like a pathological obsession with Sky, a gut instinct, a knee-jerk reaction hard-coded into the FC United DNA that has its origins at a level a long way below rational analysis. We have a problem with Sky. In fact, we think everyone has a problem with Sky, seeing them as the root cause of many of the problems that forced us eventually to turn our backs on top-level football. And just maybe we haven't forgiven Rupert Murdoch for his failed attempt to buy United in 96. But, call me an anal crosser of t's and dotter of i's who needs to pin everything down with cast-iron reasons, but I can't rely on gut instincts alone. I want to probe beneath this instinctive aversion to Sky to the thinking that lies behind it. Is our animosity well-founded or is Sky just the nearest convenient scapegoat? I think it's vital that we address this question, if for no other reason than that the whole issue of Sky TV is tying so many FC fans into knots of principle that are clearly at odds with their habits and wishes.

I realise that schizophrenia is the natural condition of your average FC fan, but rarely have we been so confused as in our feelings towards television in general and Sky in particular. The fans who sing anti-Sky songs during the

- 101 -

Our Club Our Rules

match are still happy to catch Big United on Sky in the pub before the game, and I bet a large proportion of FC fans still settle down at four o'clock on a Sunday afternoon to watch the big game of the weekend on, yes, you've guessed it, Sky. Not all, of course. There are a number of FC fans who have rigorously followed through the logic of what they see as the terrible effects of Sky on football and who have binned their Sky subscription. I certainly did. For all of six weeks. Then the cold turkey became too much. I admitted to myself that I was a hopeless, weak-willed sports addict that needed his televisual fix and took out a new subscription.

Inevitably, the morality of keeping your Sky subscription formed the subject of an early forum debate. It was interesting to read the reasons people gave for not giving it up: I'd miss the Super League; I'd miss the cricket; I'd miss La Liga; I couldn't take the football away from my little lad. Some people even used the 'pointless gesture' argument: what difference will it make if I give up Sky, I'm only one out of five million. Whatever reasons people gave, it was hard not to visualise them shifting uneasily in their chair as they tapped on the keyboard and tried not to admit that the real reason for keeping Sky was … they wanted to. And isn't that reason as valid as any other? Do we have to beat ourselves up as hopeless hypocrites because we continue to watch football on Sky? Is there no possible accommodation between the principles of FC United and Sky TV?

Let's talk practicalities for a moment. Sky is not football's biggest problem: its biggest problem – and its greatest strength - is its popularity. We're all addicted to this wonderful game. There is some irresistible magic intrinsic to a round ball, a set of goals and a patch of green that has made the game a global obsession. Sky did not create that popularity: they have simply ridden the wave of football's post –Italia 90 revival. I blame it on Gazza's tears, Fever Pitch and the ebbing tide of hooliganism. All of a sudden everyone was in love again with the beautiful game. All Sky did was put football and satellite technology together to create the powerful multi-million pound television phenomenon we see today. If it hadn't been Sky, it would have been someone else. Whether you think that the union of football and television is a marriage made in heaven or an unholy alliance, it is here to stay. Divorce is not an option. For one very good and perfectly valid reason: we don't want it to be. The reality is that we all love watching football on the box. The question is: can FC United accommodate itself to that reality?

Maybe this seems a ridiculously pompous and premature argument for a non-league club ten divisions below the Premiership and one that barely registers on Sky's radar. I wish it was – it would give us longer to iron out our contradictions – but it's not. The need to determine our position in regard to Sky could be upon us more quickly than we think. At the club AGM in March the board had to put the issue of FC's participation in the FA Vase to a vote. Apparently Sky have the rights to these matches too. They probably have the rights to my Friday lunchtime kick-about with the lads at work. Of

TV or not TV

course, they rarely exercise their right to show FA Vase matches, but they might be tempted to make an exception for FC United. Well, if I was a Sky executive, I might be tempted to fill a quiet night in the schedules next season with a live screening of FC's debut in the FA Vase. So the AGM came up with a clear and resolute … compromise. We would enter the Vase but leave open the issue of what we would do if Sky decided to televise one of our games. We were simply postponing the debate to another day. It was probably a wise decision: the instinctive aversion to Sky among FC fans would have made a rational debate impossible. It would have been fierce and passionate and, without doubt, inconclusive. The simple truth is that as a club we really haven't worked out how we feel about this issue or how we square the desire to see FC United grow and progress with the inescapable fact of Sky's involvement with football.

The principle we adopt concerning our relationship to Sky will have a fundamental effect on where the club goes, if anywhere. There are FC fans who take their rejection of Sky to its logical extreme and who would prefer to see FC forego entry to a cup or a league that might require our games to be shown on Sky. Now, Sky regularly televise National Conference games, so in effect what this hard-line stance is implying is that we should be happy to remain on the lower rungs of the football ladder, safely beyond the interested gaze of Sky executives. It's an absolutely consistent and rigorous viewpoint, but I don't think it would have the approval of the manager, the players and the majority of the fans. Playing football is about the pursuit of excellence. You strive to be successful. I think many FC fans have starry-eyed dreams of a future in which FC United are established as a football league club. If that's what we want, we will have to find a way to co-exist with Sky TV. Can we reconcile our feelings about Sky with our ambitions for our club? I find myself coming back to the same questions. Is Sky all bad? Is Sky to blame for all the ills of the modern game? And, if it isn't, who is?

Winsford United, H, 02/01/06

Sometimes everything just comes together. It's rare. Usually life doesn't lend itself to the clichéd perfection that you get in films. You know how it goes . It's a gorgeous spring morning, you have a few laughs and a few pints in the pub, stroll happily to the match, sit basking in sunshine feeling at one with the universe and watch your team … lose 1-0 to the bottom of the table. Pessimists can be a pain in the arse, but they're usually right. Well not today.

This was a Bank Holiday, this was Winsford, this was a top of the table clash. We were 11 points clear at the top but second-placed Winsford had 3 games in hand. What's more, they had really pushed us hard in the 2-2 draw at their place. Well, at Northwich Victoria's place, to be precise. We had managed to persuade several mates to attend their first FC match, so we had a magnificent seven meeting up in Wetherspoons in the centre of Bury before the game. None of the three lads attending for the first time were United fans,

Our Club Our Rules

so they had no reason to feel pre-disposed in favour of FC, though that's a pretty naïve assumption anyway. There's a few United fans out there who see FC fans as splitters or 'Judas scum' as they so charmingly put it. Still, it would be great to see if these neutral observers enjoyed the FC experience. There had been excited speculation on the forum in the lead-up to the game about the size of the crowd we might get, but ,as I looked around the pub, it seemed to me that it was quieter than normal. You try not to play the numbers game, but, hand on heart, you want to see proof that the message is spreading.

A taxi dropped us by the ground and it was soon apparent why the pub had been surprisingly quiet. Everyone had been queuing up at Gigg Lane. It looked a bit like that scene in the Killing Fields when the Americans are abandoning Hanoi. Except here everyone was trying to get in. This was the bumper crowd that we'd all been hoping for. The MRE was already showing 'house full' signs and people were now forming huge queues for the Main Stand. The next thing we know, we are being herded en masse to the turnstiles at the Cemetery End, the end opposite the MRE that is usually occupied by FC United flags and six loners. Not today. Today the Cemmy End would be almost full, and for the first time three sides of Gigg Lane would be heavily populated. A milestone day. We get in late. Many of our games have been delayed by 15 minutes in order to allow larger than expected crowds to enter the ground, and on the day we set a club record of 4328, the game kicks off promptly at 3 o'clock.

The ground is rocking on three sides, or so I'm told later by mum and dad who are sitting quietly in the middle of the main stand. In the Cemmy End we can only hear ourselves. Amazing the liberating effect alcohol has on your inhibitions and your vocal chords. It's always risky starting off a song. Always the fear that you'll belt out the first line at the top of your voice, come down a few notches on the second line as you begin to suspect that no-one is joining in, before mumbling to a standstill in line three. No such fears this time. Each time the Cemmy End had a few seconds' lull, I launched into an FC anthem: I don't care about Rio, When FC United run out to play, My eyes have seen the glory, etc And my solo immediately became a quartet and the quartet immediately became a massed choir. The Cemmy End was rocking.

It was a picture-perfect football day: dark sky, cold air, a hint of mist, the bright blur of the floodlights, the red and blue shirts, the black-green pitch. It was a script-perfect football match. Tense opening half in which Winsford and FC battled it out in midfield and both sides got forward to create chances. FC were giving a debut to Leon Mike at centre-forward. He could be the next big thing in football. And I mean big. Looked more like a tight end in American football, and was soon to be christened The Fridge by the fans. Some big men are deceptively quick and mobile. Not Leon, though. But

TV or not TV

give the lad a chance – he had, reportedly, scored goals in the Scottish Premier Division only a couple of seasons ago.

I knew something had to spoil a perfect day. And it did ten minutes into the second half when Winsford made one of their infrequent attacks and profited from a rare mistake from keeper Barry George to put themselves ahead. The whole Winsford team went berserk in front of us like a syndicate that had just won twenty million in a lottery roll-over. Calm, reasonable Paul turned to me and said: "Fair play to them. They've come here to win". Actually, he might have said: "I really hope we stuff these bastards now". I hoped so too, but was inwardly reminding myself that disappointment is good for the soul. Hadn't Winsford read the script? They were extras in our film, supposed to turn up and fight pluckily before losing gallantly.

We had less than ten minutes staring into the abyss, before Simon Carden pulled us level, after good work by … Leon Mike. Said he was a good player. Cue first rendition of the new Simon Carden song – to the tune of Octopus's Garden:

"I'd like to be,
Watching FC,
With goals from Simon Carden if he plays,
He'll knock them in,
FC'll win,
With goals from Simon Carden if he plays"

I was prepared to accept a draw - Winsford were worthy opponents. Well, apart from their habit of staying down after tackles that looked suspiciously like time-wasting. I couldn't resist a "Same old Winsford, always cheating". Everyone else preferred "Same old scousers, always cheating", though no elastic geography known to man can turn the Cheshire town of Winsford into a district of Liverpool. You know what we're like: if Scousers didn't exist, we'd have to invent them.

Leon Mike finally made way for crowd favourite Rory Patterson. Mind you, all three subs could have occupied the space left by Leon. It's too corny to imagine theatrical, flamboyant, crowd-pleaser Rory coming on to blast home the winner, isn't it? Well, you can never have too much corn. With five minutes to go, a poor kick by the keeper was turned into Rory's path. He took it in his stride before smashing the ball past the hapless keeper. Rory, in contrast, had all the hap in the world, leaping into the MRE to join the fans in mad, mind-blown, orgasmic celebration. Found out later that he nearly landed on two young kids. It's a four foot drop on to concrete too, so don't try this at home. We couldn't see the celebration from the far end and, anyway, we were too busy jumping up and down and hugging complete strangers. Spent the last five minutes in a state of greater anxiety than I have ever known at Old Trafford. Even resorted to shouts of "Defend, defend, defend" and "4-5-1, 4-5-1".

Our Club Our Rules

Filed out of the ground convinced that God is an FC fan. This was a landmark day. In years to come grizzled old men will gather for a pint and talk in misty-eyed fashion about that Winsford match. Probably grizzled old women too. Never mind grizzled, the theme for the rest of the evening was sozzled. Wandered from the Waterloo to the Swan and Cemetery to the Pack Horse chasing the buzz. Propped ourselves against the bar in the Waterloo and had a singing contest with the Middleton and Salford supporters groups in the main room. "The main room sing, we don't know why, coz after the pub, they're gonna die", "We are the barside, we're louder than you". To which they reply: "You've only got two singers" which was true. There are some days that you want to put your hands around and hold on to, to physically hold back the passage of time. But sic transit Gloria Hunniford. Ah well, we'll always have Winsford, darling.

FC United 2 Winsford United 1 (att 4328)
FC Scorers: Carden, Patterson

Reasons to be cheerful, part 1

If you're old enough, you'll remember the days when the only live domestic football match on television was the FA Cup final. I remember watching every final no matter how dire – and, believe me, Leeds against Arsenal in 72 was dire - desperate for extra time because it meant another thirty minutes of football. Apart from this annual treat, we had to feed our football habit with an hour-long highlights programme each week on BBC and ITV. And the original Match of the Day wasn't the comprehensive goal-fest it is nowadays. You were offered highlights of a single game, and if the programme director was particularly unfortunate in his choice of match, you could find yourself watching Coventry and Derby playing out a riveting nil-nil draw. Of course, this was long before satellite technology and multi-channel environments, and football had to fight for its slot in the schedules alongside sitcoms and costume dramas, and the BBC and ITV had to cater to all tastes. So there were perfectly good reasons for the restricted amount of football on telly. Nevertheless, I always felt that the BBC had an ambivalent attitude to football. Maybe it was simply because football was a working class game and the Beeb was run by middle-class Oxbridge types. That probably explains why we were more likely to switch on and find ourselves watching show-jumping from Hickstead or three-day eventing from Badminton or that non-start kick-fest from Twickers rather than football. Then came Sky, a brash Aussie upstart, free of the Beeb's middle-class snobbery, uninterested in the civilising mission of television, and keen to give us what we wanted. And what we wanted was football.

Surely no one can deny that Sky was the first television station to treat football with the importance it deserves. Suddenly a ninety-minute match was wrapped in a three-hour programme with generous allocations of time to pre- and post-match analysis and interviews. Suddenly there was a

TV or not TV

dependable supply of matches, one or two top-flight games a week and, in fairness, after a brief flirtation with fireworks and cheer-leaders, their coverage settled down into a relatively gimmick-free presentation. Let's credit Sky with realising that football was worth taking seriously, that it was valid to spend time analysing the mechanics of the game, the team selections, the tactics, the good attacking or the bad defending. Let's be clear: before Andy Gray's Boot Room no football presenter had considered the technical aspects of the game worthy of discussion. Of course, this has opened up a Pandora's box and we now have to listen to the bloke at work who never goes to a match talking about holding midfielders, playing in the hole and teams keeping their shape. Despite that, there's no denying that Sky's blanket coverage of football is a true reflection of our own obsession with the game.

Sky have raised the bar when it comes to football coverage and other channels have had to raise their game to keep up. They have tried innovative formats that really shouldn't work but which clearly do. Sky Soccer Saturday features a presenter with a quartet of ex-players watching football matches on TV monitors. We're tuning in to watch people watch football on telly. It shouldn't work – four ex-players describing the action that we are not allowed to see, sharing in-jokes and general banter, while the ever witty Geoff Stelling reads out the scores as they come in and winds up the panel. It's entertaining and it works. You know it works because, after decades providing football scores on a glorified type-writer, the BBC have copied Sky and introduced their own cut-down version of Sky Soccer Saturday. Sky have also tried other unpromising formats that have proved to be surprisingly successful. The idea of bringing in four journalists and to sit them around a table to discuss football matters sounds like a great idea ... for radio. But it was a winner on TV too. Well, in my house anyway. We started off with the dark, minimalist set of Hold The Back Page and we've now progressed to the sunny pine-clad setting of Jimmy Hill's kitchen. Whatever the setting, it's a talking-shop for football journalists and it shouldn't work, but it does.

Reasons to be cheerful: part 2

You cannot discuss the impact of Sky on football without mentioning money, and you cannot mention money without immediately acknowledging all the unfortunate consequences that money has had for the game in terms of greed and corruption and the drip-drip erosion of people's commitment to sporting values. But we'll come back to that later. Has there been no concrete benefit to football from a fan's perspective from the Sky millions? Have the people who run football squandered this historic opportunity by using the vast majority of the Sky windfall on personal wealth creation schemes? Yes, in a word, but let's try and point to something positive that has been done with this money. Some of the Sky millions have been spent on improving spectator facilities. The crumbling grounds of the late eighties have been replaced by shiny if bland new stadia, and the third-world toilet facilities of yesteryear have become the stuff of a perverse nostalgia. I quite like peeing in a toilet where the floor is not sticky with urine, where there's loo paper in the cubicle and where you can wash and dry, yes, dry your hands. I call that progress. Of course, not every modernising initiative feels like progress. I don't call it progress when clubs rip the heart out of the ground by removing the terraces and force us to sit in all-seater stadia devoid of colour and atmosphere. But you can't pin this one on Sky. The clubs were moving in that direction already. Blame the cynical marketing strategies of the big clubs. Or, here's one for you, blame the hooliganism of the 70s and 80s, the memory of which still causes the clubs to recoil in horror at the thought of bringing back terracing. There is a compromise solution, of course, that the Sky millions could be usefully spent on. They could be used to install the high-tech safe standing sections that have been successfully introduced in Germany. The clubs could fit in more spectators, friends could stand together and we might actually bring back something resembling atmosphere to matches in England.

Reasons to be cheerful: part 3

Twenty years ago a foreign player in the English league was as rare as a measured and perceptive piece of punditry from Ian Wright. Thyssen and Muhren at Ipswich, Villa and Ardiles at Tottenham and Mirandinha at Newcastle were exotic exceptions. Nowadays things have turned full circle and the media is full of agonised debates about the prospects for the national team when Arsenal are fielding sides bereft of English players. The prevailing wisdom, however, is that the influx of foreign stars has added a new and fascinating dimension to our football. They have brought elegance, intelligence and technical ability to a game that was perhaps too reliant on athleticism, spirit and character. If we accept that the contribution of these foreign stars has allowed us to watch a quality of football that we rarely saw before, then we have to acknowledge that it is the millions pumped into football by Sky that has made it possible to attract and retain these players. Of course, Italian class and French polish usually come at a price, and is it just coincidental that the incidence of diving, feigning injury and waving imaginary yellow cards has increased in recent years? Or maybe it's just a consequence of the obscene amounts of money in the game and the win-at-all-costs philosophy that goes with it. In the final analysis it's hard to argue with the judgement that the presence of Cantona, Zola, Henry and Bergkamp has enhanced our game and given us some priceless memories. And it's the Sky millions that attracted them - not the prospect of a cooked breakfast or a pint of real ale.

Reasons to be cheerful: part 4

Do you remember when the only technical wizardry on display for football matches was the slow motion replay? What a fantastic innovation it was. But

TV or not TV

it did seem that, after inventing slow motion, someone somewhere decided that football coverage had reached the pinnacle of technical perfection and that there was nowhere else to go. Well, Sky have tried hard over the years to prove to us that that's not the case. From Andy Gray's magic pen that circles players and shoots off in all directions like a hail of arrows to his tactics board that has buttons moving simultaneously to illustrate player positions as a move unfolds, there have been a number of innovations that have come in to stay or that have faded as gimmicks. You can now watch a match on Sky with a bewildering range of interactive functions: you can get match stats, replay the incidents you've missed, watch players spitting and scratching their privates on Playercam, and listen to two guys shouting incoherent nonsense in Fanzone. Yes, maybe Playercam and Fanzone are an innovation too far. Nevertheless, whether a new idea proves to be a valuable addition or a pointless gimmick, it's clear that Sky has a commitment to technical innovation and that they have shaken the established channels out of their complacency. Even the BBC have experimented with some worthwhile innovations, such as the little chequered flag that appears in the corner of the screen when a linesman flags for offside. It's hardly a major technological breakthrough but it adds to the pleasure of watching the game, and you suspect that it would not have happened without the need to match the pace of Sky's technical innovation.

Reasons to be cheerful: part 5.
Er, no, that's it. I'm struggling now.

Darwen, H, 7/01/06

"Darwen sing, we don't why, cos evolution passed them by" and don't try telling the MRE that it's Charles Darwin with an i. To be honest, this was after the lord mayor's parade and was simply an honest, competitive, no-nonsense game of football that resulted in a hard-fought win. Like many sides who visit Gigg, the Darwen lads came to battle and not to be extras in the FC United show. This was typified by the ageing pocket battleship in midfield Gordon Moore, the archetypal grizzled old pro (nothing to do with Wayne Rooney) who just keeps going because he loves playing. Some midfielders are tall, elegant strollers. This lad wasn't. One of the few players who'd struggle to look Paul Scholes in the eye, but what a gritty competitor. A bit too gritty at one point in the second half when a frustrated lunge caused knee ligament damage to goal machine Simon Carden. But, as Isaac Newton said (and he knew his football), for every action there is a corresponding and equal reaction, and player-coach Phil Power came on with ten minutes to go and exacted retribution. But credit to the Darwen lad. He jumped up, gave a wry smile and was shaking hands at the final whistle. Love football at this level.

Our Club Our Rules

The game was adorned by one of the goals of the season from Josh Howard. This is our right winger who once captained the United youth team that contained the likes of Wes Brown. To be honest, he's slumming it at this level. Touch, pace, passing, vision: he's the full package. If his strike had taken place in the Prem, Sky would have been showing it on the hour every hour for the next week. The Darwen keeper chased a long ball out of his area and down towards his left corner flag. Adie Orr raced over the turf to close him down, causing the keeper to scuff his clearance along the ground forty yards up the touchline. It went straight to Howard who kept it in play by flicking it inside with his right foot. As a defender closed him down, he transferred his weight from right to left and curled his left foot around the ball lofting it high towards goal. With the angle he must have been forty-five yards out. As Darwen defenders and keeper ran helplessly back towards goal, the ball described an elegant curve before dipping perfectly under the crossbar and bulging the back of the net. Look on ye mortals and wonder.

Less tension, less madness and less booze than against Winsford but nonetheless another fine match and another hard-earned win. Less people too, but still an excellent 3,371 in attendance. I passed an alcohol-free afternoon sitting with mum and dad in the main stand. The clear head allowed me to notice that there were a greater than usual number of TV cameras at the game. Apparently, Granada and Sky were there. Are they beginning to realise that FC is here to stay? I wonder if Sky filmed the MRE singing "When FC United run out to play, it's 3 o'clock on a Saturday, cos we don't work for Sky Sports anymore"?

FC United 2 Darwen 0 (att 3371)
FC Scorers: Howard, Carden

Reasons to be tearful: part 1

They were made for each other, the Premiership and Sky – the solution to each other's problems. By 1992 Sky had a new technology that promised huge rewards, but, a bit like 3G phone technology today, it looked like a delivery system with nothing to deliver. The chairmen of the big football clubs had a massively popular game but no obvious means of exploiting that popularity. Put the two together and everyone's a winner, apart from the seventy-two football league clubs that the big boys dropped as dead weights when they decided to form the Premier League. From the perspective of the big clubs, the creation of the Premier League was simply a matter of fairness and commonsense. Why should Arsenal and Manchester United share television revenue with lower division teams that never appear on telly and that no one wants to watch? Would Tesco share its profits with the local corner store? Their position had a certain undeniable logic in its favour, but it was a logic based on economic self-interest. Once Sky made it clear to the big clubs how much money could be made, the collective ethos of the football league went out the window. When the Premier League and Sky got

TV or not TV

together in 1992, it represented the start of an intimate, some might say incestuous, relationship that was born out of greed and that has fostered a culture of greed ever since.

Money in large amounts never brings out the best in people, and the vast sums invested in the Premiership by Sky since 1992 have had predictable consequences. Inevitably the millions swilling around the game have led to a culture of greed, in which, no matter how much you have, you always need more. So we are treated more and more often to the sight of rapacious clubs, greedy players and sleazy agents, all intent on getting their share while the getting's good. And there seems no likelihood of this gravy train coming off the rails in the near future. The Premiership has just sold the television rights for 2007-2010 to Sky for 1.3 billion. It's depressing to think that the vast bulk of this money will be used to make already rich individuals even richer. Does Thierry or Wayne or Jose or Fergie need an extra ten grand a week? Probably not, but it won't stop them taking it. When you consider what a difference Premiership clubs could make to their communities, it's hard to avoid the feeling of a wasted opportunity. These clubs are so bound up in their narrow self-interest that they simply do not see the wider community as their responsibility. Yet with their wealth and resources and their ability to reach young people they could make a significant difference. Of course, each Premiership club will point complacently at their community programmes. Thank god they do something, however little, yet it is hard to avoid the feeling that their community work is little more than politically correct tokenism and motivated more by the self-interested desire to groom a new generation of customers. Why? Because everything these clubs do is motivated by greed. They never give anything back: they simply demand more. For example, why don't the clubs use the millions provided by armchair fans via their Sky subscriptions to compensate the genuine fans who put themselves out to support the team in all kinds of weather? It's the match-going fans who have to put up with the bizarre kick-off times to suit the needs of television, so perhaps they should enjoy the compensation of reduced admission prices? But it would never occur to any Premiership club to do this. Why fleece people just the once through their TV subscriptions, when you can fleece them again through the turn-styles? Was anyone surprised to learn that Manchester United have just announced a 12% increase in the price of season tickets? What did Gordon Gekko say in Wall Street? "Greed is good. Greed works."

Reasons to be tearful: part 2

An inevitable consequence of football's new-found wealth has been the spread of casual corruption: accepted, commonplace, glossed over as unimportant and, of course, nothing you could prove – football's closed shop sees to that. It surfaces in suspicions of managers taking bungs when they sign unknown players for inflated fees. It surfaces in tales of agents pocketing half a million for making a few phone calls. It surfaces in whispers about the incestuous relationship between a football club and an agency run by the manager's son. Of course, no one is saying that corruption is new, but the problem has been exacerbated by the influx of Murdoch's millions. In the past a juicy corruption scandal might surface once in a deacade, whereas in the Premiership era stories seem to surface every few months. Hence the increasingly frequent and richly comic spectacle of a Premier League inquiry spending months in protracted investigations before producing an anodyne report that - surprise, surprise - gives the Premier League a clean bill of health. If corruption itself is spreading, then so is the cynical acceptance of it. An amoral Del Boy attitude seems to be the norm: "Dosh? Football's swimmin' in it. Get in there, my son. Fill yer boots. Everyone's at it. If you don't 'ave it, someone else will." But it's not stealing, is it? It's just Sky money, and everyone knows they've got money to burn. Yes, our money, the money we stump up in subscriptions. Trouble is, we don't seem to mind. We're hypnotised by that dazzling rectangle of green and seem to have no appetite for what goes on in the shadows. We're surprisingly tolerant. As long as people stop short of actual match-fixing, we seem happy to look on lesser forms of wrong-doing with apathy or indulgence.

Reasons to be tearful: part 3
The Premiership is the "best league in the world", as Sky delights in telling us ad nauseam. I'm not sure what criteria they use to justify this absurd claim. I think the word they're looking for is 'richest'. Or maybe 'over-hyped' or 'over-priced'. Best league in the world? It's not even the best league in the country. It's the most predictable, uncompetitive division in the football pyramid. How can you make ridiculously inflated claims for a competition that only four teams have a realistic chance of winning? In fact, make that one team since the arrival of our Russian comrade. Just for fun, I'll go out on a limb and make a reckless prediction for next season. Chelsea will win it at a canter and Arsenal, Liverpool and Manchester United will occupy the next three places. That sounds to me like a competition with serious structural flaws. Not in Sky's wonderful world of hype. We live in the best of all possible football worlds and anyone who challenges this orthodoxy is just a romantic, lunatic leftie.

It's hardly surprising that Sky is one long extended advertisement for the Premiership: it's Sky's flagship product, the root and cornerstone of its commercial success. But does anyone else feel depressed and insulted by the relentless hype and the unwillingness even to suggest that not quite everything is rosy in the Premiership garden? Sky don't do investigative journalism, do they? You don't bite the hand that feeds you, do you? Why have a documentary investigating the links between a football manager and his agent son, when you can anaesthetise the masses with hard-hitting football programmes like SoccerAM? Still, it's a public-spirited gesture from

Sky to provide programmes for the hard of thinking. Thankfully, there are some radio and television channels that still have the temerity to raise allegations of wrong-doing in football. The BBC broke the unwritten rule and screened a documentary that suggested that Alex Ferguson's son Jason had profited financially in his role as an agent from his father's position at Old Trafford. Ferguson's mature response was to boycott interviews with the BBC until a full retraction was offered. Interestingly, no retraction has been forthcoming and the boycott remains in place. He still talks to Sky, of course, where their idea of a challenging question is: "Sir Alex, are you looking forward to the new season."

So Sky's role in promoting the Premiership is two-fold. It takes the form of the constant hype that is designed to bludgeon fans into accepting their claim that the Premiership is indeed the best league in the world. But more insidiously it takes the less visible form of all the things they never say and all the programs they never make.

Reasons to be tearful: part 4

There is a conflict of interest in football. Not, as you might think, between the big clubs interested only in themselves and the football authorities concerned with the interests of the game as a whole. Don't be silly. No, the real conflict is between the armchair football supporter and the match-going fan, and it's no surprise to see where Sky stands on this one. The conflict of interest comes because Sky want to show football during those quiet slots in the schedule when their viewers have nothing better to do than watch a game of football. But having games kick off at daft o'clock shows no regard for the real fans, you know, the ones who actually lever themselves out of their armchairs to go and watch the game. The issue is complicated by the fact that most of us are both. We're match-going fans and armchair supporters, and, if it's not affecting your team, you're probably quite happy to have a live game to watch while you're eating your tea on a Saturday evening. And Monday night sounds good too after the first day back at work, when you're too knackered to do anything more useful. But it is the people we think of as true supporters – the ones who follow the team near and far through ups and downs – who pay the price for our convenience. Last season Tottenham fans had to travel to Bolton on a Monday night and West Ham fans made the long trek north to watch the Hammers play Sunderland at midday. Why? Because when it comes to balancing the requirements of match-going fans and armchair supporters, there can only be one winner. Of course, the fans don't help themselves, do they? If Sky scheduled a match for 3 a.m. on a Tuesday morning at the other end of the country, the hard-core fans would still make it a point of principle to be there. We really do encourage these people to take the piss.

Reasons to be tearful: part 5

Your mum was right: too much of anything is not good for you. Sky proves it by showing too many matches every season. Including the pay-per-view games, Sky screened 138 Premiership matches last season. That is more than a third of all Premiership games. Now, even the most brain-washed fan of the Premiership will admit that the ratio of quality to dross is not 1 in 3. Try and remember the games that have stood out over the last two seasons and you might be inclined to think that the ratio is more like 1 in 50. Even if we throw in the merely decent matches, you're lucky to see a dozen games worth watching each season. Most are mediocre, humdrum affairs that no amount of Sky spin can dress up. Over-exposure presents a genuine danger to football. Despite the game's intrinsic magic and despite our apparent addiction, no sport can survive blanket coverage without losing its special quality, and becoming banal, ordinary and stale. There's no getting round the old truth: less is more.

Reasons to be tearful: part 6

Is Sky responsible for the likes of Abramovich and Glazer? Well, after fifteen years of acting as a global promotional tool for the Premiership, the answer must be yes. To an extent. We might not like everything that Sky does, but you have to give them credit where credit's due. They have successfully convinced everyone that the Premiership is the most exciting and glamorous sporting competition in the world. It might be the triumph of hype over experience, but hype works, and inevitably the Premiership has attracted the attentions of the rich and powerful. For people like Abramovich it's an ego trip, another high-stakes game to win: he came, he saw, he was conquered. By the greatest game ever invented. For others like the Glazers the attraction is money. The old joke - How do you make a small fortune in football? Start with a big one – no longer applies. Traditionally, businessmen were happy to trade their large but obscurely earned fortunes for a bit of local celebrity. Nowadays, there's gold in them there hills and the already rich see an opportunity to become even richer. Sky proved that the combination of football and the right technology yields huge rewards. Someone like Glazer would never have bought United twenty years ago. There was no money in it. There's plenty of money in it now, and most of it comes from Sky.

Reasons to be tearful: part 7.

What is it about jester hats? What is it about a harmless piece of cheap tat: red and white cotton headwear with silver bells attached? Well, for FC fans it's a powerful symbol of the new type of support ushered in by the Premiership and Sky that has supplanted the traditional match-going culture. The jester hat is shorthand for the children of Sky, the fans who think football is simply about glamour and celebrity, the fans who sit silently next to you at games because they don't know any of your songs, the fans who

TV or not TV

take pictures of the pitch on their mobile phones, the fans who see nothing wrong in a Mexican wave, the fans who wear replica shirts but never play the game, the fans who demand the constant gratification of success and who are the first to moan when the team starts to lose, the fans who don't realise that football is as much about misery as ecstasy, the fans who have never known the chastening experience of watching their team get thumped on a miserable January afternoon, the fans who don't understand that football supporting is a metaphor for life: ups and downs, outrageous slices of luck, outrageous acts of injustice, tests of character, and simply long periods of mediocrity. At FC we think we're losing something special if we go down the route of stage-managed, happy-clappy football showbiz. We think football's worth more than: it's worthy of our best feelings.

Nelson, A, 15/01/06

So I nipped round to mum and dad's on Friday to break the bad news that I was working over the weekend and couldn't go to Accrington for the Nelson game. I hoped they wouldn't be too disappointed. Ha! Not a bit of it. "Oh, we're still going. Popping up about 12-ish, so we can have a drink in the social club and pie and peas before the game." Fine, I thought, feeling not a little put out, hope you enjoy it. These are the same people who often hummed and hawed about accepting my offer of two tickets to Old Trafford. FC United – reaching the fans other clubs can't reach. So that was that. I spent Sunday afternoon perched by my laptop poised to log on and fix the buckled wheels of industry, should I be required, and they spent Sunday afternoon cheering on another FC victory. They did kindly ring me at half-time to tell me that we were 3-0 up and that I had missed one of the goals of the season from Steve Torpey. Torps – he doesn't do tap-ins. They aggravated my sense of loss by telling me that Adie Orr now had red hair. I mean FC United home-strip red. Apparently the fans had greeted his new hair-style with a specially adapted version of the cheesy Chris de Burgh dirge: "Adie in Red". Still, it was giving me ideas. Surely anything would be an improvement on grey?

Nelson 1 FC United 3 (att 2011)
FC Scorers: Torpey(2), Mitten

Now, after all that I've said about Sky, let me say something that might surprise you: it's about time we stopped using television as a scapegoat. It's a lazy response to the problems that beset the game and it's letting the real culprits off the hook. The changes that have taken place over the last fifteen years have been done for television, not by television. Television does not control football, even though its money exerts a powerful influence. Television might put the petrol in the tank, but it does not drive the car. Nothing can be bought unless it wants to sell itself, and the people running football have consistently sent the message to Sky and others that everything

Our Club Our Rules

is up for grabs. Instead of taking the easy option of blaming all the game's ills on the pernicious effects of television, let's look for the real reasons for the current state of football. Let's look at the naked greed of the top clubs, at the weakness of the governing bodies and at the passive compliance of the fans. Yes, us, the very people who wring our hands in despair at the media-propelled commercial drift of football but who continue to stump up the money that keeps the whole frustrating greed-fest on the road.

    The country's top clubs embraced the idea of the Premiership for one reason: to extract as much television money out of their product as possible. And they have followed that logic faithfully ever since. If Sky will buy it, the Premiership will sell it. That's why it's now possible to watch over a third of Premiership matches live on Sky. Everyone knows that it's too much, but the more games you offer the more money you can demand. And Sky go along with this on the basis that the games involving the Fulhams and Boltons of this world are the price they must pay to get the matches they really want. It's understandable, though not acceptable, that individual clubs should pursue their own interests without regard for the general good of the game, but I think we are entitled to expect a little better from institutions whose raison d'etre is to protect the game from sectional interests. But they continue to make you despair. The governing bodies appear to have given up any pretence of moral guardianship and to have adopted the principle of "if you can't beat them, join them". What other motive could the FA have than that of screwing every last TV penny from their product, when they scheduled this season's four FA Cup quarter-finals over four consecutive nights of the same week? Their justification? To avoid fixture congestion in a World Cup season. Maybe I'm being a bit simple but surely that was all the more reason to play them on the same day.

    The picture in Europe is no better, although whether the G14 clubs or UEFA are most to blame, it's difficult to say. You only have to look at what they have done between them to the European Cup to see the logic of greed being followed to its ultimate conclusion. At one time the European Cup had a noble simplicity: a straight two-legged knockout format featuring one team from each country and with all matches taking place on a Wednesday night. No television mileage in that though, is there? Let's have a league stage with more matches for the big clubs and more matches to sell to TV and let's schedule them over two nights to maximise the television income. And while we're about it, let's extend entry to the competition to teams finishing as low as fourth in their championship – God forbid that that one of Europe's big boys should miss out on their slice of the TV cake. And let's give the revamped competition a grandiose name like the Champions League when it's not really a league and when most of the teams competing in it are not champions. Hence the bloated monster we see today. And let's not forget the Carling Cup of Europe, the UEFA Cup, that now schedules its matches on a Thursday when – surprise, surprise – it doesn't clash with the Champions

TV or not TV

League in the TV schedules. Even this competition introduced a league stage at its half-way point in 2004. More teams, more games, more television money. Surely somebody has to say enough is enough and have the courage to reverse this trend.

   It doesn't have to be this way. Let me give you a vision of the future that represents a happy compromise between the needs of television and the needs of football. In this brave new world the Premiership makes 50 games a season available to Sky instead of the 138 that it currently offers. That allows Sky to show one match a week with a few extra games thrown in towards the end of the season as the title chase hots up. Or cools down as Chelsea wrap the league up by Easter. The one match of the weekend will take place at 4pm on a Sunday. Sky can select the biggest match of the weekend and, being the only game shown live on TV, it becomes a television event that fans look forward to, their appetites sharpened by the week-long wait. It doesn't matter that the smaller clubs rarely feature in the live match, as a new collective agreement will see the total television revenue split evenly among the Premiership clubs. This new arrangement alleviates a multitude of problems. Firstly, the Premiership has to accept less money for fewer games. Let's say that Sky pay 250 million for TV rights instead of 1.3 billion. The era of obscene wages comes to an end and Rio and company have to rub along on twenty grand a week, the poor darlings. Does anyone have a problem with that? Secondly, we solve the problem of football's over-exposure and, suddenly, watching a match on the box or going to a game becomes special again. Thirdly, only one of the weekend's games is moved for television and the majority of fans can re-discover the joys of football at three o'clock on a Saturday. And we apply the same logic to European competition. Fewer teams in the Champions League playing fewer games and all played on a Wednesday night. Fewer UEFA Cup games and all played on a Tuesday. No more Thursday night fixtures that force the postponement of Saturday games to a Sunday. This would be a perfectly balanced relationship between television and football, and it hardly represents a Draconian reduction in football on the box. With Premiership games, FA Cup matches, European fixtures and the usual highlights programmes, there would still be plenty of football to feed our addiction. But it might also leave us more time to do other things – like write that book on the ills of top-level football. No one is saying that football on television is bad thing – five million Sky subscribers can't be wrong – but there is simply too much.

   So, who is going to help us bring about this brave new world in which there is a healthy balance between television and football? The clubs? The words "chance", "hell" and "snowball" spring to mind. They are locked into a mentality that tells them that you can never have enough money. The idea of voluntarily turning down the vast fortunes that Sky dangle in front of them is economic madness, the ravings of a starry-eyed lunatic, the preposterous suggestion of someone divorced from reality. Of course, in their reality, it makes perfect sense to pay Rio Ferdinand a hundred grand a week for kicking a football. And I'm the madman? The argument that the clubs would put forward is that slashing their income from television would mean slashing the salaries of the players which in turn would lead to a mass exodus abroad. I'm not entirely convinced about this, because English footballers are like French wines: they don't travel well. I have difficulty visualising Wayne tucking into spaghetti carbonara and sipping a nice Chianti. Historically very few English lads have settled well abroad. Most seem to have reacted like Ian Rush in the 80s who famously said that playing in Italy was "like being in a foreign country" or Luther Blissett who complained that "No matter how much money you've got, you can't seem to get any Rice Krispies". And a drastic reduction in player salaries would only return us to the position we were in the 60s and 70s when players could earn huge sums in Italy or Spain but were rarely tempted to try the experience. Denis Law and Jimmy Greaves had brief but miserable spells in Italy before coming back to England. Maybe I'm naïve but I think most players would prefer staying at home and scraping by on twenty grand a week to playing abroad for a hundred grand a week – at least if they were prepared to listen to their hearts instead of their agents. Having said all that, the top clubs are never going to give us the chance to see this little social experiment in action. Sacrifice money for a greater good, when money is the greatest good? It's not going to happen, is it?

   Maybe we can place our hopes on football's governing bodies. As guardians of the game, maybe we can rely on them to put the long-term interests of the game before profit and to make a stand against the current money madness that is ruining football. No laughing there at the back. I wouldn't place too much faith in the FA. They no longer control top-level football in this country - the Premier League does, which in effect means an elite of powerful clubs. They could perhaps assert some moral leadership by highlighting the damage that over-exposure of football on television is doing, but even this is unlikely, as they seem paranoid about taking any line that might put them on a collision course with the Premier League.

   They might also be simply deferring to the prevailing economic orthodoxy of Tony Blair's Britain: the market is king. They might not see it as their responsibility to interfere with the complex and mysterious workings of the market place. The Premier League is a willing seller, Sky is a willing buyer and the fans appear to be willing consumers. Everyone's a winner - so where's the problem? But don't they share the concern of a growing number of fans that the current dash for cash might be to the detriment of the long-term interests of the game?

   The governing body that in theory could bring about radical changes is UEFA. They could restore the Champions League to its old European Cup format: a straight knockout competition for league champions only. They could do the same to the UEFA Cup. Unfortunately, the problem with UEFA

TV or not TV

is twofold. Firstly, UEFA itself is quite happy pocketing vast sums of money either from television directly or indirectly from its official sponsors, and that's a hard habit to break. Secondly, they have to deal with pressure and veiled threats from the self-appointed elite of super-clubs known as the G14. The G14 clubs would resist any changes that implied less games and less TV revenue. There have been thinly disguised threats in the past from the G14 of breaking away and forming their own European Super League. You can understand the fear of UEFA when faced with the prospect of European football disintegrating into civil war. It's simply to keep the G14 clubs on side that UEFA have deformed their own competitions in recent years. Personally I'd like to see UEFA call the bluff of these self-important bully-boys. Let them break away and set up their own invitation-only closed super league outside the jurisdiction of UEFA and let's see who would win the battle for the hearts and minds, not to mention the euros, of the fans. Of course, only a simpleton would expect organisations as pliable and conservative as the FA and UEFA to rock the boat. But don't say I never asked.

    So who does that leave if we are going to achieve our aim of safeguarding the long-term future of this marvellous game? I suppose we'll have to rely on the most powerful group of people in the game – the fans. They always say that he who pays the piper calls the tune. It's not true in football, is it? We pay the piper – boy, do we pay the piper – but oddly, sadly, frustratingly – we seem happy to dance to their tune and then moan about it afterwards. We are football's ultimate power-brokers. We can have the football we want, if we simply exercise the power we have. I fully understand that there are many football fans out there who see nothing wrong with top-level football. They seem happy to pay ever-increasing prices to watch ever more uncompetitive matches. They will obviously not agree with my proposition that less is more: less football on television and less television money in football. I believe, however, that there is also a large body of fans who are increasingly dissatisfied with the way the game is going, and I believe we have the power to make it change direction. So what can we do? We can boycott the Premier League and we can boycott Sky. We can boycott any matches that are moved at the behest of television, always making an exception, of course, for the Sunday afternoon match that we've agreed should be televised live. We can boycott any Champions League match not played on a Wednesday night and boycott any UEFA Cup match not played on a Tuesday night. If Sky continue to show matches at daft o'clock – Saturday midday, Saturday evening, Sunday at two, etc – we boycott them by not watching. Don't dismiss this as a pointless gesture. I guarantee that it would bring about radical changes in football coverage very quickly. Half-empty stadiums and drastically reduced viewing figures are the stuff of nightmares for football club chairmen and Sky executives. Sky relies on football to bring in huge audiences to sell prime time slots to its advertisers. No viewers, no advertising revenue. We're just too nice, too English. It's time to get awkward, demanding and bolshie. We can bend Sky and the Premier League to our will if we choose to, because without our money the whole shebang is unsustainable. Football still is "the people's game", if we decide to assert our ownership.

Ashton Town, H, 21/01/06

What do they say about great teams winning when they don't play well? Well, we were a great team today. We laboured and fought and scuffed and scratched our way to a tight 2-1 win. In fairness, it's not easy playing sexy football on a ploughed field. We'll be forever grateful to Bury for giving us a home in our first season, but what has happened to a pitch that used to look like a bowling green when I was a kid. Wherever Bury's money went over the years, it didn't go on the pitch. From the top of the MRE the pitch looked like a pizza with a dozen different toppings. I was a bit concerned that our tank-like centre-back Dave Brown might get stuck in the mud, and I had visions of him being hauled out with ropes.

Credit to Ashton. They had certainly improved since the first game back in sunny September. They matched us blow for blow and a draw would not have been an injustice. The game was decided ten minutes from the end, and again it was a piece of magic from our thong-wearing wizard Steve Torpey. Finally, a ball in the box fell to the right man. He was eight yards out with the magnificent Ashton keeper looming large over him. With that unteachable mixture of skill and arrogance, Torpey dummied, watched the keeper spread himself for the anticipated point-blank blast, before caressing the ball with his instep beneath the keeper. The MRE erupted as an hour's pent-up tension spent itself. I love these tight games. Three points is three points, but some are worth more than others.

The game was drawing to a close when our promising youngster Will Ahern clashed heads with an Ashton player. It was reported afterwards that he'd had nine staples in his head, but that he should be fit for next week. Not modelled his elegant style of midfield play on Robert Pires then? I'm sure I read recently that the goatee-bearded one has just had two weeks out with split ends.

Very interesting singing episode during the second half. At the front of the MRE the chant "BNP – f**k off home" was sung for several seconds. What have the Banque Nationale de Paris done to us, I thought. Joking aside, there is a serious point to this. The forum has recently featured threads about one or two individuals spotted in the crowd with BNP badges on their jackets. There was even a rumour that someone was seen depositing leaflets on seats in the Main Stand at the last home game. These are just unsubstantiated stories so far. I personally have never seen or heard anything racist at any FC game. If these boneheads are among us, I hope they take heed and stay well away. They're preaching to the wrong audience. There's many a tough-

TV or not TV

looking lad at FC willing to give them a hands-on lesson in racial equality. Master race? You're 'aving a laugh.

FC United 2 Ashton Town 1 (att 3549)
FC Scorers: Orr, Torpey

There will be no shortage of people to tell you that any attempt to put the media genie back in the bottle is a hopelessly naive undertaking that is doomed to failure. Predictably, many of them will be the very people who make a profitable living spouting banal nothings on TV and radio. Even setting aside those who have a vested interest in seeing television wrap football even more suffocatingly in its embrace, there will also be the usual band of world-weary cynics preaching their gospel of passive acceptance and deriding any attempt to reverse the media creep of the last fifteen years as childish idealism. Of course, you can see their point. You can always see their point, as it's always a lazy expression of the bleedin' obvious. What's easier than looking around you at they way things are, throwing up your arms in resignation and telling yourself that "that's the way it is", implying that that's the way it must be. To picture reality different from the way it is now demands energy, imagination and enthusiasm – yes, all the ingredients of idealism. And it also demands that you care, and I care passionately about this beautiful, magical, thrilling game. So, I don't mind being cast in the role of Canute defying the waves. Sometimes you have to do something because it's right, not because it's effective. I have tried to offer an alternative model for the difficult relationship between football and television. I don't see an attempt to limit the amount of football on television as a Canute-like effort to turn back the waves. To me it sounds like the sanest, healthiest commonsense. And the waves that I'm defying are not the waves of progress, history and technology, they're the waves of greed, self-interest and short-termism. I don't want to see football disappear from our television screens. How credible would that suggestion be coming from someone who has spent far too many hours glued to football on the box? In fact, some FC fans should look away now, as I'm about to make an admission that might be construed as FC heresy: I don't want to give up my Sky subscription. Sky loves sport – why wouldn't it when it sells so many dishes and subscriptions? – and it has done tremendous work in promoting sports such as cricket, rugby league and darts. What I want is a subscription that costs £20 a month instead of £40 and gives me far fewer football games, but still lets me watch England thrashing the Aussies, Wigan hammering St Helens, and Phil Taylor annihilating just about everybody. Slash the amount of football and slash the cost of the subscription. That's my perfect compromise. Oh yes, and in passing it will safeguard the future of the game we all love.

Our Club Our Rules

Great Harwood Town, A, Postponed, 29/01/06

If it's Sunday, it must be Accrington, and so it was. But not for long. We arrived at the Interlink Stadium about twelve-thirty, just as the players were disembarking from the team coach. I did my usual impression of a middle-aged man looking star-struck at lads twenty years his junior, as the players filed past to look at the pitch. The Accrington ground staff, the Harwood players, the FC players, Uncle Tom Cobley and all went to look at the pitch, and thought it looked fine. Pity the referee disagreed. There had been a frost overnight and a thin strip beneath the main stand had not thawed. The game was off.

We stood around waiting for final, final confirmation. The players stood around looking unimpressed. I couldn't let the day go completely to waste. I took the chance to grab the match programme off my mum and walked up to her idol Rory Patterson to get his autograph. I mumbled something about "Cheers, Rory, it's for my mum", and he gave me that "Yeah, sure it is" look. I should have used the occasion to tip the poor lad off. "Look Rory, if you think you're being stalked by a woman old enough to be your grandmother, that'll be my mum. She's harmless, honest." Took back the programme with the signature of her favourite Irish rogue, and she was beaming. Blimey, I had worked hard on them in August to get them to go to the first home match, and now my mum was an FC groupie. My dad was disgusted, of course – I hadn't taken the chance to get him Adie Orr's autograph!

There was barely an hour to kick-off and the club officials were worried about all the people who would be turning up for the game unaware that the match was off. They shouldn't have worried. Fans still enjoyed a few pints in the Accrington social club, and fans in the Crown pub enjoyed a visit from the FC team. This is what it's like to be FC. It's not some calculating PR gesture that takes the players to the pub – they do it after every game. It's simply the desire to show that this club has a rare unity. We're just different parts of the same whole: they do the playing, we do the singing and the drinking. Best keep it that way round.

I'm wondering how far I have managed to answer my own questions. I wondered at the start if Sky was all bad and if television was responsible for all the ills of the game. I felt that our attitude to television was unbalanced and frankly contradictory. We love the game: playing it, talking about it and, of course, watching it – in the flesh and on the box, so to live at odds with television is to live at odds with ourselves. Television is a big part of football because we want it to be, and it will remain an important force in the game. I tried hard to draw up a balance sheet of the pros and cons of Sky's effect on football in recent years to show that it's not been all bad, even if the cons seemed to outnumber the pros. Even then I laboured to show where the real blame lies – with the clubs, the governing bodies, and yes, whisper it quietly, the fans whose apathy and passive compliance has allowed the other two to

TV or not TV

pursue their own agenda. It's too convenient to place all the blame on Sky. When an arsonist burns down a building, do we blame the shopkeeper who sold him the matches? The primary responsibility for football's problems lies with the people who control the game. Let's name names. It's the big boys of the Premiership and the super clubs of G14 who should be in the dock accused of greed, and it's the FA, UEFA and FIFA who should be in the dock accused of dereliction of duty and of failing to defend football against the vested interest of the clubs. And let's not let ourselves off the hook. The fans have the ultimate power in football and, if the game won't reform itself, let's flex our muscles and start voting with our feet and our zapper.

The hardest question and the one that touches me most closely is the question of FC United's relationship to television. I set out in the hope of coming up with an acceptable compromise between the demands of television and the principles of FC. I hope that I've shown that a blanket rejection of television, be it Sky or anyone else, is not a solution. In fact, our first season has already shown that the club do not reject television outright, as we have co-operated with Manchester-based station Channel M to produce a monthly programme based on events at FC. No money was involved but the club has received some priceless publicity. So we've already established the principle that television and FC United can be good for each other. What FC needs to do, and it needs to start straight away, is to develop a coherent policy on television. Let's not wait for events to catch us unprepared. If we believe as a club that television is damaging the game, we should start making that case now. The club needs to issue a policy document explaining its position on television, highlighting the damage being done to the game by its willingness to sell itself and its obsession with television income, and making the case that less is more. This is the most constructive contribution we can make in the attempt to save football from the culture of excess: initiating a debate and trying to persuade the wider football community of the soundness of our ideas. Surely this is a better way forward than boycotting matches or refusing to fulfil a fixture because the game is being shown live on Sky. Why boycott a game because it is live on Sky, when we can use it as a showcase for FC's vision of the future. Let's make sure we're there to show people that football support is about noise and passion and colour, even when you're losing – especially when you're losing. Let's treat them to our full repertoire of chants and songs and by our actions prove that terrace culture has to return to our football grounds. There's only one problem, of course. It would be such a vibrant, colourful spectacle that they'd want to show us every week!

Our Club Our Rules

February 2006
The People's Club

There was a terrible symbolism about Manchester United's decision in the 1990s to remove the words 'football club' from its badge. I wonder if the marketing genius that came up with that idea realised how much significance that single gesture had for the fans. I'm surprised they didn't go the whole hog and remove the word 'Manchester'. That would have left the stripped-down, generic brand name they really wanted. That ill-advised gesture was still prominent in the minds of the FC fans who gathered in the Central Methodist Hall in July to select the new club's badge. We had three designs to choose from, all excellent in their own way, but it's hard not to believe that the sight of the words 'Football Club United of Manchester' picked out boldly in white lettering around the outer edge of one of the badges on had no influence on people's decision. We'd never forgiven United for that betrayal.

I imagine most people's thoughts dwell on the word 'football' as the key element in that group of words. After all, it's what we do and what we love, and it's what knits everything else together. For me, however, it's the modest little word 'club' that attracts my attention and excites my emotions. It's a homely word that evokes notions of co-operation, sharing and unity. It evokes the idea of togetherness: the free association of equal partners united in a common purpose. I think we can safely say that it's been a long time since the country's top clubs thought of their fans as partners and there's certainly been nothing free about it. In his book 'The Beautiful Game' David Conn makes the point that institutions like United and Chelsea ceased to be clubs and became global business concerns a long time ago. At FC this season we've all been seduced by this feeling of togetherness, by this feeling from top to bottom, from the board members to the fans, that we're all pulling together for one purpose. Togetherness – makes a refreshing change from the us- and them-ness that seems to characterise football today.

Of course, it's easy to bandy fine-sounding words like community and togetherness, but fine words butter no parsnips. Just had to get that phrase into this book. The test of whether FC United deserves to exist and of whether FC United will continue to flourish will be in its actions. The cynics have sung different lyrics to the same tune since FC was formed last summer. At first, it was "I'll give it till Xmas" or "Wait till the cold weather sets in". Now that it has become clear that the club is an unqualified success, the words have changed to "Trouble is, as they get bigger, they'll be like all the rest". Are the cynics right? Do we have to succumb in the long run to the irresistible forces of greed and selfishness? Will our principles suffer from the eroding effect of time? No one knows what the future will be. I can only look back on the first twelve months of our existence and feel pride and admiration for so many people involved in this club who have proven time and again that the principles on which it was founded are not empty phrases. Believe me, we have buttered some parsnips this season. So this section of the book is simply intended to record the people and events that have provided a heart-warming corrective to the greed and cynicism of top-level football.

Nelson, H, 4/02/06

I thought United were supposed to be a great cup team. Not this United. Not this season. After this unexpected defeat in the Division Two Trophy at home against a side we had already beaten well twice this season, we can now concentrate on the league. This result certainly wasn't in the script. This was football at its greyest and grittiest, on a bitterly cold winter's afternoon. A war of attrition played on a pitch that resembled a First World War no-man's land. Ninety minutes of fruitless and almost chanceless attacking against a stubborn Nelson defence. Their five-man defensive system proved unbreachable, with the two wing-backs keeping our dangerous wingers Howard and Torpey under wraps for the whole game. The game went in to extra time, seriously disrupting the plans of many fans who'd expected to be in the pub by five to watch Portsmouth play Big United. And as the players slogged their way to the end of extra-time, the anti-climax of a goalless draw looked to be inevitable. We looked to have broken the deadlock when Adie Orr poked one home at the far post, only to see the linesman flag – incorrectly? – for offside.

So the last minute arrives with yet another FC corner. The ball is cleared to the tall Nelson sub who has just come on. He has the advantage of fresh legs and races up the left wing, crosses into the box to his mate who takes one touch to control it and a second to rifle it past Barry George. The Nelson chairman probably held his head in his hands – bang goes a money-spinning replay against FC United. Not that the players were bothered as they raced towards their fans and did a collective Klinsmann dive.

The magic of the cup, eh? This was the same Nelson that we had already beaten 5-0 at home and 3-1 away. This was the same Nelson that had lost 14-0 to Cammell Laird the week before. Blimey, Cammell Laird must be good.

But I loved it, even though most people agreed it was a dire match on a poor surface and was probably our worst performance of the season. Well, "that's football", as a ten-year-old lad told me as we were walking out. Brilliant, even the kids are quality.

FC United 0 Nelson 1 (att 3007)
FC scorers: Pass

Sunderland legend Len Shackleton famously included a single blank page in his autobiography entitled 'What the average director knows about football". Now, when Chaddy comes to write his FC memoirs "From window-fitter to Champions League winner", I don't think he'll be saying the same about our lot. Now, that might be because we don't actually have any directors. We have a group of eleven board members who are democratically elected by the membership and who have to stand for re-election every two years. And on the evidence so far, it seems we're pretty good at electing board members. Even so, "We've got the best board in the land" is not a chant you'll hear very often echoing round Gigg Lane, but I've got high hopes. It certainly wouldn't be undeserved. Never mind the Herculean tasks that they performed in the space of six weeks in the summer of 2005 to bring this club into existence, gain entry to the league, find a ground, recruit a team and appoint a manager, it's the little things that they have done since that prove to me that the people in charge of this club don't just talk a good game.

Maybe I've just been going to Old Trafford too long, but I don't expect to see the members of the board selling match programmes, flogging badges and scarves from an improvised stall and, best of all, standing with the rest of us on the terrace and singing the songs. Yet why should it be a surprise, when the FC board members are just fans who were willing to volunteer for an unfeasible amount of unpaid work for an invisibly small amount of reward? And that's what's refreshing about football at this level. It's not an ego trip – it's about rolling your sleeves up and mucking in. You have to be in it for love, or you wouldn't be in it all.

If one incident for me proves that the club is in good hands, it was the match against Chadderton at Gigg Lane. It was a Wednesday in November, it was wet, the pitch was a quagmire. The game was postponed early that morning. Now, when a Premiership match is postponed ten hours before kick-off, it's not a problem. You can't help but find out – from radio and television. It's a bit different when you play in the North-West Counties League – postponements don't warrant an announcement on Sky Sports or Radio Five Live. The only outlet is the internet, but not everyone has a job that allows them to surf the web several times a day. So, when the Chadderton match was called off, there was still a real possibility that people would turn up for the game. And they did. Just a few dozen fans but among them one set of lads that had travelled across from North Wales. Just as well then that FC's general manager Andy Walsh and Press Officer Jules Spencer

The People's Club

decided to form a reception committee to welcome any pour souls that had made a wasted journey. In fact, they made sure that it wasn't wasted. They met people as they arrived and took them into the restaurant at the ground and treated them to food and a few drinks. And just to take the edge off any lingering feelings of disappointment, Margy and several of the players turned up for a chat. A simple gesture, but it turned a potentially miserable trip for the fans into a memorable evening. I just wish I'd not checked the internet and turned up too.

Surely someone will write the official history of FC United one day and surely it will feature honourable mentions for the small army of people that have contributed selflessly to the success of the club in its first season. There's a collective ethos at FC that makes you reluctant to single out individuals, but there is one person whose extraordinary efforts warrant an exception: Russell Delaney. I didn't know Russell and hadn't heard his name before last summer, but he was well known among United fans and had played a big part in opposing the Murdoch and Glazer takeovers. Everyone who knew him speaks about his generosity and courage and good humour, but what amazes me is his energy. I thought I was putting myself out last summer when I travelled the ten miles into Manchester for the FC protest meetings, so anyone who drives two hundred miles up to Manchester from the south-east has my unstinting respect. When you add in the fact that Russell was making repeated journeys as a member of the FC United steering committee, was terminally ill and drove up with an oxygen cylinder in the back of his car, respect turns into humility. I hope I'd have shown the same appetite for life and the same lack of self-pity as Russell, but I'm not sure. Russell died a couple of months into the season and received a fitting ovation before the New Mills game in November. As a tribute to his good humour and enthusiasm, the club decided against the traditional minute's silence in favour of a minute's applause. I'd never seen this done before but it seemed entirely appropriate. Strange to note that Manchester United did the same thing for George Best a few weeks later. Coincidence? At the final home game of the season the players emerged for the presentation of the trophy wearing Russell Delaney t-shirts, and Rory Patterson received the Russell Delaney Player of the Season award. It's one of the characteristics of a club with soul that the past is as important as the future, and you don't forget your heroes. Russell Delaney – gone but never forgotten.

Daisy Hill, A, 3-0, 11/02/06

I love Daisy Hill. Not the team, particularly, just the name. How does a club in a macho sport like football get a name like Daisy Hill? They must have taken it from the title of an 18th century English novel: "The adventures of Daisy Hill, or how a young serving girl made her way in the world." Or am I thinking of Moll Flanders? They're probably in the league above us. Just compare a name like Daisy Hill with the names of teams in the

Our Club Our Rules

Premiership. The only name worthy of interest is Tottenham ... *Hotspur?* Now I mention it, what's that about?

After the Nelson defeat, I was a bit concerned that we might go on a bad run. I could see the headlines: "Lacka-Daisy-cal FC slip to second successive defeat" or "Whoops-a-Daisy – FC lose again". I needn't have worried. Apparently, it was a stroll in the park. I say apparently, as I was once again under house arrest due to work commitments. Thank god for t'internet. The FC website always posts match updates. It's amazing - a non-league team ten leagues below the Premiership has people logging in from New Zealand and the States to get live updates from Daisy Hill. FC United, reaching the fans that other teams can't reach.

The lads won 3-0 with goals from Howard, Chadwick and Lyons. Chaddy is our captain fantastic - we've even forgiven him a misspent youth supporting City.

Another loud vocal performance from the travelling FC army, apparently. The game was played at Chorley, and the fans seem to have taken away a fond memory of a grass embankment down one side of the pitch. No snipers on this grassy knoll, however. What is there to snipe at? Winsford lost again and we're now fourteen points clear at the top. The fat lady's not singing yet, but she's certainly loosening her stays and clearing her throat.

Daisy Hill 0 FC United 3 (att 1682)
FC scorers: Howard, Chadwick, Lyons.

Everyone knows Alex. You can't miss him at games – a lively little lad with a big smile and swaddled in his FC colours. Oh yes, you can spot him by his wheelchair too. And it's not a wheelchair you can easily miss, with its magnificent wheel trims displaying the red and yellow of the FC United badge. Alex has cerebral palsy, which weakens his limbs and keeps him in a wheelchair, but it doesn't get in the way of him following FC. He's there at every game being pushed along by father Les.

I don't know where the idea started. Possibly with a post on the forum admiring Alex's cool wheel trims. Maybe Les replied and explained that, however slick his current chair, what Alex really needed was a high-tech motorised wheelchair that would allow him to move around unattended and in an upright position. No one wants to sit down at FC. And that was that: a cause was born – United for Alex. The new wheelchair would not come cheap – a daunting fifteen thousand pounds – but there was never any real doubt that the fans at FC would raise it. Bucket collections, fun runs and an auction of FC and Man United memorabilia kept the money pouring in and proved that the words 'FC family' was more than just a trite phrase. People were determined to get Alex that state-of –the-art dream machine. Maybe none more so than Megastall Geoff and Kitman George. These guys made the rest of us feel old and past it when they biked around every ground in the North-West Counties Division Two inside four days. That was a 450-mile cycle ride that culminated in their arrival at Gigg Lane before the last home game of the season. I got tired just following their progress on the internet. George and Geoff, we salute you, which is very appropriate really given that George is a sergeant in the army. So, Alex now has his new wheels, which we all look forward to seeing next season – complete with FC wheel trims, of course.

This is what people in a real club do: they club together. It's not about doing it for show or scoring points. It's about simply responding to that inherent human impulse to muck in and help each other. I'm starting to feel uncomfortable about continually stating the bleedin' obvious - though I don't know why, it's never stopped me before – but here we go again: it's better to give than to receive. Maybe the people running football with their lowest common denominator view of human nature need to be reminded.

And it's not just a case of helping your own. At the end of a long season the players and fans of FC still found the time and the energy and the money to help two lads who had no link to FC United. Over a thousand fans travelled down to Telford for a fund-raiser in aid of Man United fan Jamie Turner. Jamie had been attacked at Southampton a year before and suffered serious head injuries. He's had several operations and is still convalescing and FC were proud to be able to help him. Closer to home a young lad called Chris McGuirk found himself in a wheelchair after an accident playing rugby. Once again over a thousand FC fans turned out on a showery May bank holiday to watch FC play a team of local celebrities. Of course, if FC "should play in Rome or Mandalay, we'll be there" and at the moment we just don't want this season to end, but it's more than that. Helping others – it's a buzz.

Blackpool Mechanics, A, 18/02/06

Blackpool, beer and 4,000 FC fans: an explosive mix. Just light the blue touch-paper and stand back. And sure enough, it exploded – in a joyous multi-coloured, many-voiced carnival of football fandom. Streets that ran red and white with bar scarves and football tops, a Mortensen Stand that bounced up and down for ninety minutes and pubs that throbbed with the hoarse singing of grinning, delirious FC-ers in every stage of inebriation. They weren't just drunk on beer. They were drunk on the craic, on the friendship, on the good-natured madness, they were drunk on FC. Saturday night in the Old Bridge pub rocked to the sound of an FC knees-up. Who cared – who remembered – that Big United had slipped limply out of the cup at Anfield? Not the fans who adapted the old Spirit in the Sky classic:
"We won't pay Glazer or work for Sky,
Still sing City's gonna die,
Two Uniteds, but the soul is one,
As the Busby Babes carry on"

Our Club Our Rules

And carry on they did, and on, and on. For what seemed like forever. The rhythm seemed to cast a captive spell, as the same four lines merged seamlessly into the next repetition. Talk about trance music. It was a gathering of the FC clan in all its diversity: the daft young lads, the daft middle-aged blokes, the pretty wives, the pretty girlfriends, the young kids, families, couples, groups of mates, fans from Norway, fans from Poland, the FC players, all mixing euphorically in the FC melting-pot. A joyful madness. It's a love thing.

The weekend had started on the Friday evening. To celebrate the momentous occasion of FC's first Euro away trip – Blackpool's as close as we'll get – many of us were making a weekend of it. And we were coming mob-handed. Well, if you call me, Shelagh and mum and dad a mob. Left work early, picked up my better half en route, then straight up the M6 to that mecca of junk food, tasteless tack and loose women. Local FC fans had arranged with the landlord of the Old Bridge pub that this would be our base for the weekend. They were happy to have us, and we were happy to be had. The whole pub, including the function room at the back, was given over to FC. The fans were up for the craic and the bar staff were welcoming. Nothing bar a sudden shortage of beer could spoil the weekend. And nothing did.

We found a little corner of the function room early on Friday night, and were soon chatting to the Warsaw Reds. They had flown in from Poland for four days to treat Blackpool to their very own brand of East European madness. One of the lads Filip told us about their trip to the Big United game in Milan last season. They had hired a minibus from Warsaw to the airport in Katowice – a three-hour trip. Er, not in the middle of the Polish winter. Fourteen hours later they were stranded half-way with no hope of making their flight. So what would you do? Shrug philosophically and make your way home? Not these lads. They flagged down a passing taxi-driver and asked him to drive them to … Milan. And he did. At a cost of seven hundred pounds. All that to see AC Milan dump an off-colour United out of the Champions League. Maybe the prospect of two days of alcohol-fuelled lunacy with the Red Army was the real attraction. And now they're confirmed FC fans. They know where the craic is. Filip, what a guy. Speaks better English than most FC fans, but has never had a lesson or been to England before. Was he having me on? Then he gets up and kisses the hand of Shelagh and my mum before wandering off! I can almost forgive him for referring to my dad as my brother. Almost, but not quite.

And by ten-thirty the Warsaw Reds had been joined by the Scandinavian branch in the form of Voxra. That's a charming and sophisticated Norwegian lady, not a flaxen-haired Norse goddess. Mind you, thinking about it …

Re-learnt a lesson I should have known by heart: never drink strong lager on an empty stomach. Was speaking Venusian by the end of the evening. So perhaps it wasn't the best idea I've ever had to insist on giving an interview

- 130 -

The People's Club

to a Granada TV crew. My god, if that ever appears on TV, the few people who still think I'm grown-up will be quickly disabused.

Saturday morning arrived and brought with it a brisk walk up the prom in search of the mass kick-about on the beach that had been mentioned on the forum during the week. Sure enough, in the shadow of Blackpool Tower about a hundred kids, lads and dads were chasing a ball across the beach. Including Filip, looking bright and breezy. Jeez, what kind of constitution do these Poles have? Parliamentary democracy, I believe, he-he. I slipped smoothly into a holding role in front of our back fifteen, and then gave it up in favour of racing about a like a looney just trying to get a touch of the ball. Still, I think I showed enough cultured touches for people to get the message back to Margy that I could still do a job for the team ... you know, carry the oranges, clean the boots.

Met up with Mark at the beach football. He had driven down early that morning and booked a B&B for the night. He was anxiously checking his watch, determined that we should all be safely ensconced in a pub for the kick-off of the Liverpool-United game. I think two hours riding donkeys or playing bingo would have been better. An ugly, bad-tempered game short on quality ended with Liverpool winning 1-0. Is it strange to admit that I found the game boring, couldn't get excited, and didn't care about the result? Can people say that I never really loved United? They can say it, but it wouldn't make it true. But it is true that I am now completely indifferent. As Wilfred Owen said: "it touches me now like some queer disease".

We left the pub and joined everyone else streaming towards Bloomfield Road. I held my breath when I saw a bloke walking towards us wearing a Liverpool shirt. Happily, nothing worse than a few venomous insults flew his way. There were chants of "96 wasn't enough" – a reference to the Liverpool fans that died at Hillsborough. It's disgusting. We go bezerk about neanderthals doing aeroplane gestures and singing Munich songs, and then we sink to their level and sing shite like this. It was the only bum note of the weekend.

The approach to the ground was jammed with hordes of FC fans forming long queues at every turn-style. A brilliant blue sky beamed down on rows of laughing faces as people queued patiently but noisily to get in. The strains of "I don't care about Rio" rippled from row to row. Bemused stewards looked on like people on a beach watching the approach of a tsunami, as waves of fans poured through the turn-styles. Not surprisingly, the start was delayed.

Talk about a game of two halves. The first half saw FC pour forward, but to no effect. The ball went forward, didn't stick, and came right back. Even our returning hero Rory Patterson was struggling to get on the ball. Blackpool saw less of the ball but made more of it when they did, and it was no surprise and certainly no injustice when a diving header put them one up before the break. Oh dear, was the party about to fall flat? After a moment's shocked silence, the whole of the packed Mortensen End blasted out a defiant: "We told you not to score" in anticipation of an FC comeback. Well, there was no comeback before half-time, as the Mechanics went off with a deserved lead.

At half-time Shelagh was reminding me that things come in threes. Wigan Warriors had lost to Leeds Rhinos last night, Big United had lost to Liverpool at lunchtime, and ... FC could be about to lose to Blackpool Mechanics. Thank god Margy and the boys aren't superstitious. They came out a different side in the second half. As this was Blackpool, maybe Margy gave them the "we'll fight them on the beaches" speech. Whatever he said, his real master-stroke was to give the team an injection of Power, Phil Power, our veteran player-coach. Phil the Power came on to replace debutant Simon Band at centre-forward. There's no substitute for experience, especially when it's coupled with skill, aggression and sheer football nous. Phil gave a master-class in how to lead the line. Where in the first half everything had been breaking down on the edge of the box, now it was sticking, and Phil was bringing the FC tricksters Patterson, Torpey and Howard into play. Two Patterson penalties and other goals from Chadwick and Ahern kept the party swinging, as FC ran out 4-2 winners. Oh, we do like to be beside the seaside, oh, we do like to beside the sea ...

Unfortunately, a few dozen FC fans couldn't resist the temptation to invade the pitch at full-time. Maybe most were daft young lads caught up in the excitement of the moment, but that doesn't excuse the middle-aged men shoving the stewards aside and running on to the pitch for their ten seconds of fame. FC might be an escape from the sterile regimentation of the Premiership, but it's not a charter to do exactly what you want and sod everyone else. The rule is clear: stay off the pitch. The rule is not for bending. FC might be all about 'our club, our rules' but it's their league, their regulations. They dock you points at the drop of a hat in the lower leagues.

But a few people acting up is not the abiding memory of this weekend in Blackpool. The abiding memory is of a noisy, happy, expanding FC family bringing fun and good-natured lunacy back to football. The Blackpool weekend will go down in FC folklore, and in years to come we can tell people: we were there.

Blackpool Mechanics 2 FC United 4 (att 4300)
FC Scorers: Chadwick, Ahern, Patterson(2)

Over the years at Old Trafford we've got used to the idea of players and fans living in separate universes and never the twain shall meet, so the first season of FC United has been a culture shock. When you watch top-level football, you accept the idea that football supporting is a one-sided affair: you supply the encouragement and the praise and the adolescent infatuation – even in middle age - and, oh yes, the money, and they, er, play football. You expect the fans to look in starry-eyed wonder at their heroes on the pitch living the dreams that they will never get to realise. You don't expect to see the players looking in wonder at the terraces and wishing they could join you.

The People's Club

That doesn't happen. Not unless you live in the alternative football universe of FC United where normal football logic has been turned on its head. The fans at FC have created a terrace culture that is so noisy and colourful and funny and infectious that the lads on the pitch have been envying us. I think they feel they're missing out on a part of the FC experience by just playing.

There have been several instances of players joining the fans on the terraces for a match, but I keep going back to the game against Castleton Gabriels. Cassy Gabs had moved the game to Radcliffe Borough to accommodate the expected bumper crowd, and they weren't disappointed as the turn-out fell two short of the 2500 capacity. I turned up at the social club about two-thirty after a few drinks in town and the large room was already a good-natured riot of singing FC fans. And players. I spotted three of them, Steve Torpey, Tony Coyne and Scott Holt, over to my right having a pint and singing songs and generally indistinguishable from the group of fans surrounding them. Now, I knew that the football culture at FC was subtly different from that of other clubs and that we had put the emphasis back on football as fun but even I thought that this was a surprisingly lax pre-match preparation. Of course, they were taking advantage of their injuries to enjoy the match in the company of the affectionate lunatics on the terraces. Did Liverpool supporter Torps think that this was such a good idea when the fans made him stand on the table and sing "If you all hate Scousers, clap your hands"? It didn't bother him a jot. After the pre-match session in the social club fans and players packed into the temporary stand behind the goals. I remember Torps walking across the pitch in front of us at half-time to an affectionate chorus of "You scouse bastard". Let social commentators beware – you'll never understand football culture without a keen nose for post-modern irony.

I wonder if the players realised how important their decision to watch the game with the fans was. It was one of those little things that appear insignificant in themselves but that, when added together, define the culture of a football club. It binds the fans to the team. It reinforces the feeling of being in it together, blurs the distinction between players and fans and erodes those barriers that distance fans from their team and their club at the highest level. What made the day special for the fans was the knowledge that the players were not on a mission, not making a political gesture, that they were simply doing what they wanted. They just fancied having the craic with the fans, because they are fans too. Every single home match Margy's programme notes feature a word of praise for the 'incredible FC fans' and emphasise the importance of the support to the team, but no amount of words can express this appreciation as powerfully as the choice of Torps, TC and Scotty Holt to stand with the fans on the terrace. And you know how much it means to the fans when they come on the forum afterwards and slate Torps for his dress sense. I mean, a shirt and tie with an acrylic jumper and trainers. Steve, where's your Armani and bling, mate?

Our Club Our Rules

Holker Old Boys, H, 25/02/06

How do you follow that weekend in Blackpool? By a week in rehab judging by the bloated, drink-sodden faces we left behind us in the Old Bridge. I know these lads worship George Best, but at the rate they're going, they'll be meeting him before the end of the season. Anyway, back to a bread and butter North-West Counties match day. It's a home game, so we must be at … Moss Lane in Altrincham. A change of venue enforced because of a beer festival taking place at Gigg Lane. That's an official beer festival, not the unofficial beer festival that takes place every time FC play. It was arranged before Bury and FC came to an agreement over ground-sharing, so we can't complain. In fact, many FC fans were clapping their hands in appreciation, as they usually trek up to Bury from South Manchester every fortnight, and Altrincham is on their door step. For me, it meant that the expedition to far-flung corners of Greater Manchester continued.

Arrived in Alty about one o'clock and headed for the Bridge Inn. The Bridge in Alty bore no resemblance to its almost namesake in Blackpool – about a dozen regulars having a natter or picking horses from the paper. But by the time I was joined by Mark and Rob and Pete, it was filling up with FC fans. Pete's another OT regular who was taking in his first FC game. Several pints later we were walking down a cold but bright Moss Lane to the ground, a quaint little ground with a decent-sized main stand and terracing on three sides.

The game itself proved to be a run-of-the-mill affair. At the end of a laboured first half FC nudged in front with a goal from Josh Howard. The second half saw a competent if unspectacular display from the lads and, despite the minor blip of a well-taken Holker equaliser, ended in a routine 4-1 win for FC. It was crowned by a solo goal from clown prince Rory who twisted past a couple of defenders before slotting the keeper. There was a definite after-the-Lord-Mayor's-parade feel to the afternoon both on the pitch and off it, as both players and fans gave a muted performance. On the occasions when the fans were singing, I found myself irritated to hear so many old United songs, and songs in honour of Solskjaer and Cantona instead of Torpey and Patterson. We'll never forget our shared United past, but while we're watching FC, let's sing our hearts for the lads – our lads, the ones in the FC shirts. I was encouraged by a little cluster of fans stood near me in the first half who had their own set of superb songs for FC players. How about "Billy Mac, you are a centre-back" to the old Supremes classic for Billy McCartney. And even better "The answer, my friends, is Howard on the wing" for Josh. Magnificent.

After the match I didn't ask Pete directly what he thought of FC. He might have given me the wrong answer. You know what it's like when you're potty about a girl and think she's got the face of an angel. You ask for your mate's

The People's Club

opinion, and he says: yeah, not bad, wouldn't kick her out of bed. It's too bruising for the sensitive soul of a poet.

The day ended with me jumping on a train to Stockport, though no one told the driver and he took me to Manchester Victoria instead. I must stop drinking when I go to games.

FC United 4 Holker Old Boys 1 (att 3159)
FC Scorers: Howard, Simms, Ahern, Patterson

Great Harwood, A, 27/02/06

I'm not sure about great but they were pretty good. Or maybe we were pretty ordinary. The truth was probably somewhere in between. We were back in Accrington again at the Interlink stadium. I'm tempted to say it was starting to feel like a second home, but I associate home with concepts like warmth and comfort, and this was a bitter winter's night with heavy showers and hints of snow. We sat in the main stand among the Great Harwood fans. As the game started I looked to my left and saw an old guy buttoned up against the cold. A wave of fellow-feeling swept over me – grassroots football, eh, old blokes who've watched their local team for half a century turning up in all kinds of weather for the love of the game - until he started to come out with an uninterrupted stream of biased, mean-spirited comments on everything FC. We were just a team of big-city fancy-dans. Miserable old git. But maybe he had a point on the night.

Despite an early penalty from Rory, we never settled into any rhythm. Harwood spent the first twenty minutes kicking anything in white that moved and then settled down to play some fluent football. When they equalised with a soft near-post header from a corner towards the end, we couldn't complain. We had had chances in the second half – Rory had ballooned one over an open goal from six yards – and the ref had denied us a stonewall penalty, but a draw was fair. We had struggled to establish any control in midfield where young Will Ahern and Chris Simms had been out-muscled by a very fit Harwood side.

This was far and away our lowest crowd of the season, which was a real shame for Harwood, as they were banking on the match takings to make good the damage done to their ground by a fire last season. But it was a Monday night, and a cold one, and Accrington is not the easiest place to get to. Credit to those of us who made it, and especially to the lunatics who stood on the open terrace behind the nets and experienced all four seasons in one night. In fact, make that three seasons – there was no hint of summer about it. And I'm beginning to think Accrington is a bogey ground for me. Three visits this season and I've not seen us win yet.

Great Harwood Town 1 FC United 1 (att 1028)
FC scorers: Patterson

Our Club Our Rules

You can talk all you want about fine-sounding abstractions such as community and co-operation and ownership, but ultimately an institution will stand or fall on the people that comprise it. A statement of principle can inspire and enthuse but that feeling can quickly turn to disillusionment if the day-to-day reality is a contradiction of those principles. Your splendid values become a mockery and an accusation if you can't live up to them. Judge us on what we do, not what we say. FC United will stand or fall on the quality of the people: in the boardroom, on the pitch and in the stands. All I can say at this stage is that we have a made a wonderful start, that the board have been sure-footed in their decisions, that the players have played joyous, celebratory football and the fans have been spreading a carnival atmosphere across the North-West.

The club feels like a family. Red Army veterans with decades of watching United home and away in England and in Europe have been shaking their heads in happy disbelief this season. They have been on the forum telling each other that they have made more friends in one season at FC than in forty years at Old Trafford. Other fans who went to Old Trafford for years simply to watch a game of football have realised that the game is just part of a much bigger experience. How many times this season have I had to remind myself that I had a football game to watch? When the party is this good, it can't be spoiled by the fickleness of the football gods. It's always a good day – win, lose or draw. FC take more fans away than most Premiership clubs but there has scarcely been an incident worth recording this season. Is it because we are a better class of football fan? No, of course not. It's simply because we're so bloody happy. As Friedrich Nietzsche – a tricky right-winger and a favourite with German hoolies in the thirties – pointed out: happiness makes you virtuous, not vice versa. And he knew his fussball.

March 2006
Till the fat lady sings

Everything has to start somewhere: even movements that go on to make a mark on the world often begin in humble surroundings. I was reminded of this the other day while padding along behind the shopping centre in Rochdale. There's a little cobbled street directly facing the entrance to the unlovely concrete multi-storey and you'd miss it entirely if not for the large plaque on the side wall of the first building in the street. If you take time to read it, it tells you that:

On December 21st 1844
The Rochdale Equitable Pioneers Society
commenced trading in this building
thereby launching the
worldwide co-operative movement

Did the gentlemen that opened the first co-op in 1844 think that their humble movement would prosper and still be going strong 160 years later? Probably not. Especially as there would have been the usual chorus of hard-headed realists telling them that their little experiment in social collaboration was utopian nonsense and doomed to failure. Why? Because it wilfully ignored people's innate capacity for greed and selfishness. Because it implied faith in people's ability to co-operate in the pursuit of a shared purpose. Because it expected too much of people. Not something the cynics could ever be accused of. The co-operative movement was driven by the conviction that there was a better way of doing things, that the crude, ruthless mechanisms of capitalism were not the only model of social interaction. The more you think about the co-operative movement, the more it sounds like FC United. After all, what better description could there be of FC United than a co-operative self-help society? So in fifty years time we can all look forward to seeing a plaque on the wall of the Central Methodist Hall in Manchester proudly announcing:

Our Club Our Rules
On 5th July 2005
In this hall was formed
the world-famous football club
FC United of Manchester
dedicated to the idea that football
truly is the people's game

Or can we? Will FC United have flourished to become the successful model of a new type of football club predicated on the belief that the aim of football is football and that the strength of a club is not profits but people? Or will it be it the subject of wistful reminiscence, a well-intentioned dream that dazzled briefly before fading like a ripple on a pond? Even a brilliant debut is no guarantee of longevity. But that FC United have made a brilliant debut, there can be little doubt. Success on the pitch, ever-increasing attendances, plaudits from the media, financial rude health and a trail of good will left in our wake as we have taken the FC football carnival across the north-west of England. A tide of anger and passion and enthusiasm has swept us along, carrying us up and over the occasional setback and moments of self-doubt to deposit us, breathless and euphoric, at the season's end. It's been emotional. And we can look back on our achievement with a justified pride: it's no small thing to have defied the forces of lethargy, inertia, apathy and cynicism. In May 2005 FC United wasn't even a glint in a disgruntled United fan's eye, and now it's a vital and undeniable reality. I can't imagine the football landscape without it. So maybe we're entitled to bask in a few moments of self-congratulation. Aye, a few moments, but then it's back to work.

History is a distorting mirror: everything seems inevitable looking back. Nothing seems inevitable looking forward. Life doesn't do guarantees. The world is littered with buildings that might have boasted commemorative plaques, but don't – all the buildings that hosted the first meeting of people fired with good intentions and ambitious plans, buildings that saw the birth of movements that faded without trace after a promising start. That's the problem – you don't see the plaques that aren't there. Failure is the norm, but we only remember the successes. So if we want to be able to point our grandkids to that FC United plaque in the future, we have to beware of complacency. As a great England manager once said: "This is not the end. It is not even the beginning of the end. It is only the end of the beginning." You probably know him - he wore a hat and smoked a big cigar. No, it wasn't Malcolm Allison.

Flixton, H, 15/03/06

Over two weeks without a game and it was having an effect on the FC morale. There had been some strangely pessimistic posts on the FC forum – it wouldn't last, it was running out of steam, it was doomed to fail – and this was three weeks after four thousand FC fans had enjoyed a carnival

Till the fat lady sings

atmosphere in Blackpool. Very odd. The problem is that for teams at our level, if you're not playing matches, you cease to exist. And while FC have not been playing, Big United have been on Sky three times, including a win in the Carling Cup Final against Wigan. So for some fans Big United seem real because TV validates them and proves their reality, while FC United, in the absence of matches, seems like some weird and ridiculous dream.

Well for some of us FC is the new reality and we turned up at Gigg Lane in the bitter cold to see them face a stiff test against Flixton. I could see it was one of our lower crowds despite the fact there were no other contending football attractions. I'm not sure it was due simply to the bitterly cold weather conditions. Are the doom-mongers and pessimists having an effect? Has one glorious Carling Cup triumph overcoming the likes of Birmingham, Blackburn and Wigan been enough to make the schizophrenics among us see the error of their ways and go running back to Old Trafford with their FC bar scarves between their legs? I refuse to believe it. People are better than that.

The game itself was a cracker and Flixton did us the service of highlighting just where our weaknesses lie. The defence lumbered, the midfield blundered and the attack misfired. Flixton exploited our lack of pace at the back time and again, as our defenders turned like oil tankers. Flixton passed the ball with more fluency and assurance in midfield, and up front they were denied by two point-blank saves from Barrie George, before taking the lead – to no-one's great surprise. We also had chances but our play was spasmodic rather than fluent. A one-goal deficit at half-time became a two-goal deficit within minutes of the restart, as a hopeful through ball was allowed to find its way to the Flixton centre-forward who ran on to score nonchalantly as Barrie George went to ground and Billy McCartney floundered in his wake. Oh dear, my mum said there would be days like this. Two down at home, clearly second best, the bitter cold seeping through my bones - this is when you start to wax lyrical about the spiritual benefits of suffering. The encouraging thing was that the crowd rallied behind the lads who were clearly having a bad day at the office. The singing did not falter and the lads responded and gave the Flixton goal the thirty-minute sustained battering that the fans demanded. The introduction of Spencer and Carden into midfield and the entrance of debutant Dave Swarbrick tilted the game in our favour. Twice the ball was booted clear six inches from the Flixton goal-line, Adie Orr blasted a glorious chance over from eight yards, and Rory missed a penalty. We weren't going to score tonight, and this was largely down to a commanding performance from the tall Flixton keeper who defied both the FC attack and the massed ranks of the MRE.

We were wrong. We did score, when Chaddy dived low to head home. Cue riotous scene in the back of the Flixton net. Keeper instinctively wraps himself round the ball as Chaddy and four other FC lads pile in to retrieve it to get the game started again – they know time is running out. The five FC lads are followed into the net by about eight Flixton defenders trying to protect their keeper. I make that about fourteen blue and red shirts in the back of the Flixton net soon to be followed by the referee trying to restore order. Two minutes of mayhem later Chaddy is running towards the centre-circle with ball in hand while the referee is booking ... the Flixton keeper! Presumably for sticking a chin on Chaddy's knee. Worth the admission fee alone.

The game restarted and FC swarmed forward for the final few minutes but without success. The last hope faded when the Flixton keeper tipped the kitchen sink round the post in injury time. Final whistle goes and the first thing I see is Chaddy and the keeper shaking hands. Don't you love football at this level.

Oh well, let's hope the team and the crowd make a comeback on Saturday against Leek CSOB.

FC United 1 Flixton 2 (att 1924)
FC Scorers: Chadwick

Pitfall 1: Second season syndrome

Let's be honest, it's human nature. We throw ourselves into something new with an energy and an intensity that simply cannot be maintained. The beginning is always the best bit, the period we look back to longingly when things have settled into a comfy routine. Hence all the letters to Auntie Glenda asking for tips on how to put the magic back into a relationship. Not that I'm suggesting that the FC adventure has reached the pipe and slippers stage already or that FC fans should be getting out the nurse's uniforms just yet, but we do need to prepare ourselves for the fact that the FC experience this season will have a subtly different flavour to it. We all remember the first days of a relationship when the excitement is tempered by nervous uncertainty about how long it will last, and when the absence of guarantees gives every date an added edge. It's been like that this season for FC United fans, especially at the start. We wondered how many would turn up for the very first match at Leigh. We wondered how many would travel up to Gigg Lane for our first home game. We worried how many would come back after our first defeat against Norton. We worried how many would turn up when there was a competing attraction at Old Trafford. We did a lot of worrying. Even a week after the amazing Euro away tie at Blackpool when over 4,000 fans had turned out for FC, there were posts on the fans' forum claiming that FC had run its course. It has been a season of doubts and insecurity, but it's precisely those things that have given each triumph – the astonishing crowd at the last home game, the on-field success, the accolade of Non-league Team of the Season – an added sweetness.

But there can never be another first season. The summer of 2005 was a time of madness. We lived in permanent suspense, not knowing whether we would have a team or a manager, a ground to play at or a league to play in. The first season has been a season of constant firsts. The first sighting of the

Till the fat lady sings

lads running out in the red of FC United; waiting until our fourth outing to see the first FC goal courtesy of a Steve Torpey scorcher; 2,500 trekking out to Leek in a downpour to see FC's first league game; playing Padiham in balmy sunshine a week later in our first game at Gigg Lane; our first "Euro away" weekend in Blackpool; our first trophy; our first genuine European away tie that saw 500 of the FC faithful join 7,000 Lokomotiv Leipzig fans on an unforgettable night at the Bruno Plache Stadium. In fact, every week felt like the first time. And there will be other firsts to look forward to in our second season – a debut in the FA Vase, a true Manchester derby when FC play Maine Road, new reserve and youth teams to support, the return against Leipzig at Gigg Lane – but, inevitably, that feeling of leaping into the unknown won't be quite as intense. Actually, ignore everything I've just written in this paragraph. Just listing all the firsts that we can look forward to next season has given me the same feeling of giddy excitement that I had twelve months ago. I don't think that second season-itis is going to be a problem. Maybe I should come back in eight years' time with warnings about tenth season syndrome. Shouldn't the novelty be wearing off by then?

Nevertheless, some things will change. Things that struck us as extraordinary at the start of the season and that we became quite blasé about by April. We got used to being media stars. They all came to Gigg Lane eventually to see what the fuss was about: local station Channel M, Sky Sports, Canal Plus from France, crews from Holland, Germany and Russia. We got used to seeing ourselves being interviewed on television – even those of us with a great face for radio. The written press didn't lag behind either, as the tabloid press, the Sunday papers and a whole range of magazines came, saw and were conquered and went away to write articles undiluted in their praise for the FC phenomenon. The Guardian and the Manchester Evening News even featured a regular FC United column. All of this media attention was welcome and deserved – was there a bigger football story than FC United this season? But we must expect to spend less time in the media spotlight next season. The media has the attention span of a goldfish: it picks things up and then drops them again just as quickly when the novelty wears off. We have to accept that we might be old news by next season. That's fine as long as we don't allow the reduced media attention to awaken our insecurities and to stir up ridiculous thoughts of FC United "running out of steam". We don't need the media to validate what we're doing at FC. We're not the Beckhams – we don't have to see ourselves in the media everyday just to prove we exist. We just have to settle down to being a normal football club. Did I say 'normal'? What I meant was, we just have to go quietly about our business of creating the kind of club that football has never seen before, the kind of fans' club that will be the norm in the future.

On the pitch too things could be rather different in our second season. This season we carried all before us. Well, apart from defeat in the Supporters Direct Cup, defeat in the North-West Counties League Cup and defeat in the

Our Club Our Rules

North-West Counties Division Two Trophy! But we carried all before us in the one that mattered. Our cup reverses allowed us in time-honoured fashion to concentrate on the league and our powers of concentration were so impressive that the trophy was secured several weeks before the end of the season. And let's not be coy, everyone loves a winner. Yes, the win at all costs attitude is blighting the game at the top level, but winning is wonderful when you achieve it honestly and fairly, and provided you know how to lose too. It's impossible to underestimate how important it was for FC United to get off to a winning start in its first season. It created a momentum that grew through the season and resulted in that record-breaking crowd at the final home game. It was no coincidence that this astonishing attendance figure coincided with FC being presented with the North-West Counties Division Two trophy. Why deny the obvious truth: people love success, and the desire to share in the post-match celebrations swelled the crowd that day. One of the ironies of success, however, is that you've earned the right to make life harder for yourself, ie. you've earned the chance to play better teams next season. I have no doubts that we will acquit ourselves well in Division One and that we will enjoy some magnificent football, but we might not win. Thank god the all-conquering Cammell Laird have been promoted out of this division, but that still leaves plenty of sides capable of giving us the run-around. It will be hard. It was hard this year – don't be fooled by what looks like a triumphal march to the title. But, of course, we did win, and often. A draw and a defeat represented a bad patch this season. But how will people react next season, if FC go six games without a win and are languishing in mid-table? How will they react after a 4-0 drubbing at Maine Road in the Manchester derby? It could happen. It will be a test of our credentials as fans. We think we're a breed apart from those Johnny-come-lately United fans who have been spoiled by success. We think that real supporters stay committed to their team though thick and thin, especially thin. But we're being naive if we don't accept that some of the 6,000 against Harwood were there because they preferred a winning FC to a faltering United. Maybe in recent years we've all got a little too addicted to success. Even this season an unexpected cup defeat to Nelson generated a few big-time-Charlie grumbles on the forum. So, if we don't carry all before us next season, I hope we don't hear the sound of toys being tossed petulantly out of prams, and it will be fascinating to see if an absence of silverware checks the growth of our fan base.

Leek CSOB, H, 18/03/06

Gloves, hat, scarf, vest, t-shirt, jumper, big coat. After Flixton on Wednesday I was taking no chances at Ice Station Gigg. Predictably, it turned out to be a mild, sunlit spring afternoon that meant I could keep my woolly hat in my pocket. Thank goodness for that. Hats don't work for me. They make me look like a village idiot, and I can manage that without props.

Till the fat lady sings

This was a match that brought back recent memories for many fans – memories of monsoon conditions in Staffordshire back in August when Leek were our opponents in our first ever competitive match. Not for me, of course, as I was confined to the house by work. For me it brought back memories of crackly phone updates from Mark, his shouts drowned out by raucous singing. Still, a 5-2 win had been an auspicious start. Would Leek be as obliging today, and provide the morale-boosting win that we needed? We might be well clear at the top of the table, but a draw and a defeat in out last two games had some people talking about Devon Loch. Pessimism – a football's fans natural condition.

Happily the opposition defence lived up to its name – it was Leeky. The avalanche began after four minutes when FC's iconic striker, Phil 'The Tan' Power, poked home from close range, and inside ten minutes FC were 2-0 to the good and in the comfort zone, with any thought of promotion jitters consigned to the dustbin. I don't want to compare the Leek boys to Welsh vegetables – oops, back to Robbie Savage again – but they were just to the taste of an FC side with a point to prove. Rory was skinning them, Torpey was roasting them, and the Power was having them for breakfast. Apparently Rory had been on the fans forum this week and he must have read the comments about his "petulant, Billy Big-time performance" against Flixton, when he'd seemed more intent on winding up officials and opponents than making an effective contribution. Today he showed us what we already knew – that the boy can play. Pace, skill and a flair for the spectacular. He completed a hat-trick in the second half with a strike from twenty-five yards which I can only describe as an "exocet". God knows how we used to describe that type of strike before the Falklands War. The ball was headed clear from a corner into the path of Rory who drew back his hammer of a right foot before drilling the ball hard and fast past stunned defenders and into the top of the net. All the Leek keeper could have known about it was a whistling noise past his right ear and singed sideburns. If the goal was magnificent, so was his celebration, or lack of it. He just stood there chest out glaring at the MRE as if demanding a grovelling apology from all those who had dared to doubt his brilliance. Think Cantona, haughty, imperious, contemptuous, against Sunderland about ten years ago. That boy Rory is pure theatre. Of course, it's theatre of the absurd sometimes, but just as often it's Shakespearian majesty.

It finished 8-1 to FC, the only surprise being that Leek didn't get nil. Their goal was also honed on the FC training pitch. A long punt up field was headed back to the keeper by Chaddy. Unfortunately, the keeper had rushed out of his area and couldn't pick it up. Cue the Keystone Cops: keeper smashes the ball straight into Chaddy's mush, ball rebounds off a dazed Chaddy beyond the keeper, grateful Leek striker nips round the keeper and taps the ball into an empty net. You can laugh about it when you're 5-0 up. The keeper, by the way, was Phil Melville who had come in to give Barry

George a rest and to show Barry how a more experienced keeper organises his defence! Also, he's a bit on the portly side, Phil, which meant he got the "You fat bastard" treatment that we usually reserve for away keepers. I could understand his hurt expression. After all, we never sing it for Barry, and he's not exactly waif-like.

At least I've finally found out what CSOB stands for: Can't Stop Our Boys!

FC United 8 Leek CSOB 1 (att 2559)
FC Scorers: Power(2), Swarbrick, Torpey, Patterson(3), Simms

Pitfall 2: Manchester United do well.

FC United grew out of Manchester United and, however we define our allegiance now, we were all United fans twelve months ago. A year is a long time in football – ninety minutes is a long time if you're watching Aston Villa – and extraordinary things have happened over that period. Many of us are wondering just how we managed before FC. How did we not see the yawning void in our football world that was waiting for the creation of FC United? For many of us there is no going back. If the future was to betray us and FC United faded away to become a footnote to history, we wouldn't recant our sins and run back chastened to Old Trafford. But some would. In fact, some FC fans have never left – spiritually. FC United is a temporary haven for their Redness until the glorious day when the American occupying force has been sent packing. Blimey, makes OT sound like Iraq. Mind you, "shock and awe" neatly sums up what many United fans felt last summer.

But let's look at a scenario that very few of us have considered. What if the worst predictions about the Glazers were to prove unfounded? What if they found some way of making their ambitious financial plans work, while at the same time delivering continued on-field success? What if they showed themselves respectful of United traditions and resisted the temptation to turn Old Trafford into the "Budweiser Soccerdome"? What if they managed to exploit their prize asset without hiking up admission prices every season? Finally, what if they pulled off the logic-defying trick of making their sums add up, while continuing to give the fans big names and big trophies? Would a proportion of FC fans for whom Glazer is the main problem revise their opinions? Perhaps these fans do not have a problem with millionaire footballers, uncompetitive leagues, Premiership greed and a media-dominated sport. If the Glazers were to prove themselves acceptable guardians of the United tradition, how many FC fans would abandon their bit on the side – however sexy and warm and funny – and go back to the missus? I mean, most blokes can be tempted into having a fling, but they don't usually leave their wives, do they? If an upturn in United's fortunes was to coincide with a fallow period for FC, would we see a leakage of support back to Old Trafford. It's possible, because, as amazing as it seems, there are some fans who would rather watch some kid called Rooney rather than our very own master of mischief, Rory Patterson.

Pitfall 3: Manchester United do badly.

It is possible that rumours of Manchester United's demise might be premature, but the portents are worrying for the suits at Old Trafford. There's a new kid in town, some flash foreigner with more money than he can spend, who's found the best toy that money can buy and who shows no sign of getting bored with it at present. The Glazer resources pale into insignificance alongside the Abramovich billions, and in a football world that allows billionaires to bankroll a football club, it seems likely, even probable, that Chelsea will dominate football for as long as they want to. They probably wouldn't admit it, but the people in charge at Old Trafford know as well as the fans that they've come down in the world, that they are competing with Arsenal and Liverpool rather than Chelsea, and that in transfer terms they are picking up the crumbs that fall from Roman's table. There's a real possibility that the glory days are over for United – and everybody else - in the short-term, at least until Roman finds a new interest. It will be interesting to see the effect of this on a generation of United fans that have gorged on success for the last fifteen years. Are the current Old Trafford faithful made of the same stuff as the thousands who continued to pack the ground in the seventies after United's disastrous relegation to Division Two?

Will FC be the obvious beneficiary of a downturn in United's fortunes? Possibly. It's not too difficult to imagine some United fans finding it increasingly difficult to justify paying Premiership prices to watch a team that is a pale shadow of recent trophy-winning sides. They won't stop supporting United, but they might reason that it makes more sense to get their live football fix watching Little United for £7 a game, while continuing to watch Big United on Sky television. Why pay over £600 for a season ticket to watch United perform as a support act to the Chelsea All Stars, watching games in a subdued stadium alongside passive fans, when you could be at Gigg Lane enjoying the colour and the noise and the passion, and roaring on FC in a genuinely competitive match in a genuinely competitive league? All for a fraction of the cost. Perhaps some United fans are making this kind of calculation already. Perhaps only renewed United success will keep them on board. But if that success fails to arrive, might we see a leakage of fans from Old Trafford to Gigg Lane?

So why would that represent a potential pitfall for FC United? Don't we want our mates who still go to OT to come down and sample the FC experience for themselves? Of course we do. I just want them to come for the right reasons. I'm wary of the fans who might come because Big United stop winning. I'm wary of the fans who might come with a patronising "It's not the real thing but it'll do until things pick up again at Old Trafford" attitude. I'm wary of the fans who might come with Billy big-time attitudes and slag off the lads when things don't go our way. In short, I'm wary of fans coming along who don't sufficiently love this extraordinary club or properly appreciate the unique football culture that has been created in the space of a single season. It is a culture suffused with the values of the club: democracy, participation and ownership. It is a culture that has its own flavour: humour, bolshieness and good-natured lunacy. It is a culture that expresses itself in standing up and singing, in chanting, in laughing at ourselves, in doing the worst bloody congas in the world, in making every game into an excuse for a party – win, lose or draw. It's something that continually amazes me and delights me and that fills me with pride. Don't get me wrong - there is no desire to keep FC as "our thing", an exclusive club for the few who were there at the start, but there is a legitimate fear that this special brew could get watered down. Many FC fans left Old Trafford because they could no longer stomach the soulless "Theatre of Dreams" match-day experience, where too many supporters sit and moan instead of playing an active part in urging the team on. They don't want to see that replicated at FC. Of course, there's a place at FC for the fans who simply want to come down and enjoy the football and drink in the atmosphere created by others – you don't have to be a loud-singing, hard-drinking football extrovert to be an FC fan – but it would be tragic if the FC culture of support as noisy, colourful participation was gradually eroded into the culture of passive consumption that plagues Premiership football.

So, what message are we sending out to football fans, Reds and others, that might be considering giving FC United a try? The message that everyone is welcome, that FC might be an extended family but it's no insular little clan. I want this club to grow and grow. After all, I'm evangelising for a football reformation in which clubs re-bind themselves to their communities, a reformation in which football clubs use the unifying power of football to combat the trend towards social dislocation and isolation. But I want the fans that come to FC to 'get' what FC United is all about. I want them to understand what we are for and what we are against. I want them to understand that FC is the expression of certain principles that you are proud to stay loyal to, regardless of the vagaries of success or failure on the football field. Come down to Gigg Lane and actively support, get together with the fans in pub, join your local supporters branch, become a member and vote at the AGM, offer your services to the club as a volunteer – join the revolution. Oh yes, and come and see some cracking football too. I'll make a practical suggestion here, just in case this extended FC United love poem ever falls under the gaze of the marvellous Mr. Walsh. Andy, let's have some embossed membership cards with a statement of FC principles on the back. As a starter, I'll offer:

> FC United – it's about football, it's about fun, it's about people.

Till the fat lady sings

Now I've started, I can't stop. What about:

FC United: do not ask what your club can do for you – ask what you can do for your club.

Mind you, I am the person who came up with the ineffably naff Fans United as a name for the club!

Oldham, A, 1-0, 22/03/06

You can't have fillet steak every meal. Sometimes you have to make do with turkey twizzlers. Still, it was great to visit another new ground on our first-season travels. Boundary Park is famous among football fans as one of the coldest grounds in the country. I watched Oldham play City there about twenty years ago and I'm still trying to get warm. You think of Greater Manchester as a featureless, flat plain, so it's surprising to learn that Boundary Park is the second highest ground in the country, just behind ... The Hawthorns. How does that work? Isn't the Midlands below Manchester on the map?

Anyway, back to Wednesday night. It was cold, of course, but not cold enough to bring back nightmare memories of Gigg Lane a week before. I sat in the main stand with mum and dad about five rows back from a lunatic Oldham Town fan. He kept us all entertained by booing every FC player, shouting "cheat, cheat, cheat" every time the referee gave a decision our way, and singing "Top of the league, you're 'avin' a laugh". We certainly were. At him. In fairness, I think he was related to one of the players and was only doing his best to get behind his lads, but you just knew that he'd spend the rest of the week telling everyone he knows that "FC are rubbish, over-rated, will get pasted every week next season, and the ref gives 'em everything". I just felt sorry for his wife who sat quietly beside him. Or was it his nurse?

I thought we might come a cropper in this match. Oldham Town had been unlucky to lose 1-0 at Gigg Lane after running us ragged for forty-five minutes. They're a very young side with plenty of skill and pace and, more importantly, they're a footballing side. As it turned out, they were more conservative tonight than in the first match and, though they were neat and skilful at the back and in midfield, they rarely got enough men forward to cause us problems. The Power continued to lead the line with intelligence, while Torpey, Patterson and Swarbrick buzzed around him dangerously. But it was a game of few chances. It took a goal from a corner to win the game, when Chaddy used that right knee so familiar to opposition centre-forwards to more constructive effect and looped a strange shot into the top corner. Though Spencer and Ahern generally controlled midfield, the game stayed in the balance and Oldham always had a goal in them. Rory could have given us a more relaxed last ten minutes but he continues to pile up contenders for the miss of the season competition, waltzing round the keeper only to blast high and wide.

Respect to the young Oldham lads – they're going to be a cracking team in a few years time, if they stick together. Another hard-earned three points and one hand on that Division Two trophy. As the fans have started singing: "We'll win the football league again – this time at Padiham". Which is not strictly true, as Padiham have moved the last game of the season twenty miles away … to Boundary Park.

Oldham Town 0 FC United 1 (att 1767)
FC Scorers: Chadwick

Pitfall 4: we lose our way

That FC United is currently in safe hands, there can be no doubt. All the contacts that I have enjoyed with people at the club throughout the season – members of the board, the management and players, volunteers, and, last but never least, the fans – have filled me with pride and convinced me that we have been incredibly fortunate in the people that FC United has brought together. Without exception the people running this club are the most modest, principled and down-to-earth people you could want to meet. Not to mention, talented. We are truly bloody lucky. You only have to read the programme notes written by Margy to realise that the individuals in charge of FC's fortunes are just fans with a few extra responsibilities. It seems extraordinary to me that the instincts of the board are so sure-footed that time and again their decisions have seemed incontestably right. A succession of choices - enlisting the Bhopal Appeal as the club sponsor, naming the Player of the Season award in honour of Russell Delaney, allowing kids in for nothing at certain home games, boycotting post-match hospitality at Darwen because their board refused to sell concessionary tickets, accepting invitations to play in fund-raisers for good causes, putting all major decisions to the vote of the membership, employing a community development officer, setting up youth and reserve teams – have not only been faithful to the principles of FC United, but have actually shown how those principles can work in practice.

Another safeguard for the future of the club is the existence of an articulate and opinionated membership. The fans' forum acts as the unofficial watchdog over club affairs, and nothing seems to happen at the club without it being reported on the forum. The fans have such a passionate commitment to the club that they are sensitive to what they consider even a minor deviation from the club's principles. At the last home game of the season a mischief-maker from up the road at Old Trafford tried to sour the carnival atmosphere by handing out leaflets alleging that FC board members were cashing in on their position by selling FC t-shirts. Two FC United board members had been running a t-shirt company for several years and had made Manchester United t-shirts – indeed, still do – long before FC United had come along. Their only 'crime' now was to be producing FC t-shirts. The shirts were not being promoted as official club merchandise. They were simply t-shirts that FC fans might or might not wish to buy. They were not sold via the club shop or the match-day megastall and any individual, FC fan or not, could have done exactly the same thing. The leaflet omitted to mention, of course, that a generous proportion of the money from each sale went to the club – a freely given donation from the afore-mentioned board members. The forum picked up this issue and a fierce debate ensued for several days. Some fans regretted what they saw as a conflict of interest. Some fans dismissed the whole thing as mischief-making. Some fans argued that it was taking principle to a ridiculously precious pitch and creating a problem where one did not exist, and some fans reminded people that these allegations originated with an individual who had spent years making his living from United-related ventures and who saw FC as a threat to his business. It really didn't matter whether this debate was a case of making a mountain out of a molehill or not, the important and healthy thing was that the debate was taking place. You can't get away with anything. As long as the fans continue to scrutinise everything at FC, we will continue to prosper. Only apathy can hurt us.

So, why have I raised the possibility of FC United losing its way? Not because I think it can happen or will happen in the foreseeable future, but simply because I am so proud of what this club is that it does no harm to play the devil's advocate now and again. Let's talk about some of the ways that this club could lose its unique culture. We might get too obsessed with success. What if the board came to us next season and said that we can guarantee successive promotions for the next few seasons by paying the highest wages and attracting the best non-league players? All we have to do is double the price of season tickets, accept shirt sponsorship, cut back on our investment on community projects and bring out a new FC United kit every season. Would any FC fans agree to that Faustian pact? At the moment, it would have a snowball's chance in hell. At the moment rigid adherence to our principles sets the boundaries for our success on the football field. We won't pay more than we can afford on the team. We won't sacrifice money set aside to pay for the things we believe in to buy success. Success within our principles, not at the expense of them. Otherwise, how long would it be before FC morphed into everything we have turned out backs on? If it quacks like a duck, walks like a duck and swims like a duck, it's a duck. If we behaved like any other club fixated on success at all costs and obsessed with the need to make money to pay for that success, because that's where that fixation leads to, would it be any consolation to be a democratic, fan-owned football club? It might be an improvement on the clubs cum businesses owned by profiteering individuals that dominate football now, but we would be quibbling about small differences. FC would have ceased to be the ideal that I believe in now.

Staying faithful to its principles will not hinder FC's growth. Just the

Our Club Our Rules

opposite. By having a unique identity and by offering football fans a genuine alternative to today's Premiership clubs, FC United can guarantee its expansion and its longevity. Football clubs have spent years insulting the intelligence of their fans. We can show that there is another way. The fans can surprise the cynics by showing that given a choice between success and principle, they might actually understand that you can buy success at too high a price. If the board at FC came to the fans and said that we could sign European superstar Carlos Kickaball but it meant upping admission prices, I hope I could rely on the fans to give the idea a resounding thumbs-down. If the day comes when the fans decide otherwise, I might have to go and … form a breakaway club.

New Mills, A, 25/03/06
"We've got a ticket to Hyde, and we don't care" to paraphrase the Fab Four. But it was off to Ewen Fields to watch the Fab Eleven take on New Mills. We're in touching distance of the league title now, but perversely it's getting harder to suppress our impatience. Postponements are frequent at this level and the table makes bizarre reading by the end of March. You have to do a careful double-take when looking at it. You think: "Fantastic, 24 points clear and only six games to go". Well, make that fourteen games to go for teams like Nelson. If they win their eight, yes, eight games in hand, they'll only be nine points behind us. Not exactly breathing down our neck, but still uncomfortably close for a paranoid football fan. Is there any other kind? They're not likely to win all their games in hand, to be honest - they've got eight games a week in May.

Ewen Fields is a tidy little ground: one small but handsome main stand and covered terracing on the other three sides. We were grateful for that cover when the rain poured down in the second half. Not that the rain dampened any spirits among the FC faithful behind the goal. A dull second half on the pitch was enlivened off it by a ten-minute version of "Won't pay Glazer or work for Sky" - each repetition given the thumping accompaniment of hands drumming against the corrugated metal at the back of stand. It sounded like a tribe of warriors working themselves into a trance before going into battle. "I don't care about Rio" might have been the original FC anthem, but this chant might supplant it by the end of the season. You can see why it's proved a big hit with the fans: it unites the feelings of many people for both FC and Big United.

On the field New Mills were the only side showing any fluency in the first forty-five minutes. They passed well through midfield without ever suggesting a goal was imminent, while we barely strung three passes together, hardly created a chance, and … went in at the break 2-0 up, courtesy of Joz Mitten and Rory. Who said football was fair? Great turn and finish by Joz who works selflessly up front and deserves every goal he gets.

Mark had brought his lovely missus Rachael with him for her first taste of

Till the fat lady sings

FC. Now, Mark might not be a member of the NWAF (No Women At Football) party, but I think after Saturday Rachael certainly is. She admitted to me at half-time that she was "not exactly enthralled", and all I could do was agree with her. At least I could reassure her that FC were kicking towards us in the second half and that we were guaranteed a close-up view of a few FC goals. Until Rory decided to re-write the script by getting himself sent off. He does like to engage the officials in conversation on football-related topics.

So with half an hour to go we sat back and waited for a New Mills onslaught that never came. The defence coped comfortably and Phil Melville made a couple of excellent saves from long-range shots. In fact, it was FC that missed the best chances. I think we were suffering from a Power shortage. The aging maestro has that ability to make others play. Still, that's three points closer to first-season glory.

New Mills 0 FC United 2
FC scorers: Mitten, Patterson

Maybe it's because our first season has exceeded the wildest expectations of the cheeriest optimist that I'm inclined to sound a cautionary note now. It's not life, is it, for things to move ever onwards and upwards without a few setbacks along the way, and without doubt FC will experience its difficult moments. But that's what you want: it builds character, and it will make the club stronger. There will be challenges ahead, and how we meet them will determine our success. No pain, no gain. No challenge, no glory.

Maybe our biggest challenge lies in not shooting ourselves in the foot and frittering away the good will that we've built up in our first twelve months. More than a few people, not all of them FC detractors, confidently predicted that we would sabotage our own cause by stirring up trouble and making ourselves unwelcome wherever we went. How fantastic it feels now to look back on the season having proved them wrong. Large numbers of fans have followed the team home and away this season and, despite indulging in a dry sherry or two, there has barely been an incident worthy of note. In fact, the opposite has usually been the case, and we have come away from games with the praise of the local police and landlords ringing in our ears. Yes, circumstances have helped: an absence of opposition fans and an absence of painful defeats. So, not much in the way of provocation and not much in the way of disappointment. But provocation and disappointment will inevitably come our way at some stage in the future – that's the nature of football – and we must show the same good humour that we have displayed so far. There have already been signs that the occasional moron will try and provoke us by singing Munich songs – something guaranteed to excite an aggressive, knee-jerk reaction from United fans (and most FC fans remain United fans at heart). We have to rise above it. However counter-instinctive and difficult it may be, we have to rise above it and treat the idiots with indifference or even the caustic wit that we are already famous for. They'll soon get the message that FC fans can't be provoked. If we give in to our worst instincts and react aggressively, the damage that we do to the image of the club could be huge and irrecoverable. There are plenty of journalists out there waiting for an opportunity to un-mask the self-righteous impostors at FC who, when they don't get everything their own way, revert to type and turn into a football rabble. We have to make sure that we never give them the chance to write that story. That's the ongoing challenge. And there's more at stake than the fortunes of FC United. What's at stake is the idea that football fans have moved on from the ugliness and stupidity of the hooligan heyday of the seventies, that there is an alternative to the all-seated, heavily policed, over-stewarded Premiership experience, that fans can be lively, noisy and passionate about their team, have a few drinks before the game and stand together on a terrace without degenerating into an unruly, aggressive mob. There is an alternative to the Premiership nanny state but we're not going to convince anyone if we go round acting like Asbo-wallahs auditioning for Shameless.

Another difficult moment could come when Malcolm Glazer decides to sell up at Old Trafford. I don't think anyone at this stage could predict what effect this would have on the fortunes of FC. Some of the fans who walked away last summer didn't get beyond Glazer and the debts that he saddled the club with. General concerns about the state of top-level football probably played no part in their decision to join FC United. So, if Glazer sells United to a home-grown, pure-bred English billionaire with the funds to pay off the club's debts and the resources to compete with Abramovich's Chelsea, presumably their reason for being at FC United will disappear. It would be extremely interesting to see how many FC fans returned to the United fold in those circumstances. Maybe I'm blinkered by my FC-tinted spectacles, but I don't think it would be a large percentage, and at least we would have the compensation of knowing that the fans who stayed were fully committed to the principles of FC United. And every season that Glazer remains at Old Trafford is an opportunity, another season in which FC can continue to develop into the model of what a football club can be. If FC remains a genuine alternative to the type of club that currently dominates the Premiership, events at Old Trafford will have less and less relevance for the development of the club. By the time that Glazer leaves Old Trafford, we might have built something so powerful at FC that no one wants to walk away.

What else could sabotage the onward march of FC United? What about a high-profile defection? Let me share with you the recurrent nightmare that wakes me up in the early hours of the morning, eyes fixed in horror on the ceiling, duvet flung off the bed and the sheets soaked with sweat. No, it's not the thought of being trapped in a lift with Jade Goody. I'm watching breakfast TV, enjoying Sian Williams's winsome ways and eating my bowl

Till the fat lady sings

of Morrison's frosted cornflakes, when a familiar face suddenly appears on screen. My befuddled wits achieve a modicum of clarity and I realise that it's FC's general manager Andy Walsh. I turn up the sound just in time to catch Andy saying: "I'm going back to Old Trafford. It's all been a terrible mistake. Mr. Glazer is the future of football. We're just a bunch of misguided romantics harking back to a past that never existed. Forgive me, Malcolm, for I have sinned." Right, that's it, I must stop eating cheese before I go to bed.

Our Club Our Rules

April 2006
The ties that bind

It's six o'clock on Saturday April 22nd and the forecourt of the Swan and Cemetery pub is thronged with groups of grinning fans. Waves and smiles pass back and forth across the crowd as faces recognise other faces, and expectant looks are cast down Manchester Road in the direction of Gigg Lane. People are spilling over into the road and cars are edging through them, trailing bar-scarves and sounding celebratory horns. Then there is a stirring in the crowd and a ripple of movement, and the waiting is finally over. The bright red bulk of an open-top bus has turned into view and is gliding slowly towards us. The happy mass of fans that was simmering quietly comes to the boil in a roar of song as the bus turns into the pub car park. The top deck is a disordered scramble of players and wives and kids. Mobile phones are suddenly everywhere, held aloft to capture the moment. But it's not the fans snapping away on their mobiles – it's the players who look as though they can't believe the dream they are living and who are pointing them at the waving, dancing, singing mob below. The players have the wide grins of kids on Christmas morning as they join the rest of us in a chorus of: "Championes, Championes".

What follows for the players is what they've been doing all season: partying with the fans. The lads are mobbed as they pile off the bus, and they happily give themselves up to the crowd. Every fan seems to want a picture with every player. There's an endless queue of people to have their picture taken with Chaddy and the North-West Counties Division Two trophy. A hundred obliging poses later, a flagging Chaddy is shouting: "Get Torpey. He'll do some pictures." Rory is on the pub steps doing an interview. Joz Mitten has a red and white wig on and is talking excitedly about converting to centre-back next season. Middle-aged men are cadging pens to go and stand in line with kids to get autographs off Chaddy, Torpey or any player that comes within reach. George the kit man is showing pics of his 4-day, 450-mile sponsored bike ride round every ground in the NWCL Division Two to raise money for Alex's motorised wheelchair. I'm sat round the back

The ties that bind

on the pub terrace with David and Guy and Mike smiling like an idiot and drinking in the giddy scenes around me. Before long defender Rob Nugent's face appears at the open pub window and starts shouting the FC version of Anarchy in the UK: "I am an FC fan. I am Mancunian. I know what I want and I know how to gerrit. I wanna destroy Glazer and Sky. I wanna be-eeee … at FC". Two minutes later board member Scott Fletcher is bouncing out onto the terrace singing the same song. Meanwhile general manager Andy Walsh is standing close by looking slightly drained and probably wondering what he's started.

When we wander indoors, the singing is in full flow. It won't falter for the next two hours. The fans are a few pints ahead of the players, but the players look determined to catch up. Football and alcohol. A combustible mix, eh? Not here. Not tonight. In fact, not ever when it comes to FC. The pub is wall-to-wall grins. Soon the irrepressible kit man George is up on a table conducting the choir. Then he's joined by a pretty young girl. It's the daughter of Russell Delaney. There are tears in the eyes of tough-looking blokes as they look at his daughter and sing "Will never die, will never die, will never die, will never die, we'll keep the red flag flying high, cos Man United will never die."

The players are talking to anyone that wants to chat, and that seems to be everyone. Assistant manager Phil Power, looking as dapper as ever, comes over to chat to us. He's soft-spoken and a gentleman off the pitch, but a force of nature on it. He's been sent off today after some histrionics from the opposing full-back induced the ref to produce a red card. He has a little grin on his face as he tells us about waiting for the lad in the tunnel at full-time. I think they had what is described in diplomatic parlance as a frank exchange of views. Defender Dave Brown accepts a pint from us and chats with David about the local Heywood Sunday league sides they've both played for. He's busy praising the players' player of the year Steve Spencer, when Spenners, as he calls him, suddenly strolls up. I've raved about Steve all season and now I get fifteen minutes of chat with him that proves his manner mirrors his football: modest, level-headed and intelligent. A cracking lad. Then I'm launching into a chorus of "O Gareth Ormes is our left back", when Dave and Mike and Guy start laughing and point over my shoulder. I turn round to see a laughing Gareth Ormes who immediately bursts into a rendition of his own song. Minutes later Rory is standing next to our little group at the bar looking a picture in his black blazer, club tie and blue plastic hat. He spots Mike's County Cork gaelic football top, rolls his eyes, shakes his head and announces in his broad Irish brogue: "Tyrone's better." Ten minutes after I'm in the loo and telling striker Adie Orr at the next urinal that he's my dad's favourite player. I'm like a kid in a sweet shop.

It's just mad – the happiest piss-up you can imagine. You can feel the waves of love radiating out from this noisy little pub. Daft snippets of phrases are slipping across my mind as my brain tries to put a label on it … If

Our Club Our Rules

Carlsberg did football clubs ... This is how it feels to be FC, this is how it feels to be home ... Consider yourself FC, consider yourself one of the family ...

Cheadle Town, H, 01/04/06

Not so much Jim'll Fix It as Jules'll Fix It. One email to the club's press officer Jules Spencer was all it took to get permission for my sister Karen to attend the match as a press photographer and use FC United as the subject of her college project. The club that likes to say Yes. Makes a change from the clubs that like to say "Sod off, we're busy". Of course, I had to go with her and act as her guide. A purely altruistic gesture on my part and in no way motivated by the desire to get up close and personal with my football heroes. Up close and personal in a manly way, of course.

We got there early as she was keen to get pictures of the various match day volunteers doing their bit in the build-up to the game. Cue a string of bemused programme sellers, turn-style operators, catering staff and stewards trying to work out why somebody wanted their picture. Not to mention the players that we intercepted in the car park or the players' lounge. I was trying hard to keep that note of schoolboy excitement out of my voice as I accosted Rory, Steve Spencer, Dave Brown, Chaddy, Steve Torpey and Phil Power. Tried to sound cool as I traded football snippets with the lads. Rory had been for a trial with Grimsby in mid-week. "Are you staying with us, Rory?" I think he said yes. "Hope those legs will keep going for another five years, Phil". I think he just smiled. Steve Torpey borrowed a pen off my sister, the Power joked about the light bouncing off his bald head, and Chaddy showed us how to find our way into the main stand. In a word, they were superb: friendly, down-to-earth, obliging. Even Chaddy didn't take offence when I told my sister that he was our captain, and she asked whether he played football. This was her first football match. He just laughed and said: "Not very often according to some people".

That press pass certainly opens doors, and we found ourselves pitchside as the players warmed up. Karen gets a picture of Margy looking dapper in his match day suit – "My fifty-quid suit" says he. I'm in my element discussing the possibility of Grimsby signing Rory or Will Ahern, talking about heavy pitches and asking how we'll do next season with the great man himself. I felt like a kid on Jim'll Fix It.

No chance, however, for Karen to get a picture of the MRE in full flow. No, nothing to do with an unusually subdued performance from FC faithful. It was down to the fact that the MRE was closed for maintenance. Rumour has it that a season-long hammering from FC hands has loosened the corrugated iron panels at the back of the stand. So we had no fans behind either goal as the MRE hordes re-located to the south stand. It did seem to dissipate the atmosphere slightly.

The ties that bind

The game itself threw up one hero. Unfortunately for us, he played for Cheadle. Step forward and take a bow Cheadle defender Ashley Stokes. The Cheadle keeper was injured early on and they had no reserve keeper. Their manager told me afterwards that this young lad was quick to volunteer. Seventeen years old and nine stone wet through, but tough as old boots. As Cheadle held on doggedly to a 1-0 lead, he stood up to every cross, shot and challenge with a bravery bordering on recklessness. After one second half scramble he lay shaking on his six-yard line – the way people do when they're badly injured and in shock. I went cold for second. Until he jumped up and carried on. Minutes later blood ran down the side of his head as an FC boot landed studs first on his left ear. But he made it to the final whistle. The only surprise was that we managed to get one past him, when Chris Simms leaped high to head home from close range. I keep seeing this at FC games - unsung heroes who embody everything that football should be about: skill, character and courage. North-West Counties Division Two, I salute you.

I wish I could say the same for the referee, Mr. Hussain. I know it's a difficult job, but he made it look impossible. How he turned down a stonewall penalty in the first half when Dave Swarbrick slalomed through the Cheadle defence before being attacked with a machete, I'll never know. Had he made up his mind to avoid any possible accusation of being a homer by giving Cheadle every decision going? Let's be kind to a fellow human being and just say he had a bad day at the office. Which you and I never have, of course.

So it looks as though we'll get them in singles. Another tough battle and one more point closer to our first trophy. The afternoon ended with FC fans helping the Bury groundsman replace divots in the muddy pitch. The fans had responded to a request to bring garden forks to the game to help repair the pitch. Nice to see the appeal didn't fall on deaf ears.

FC United 1 Cheadle Town 1 (att 2713)
FC Scorers: Simms

Being a multi-millionaire footballer doesn't make you a bad person, but it can't do much for the development of character. The wonder is not that footballers occasionally behave badly, the wonder is that they don't behave worse. How can you avoid having your head turned upside down when you're earning a hundred grand a week? And what on earth can you spend it on? Just how many flash cars, Hugo Boss suits and pieces of bling can one person buy? Just what does your average Premiership footballer do with his money? Not very much is the answer, probably. After a certain amount, it's just more, isn't it? The trouble is, you don't turn money down, when people are throwing it at you. Put yourself in their position. Would we turn it down, if it was offered to us? No, because money has this pernicious effect: no matter how much you have, you always think you need more. But are we really doing these lads a favour by giving them what they think they want?

Our Club Our Rules

The sensible, dull Shearer types probably do nothing with their money, saved from themselves by a lack of imagination. Their advisors place it in an off-shore account, where it accumulates pointlessly. But what about the daft lads, the silly, wild, immature ones transformed into millionaires overnight? Is it any wonder some of them are tempted by drink and drugs and gambling? You've got thousands of quid in your pocket that demands to be spent. Your trophy girlfriend will doubtless do her bit, but you've still got more dosh than you know what to do with. So you end up spending it on pointless crap like a fleet of expensive cars. And what will be the next must-have life style accessory for today's footballers? Cosmetic surgery? You heard it here first.

So a Premiership journeyman earns more in a week then a nurse earns in a year. It's not right, is it? I'll never feel comfortable about that. Of course, the realists spout glib nonsense about market forces. It's supply and demand, innit? Except it isn't. That's why most of England's football clubs are massively indebted. Clubs don't work on sound economic principles. They don't pay what they can: they pay what it takes. They're in it to win it. They chase the dream. Sometimes, as in the case of Leeds United, they fly too close to the sun and crash and burn. Clubs get seduced by their own ambition. Clubs allow themselves to be blackmailed by players. As contract talks reach an impasse, star player is spotted meeting the officials of a rival club in some discreet spot like a crowded restaurant. Star player's agent crops up in the tabloids with the timely news that there is interest from Real Madrid. Desperate for the success that will maintain its revenue levels, the club caves in to star player's exorbitant demands. Cue press conference, a signing of contracts, smiles for the camera and star player announcing that it was never about money, simply a question of whether the club's ambitions matched his own. And the cynicism of the fans ratchets up another notch. But we're not innocent. We play our part in turning young men into millionaires. We allow the club to blackmail us. The club challenges our ambitions. If you want success, you've got to pay what it takes. That wage bill needs paying, so up goes the price of your season ticket by ten per cent. Never mind that inflation is running at two per cent and that your annual pay increase is hobbling along at nought per cent. So we grumble. Then we pay. Our very strengths – loyalty to our club and an insatiable love of football – are also our weakness. So we arrive at a situation where a Premiership mediocrity – a Savage rather than a Rooney – is pocketing over a million a year in salary and bonuses. Is this the best use of our money?

So we have a new breed of footballer earning unprecedented amounts of money. But it's not just the players that have changed as their salaries have rocketed: the variable on the other side of the fan-player equation seems to have changed too. There's a socio-economic explanation of the way football's changing. The working-class fan is being replaced by the middle-class supporter. Of course, the glamour and success and the machinery of hype attracts the nouveau fan, the event junkie, the aspirational supporter, but

The ties that bind

I think the truth is more subtle than this. The working class fan himself is becoming that middle-class supporter. We're all more prosperous these days. The change is within us. We're now paying big money to watch players on big money and inevitably our attitudes have changed. There's a dwindling fund of good will when players don't perform. We're less patient with under-performing superstars. There is no longer a simple wish for success, there is now an expectation, nay, a demand for success. We pay to watch our team win and we grumble when they don't. Whereas in the past the barren years became an opportunity to re-affirm your loyalty, nowadays it seems to be a pretext to get on the radio and denounce the players as over-paid, over-rated, can't-be-arsed mercenaries. If you're earning big bucks, you'd better be winning.

Norton United, A, 09/04/06

I'm starting to feel guilty about this. Every time FC have a long away trip to the frozen wastes of Barrow or the darkest depths of the Potteries, I'm always on work duty and can't go. Still, I did go to Eccleshall away at Stafford, so I have suffered for the cause this season. I had a bad feeling about this game. I always do when I'm not there and can't do anything to help. I always feel my presence can stop the worst happening – despite the overwhelming weight of evidence to the contrary over the years. Were Norton going to be the first team to assume the mantle of FC United's bogey side? They had already shocked us at Gigg Lane in October by winning 2-1. Could they complete a famous double at Vale Park in April?

The reports tell me that it was a game of two halves: winter snowstorm in the first half, spring sunshine in the second. Well, we must be an all-weather team, as we came away 3-1 winners. A goal up at half time, we survived a second half wobble when Norton missed a penalty and then equalised, to run out easy winners. Well, it looked easy from the comfort of my front room watching the updates on the web site telling me that Torpey had nudged us in front and that a Norton own goal had made it safe.

Surely we've got one hand and three fingers and a thumb from the other on the trophy by now.

Norton United 1 FC United 3 (att 1284)
FC Scorers: Howard, Mitten, o.g.

It's hard to warm to multi-millionaires. The crazy money at the top of the game is taking the players ever further from the fans. The opportunities for contact between players and fans get fewer every season. We're expected to feel pathetically grateful for a brief stage-managed appearance when a twenty year-old turns up to sign copies of his autobiography. Access to these valuable assets is carefully controlled. The fame and the hype and the money have placed the players in some strange bubble. They can't live normal lives or have normal contact with the fans. And all the time the gap between players and fans continues to widen. We live in the real world of jobs and mortgages and difficult choices and your Premiership superstar lives on Planet Football.

At United not too many years ago it was still possible to turn up at the Cliff and watch the players train. You could politely mob the players as they walked from their cars to the training block, get autographs and pictures and exchange a few words. Now they've moved to a swish training complex in the Cheshire countryside and that simple, informal access is no longer possible. It's just another example of how the bond between fans and players is being eroded. The new training complex at Carrington is located half a mile down a country lane, and access to it is denied by a manned security post. So whereas before you could shake hands with Eric and Hughesy as they arrived for training, now all you can do is wait by the entrance for a flash of Rio as he speeds away in his blacked-out SUV, sun-glasses on, hooked up to his ipod or his blue-tooth mobile, as he races off to his gated mansion in the Cheshire countryside. And if the great man ventures out at night, you'll be lucky to catch a glimpse of his extravagantly coiffured bonce beyond a phalanx of minders as he's led off to a fan-free VIP area. My God, what tales we'll have to tell our grandkids in years to come: "Oh yes, what a night that was. I actually spoke to one of Rio's minders."

I'm not worried that Rio doesn't care about me. Why should he? The worrying thing is that it's getting harder to care about Rio.

Chadderton, H, 12/04/06

Nothing succeeds like success, and the knowledge that a win over Chadderton would guarantee promotion in our first season had brought us increased media attention. As well as increasing coverage from the Manchester Evening News and local TV station Channel M, national TV and radio was showing interest and tonight's game had warranted a mention on Five Live and Breakfast TV's north-west news slot. Quite right too for the greatest story in world football this year.

Would the players fluff their lines? Would Chadderton turn out to be a team of superstars and play us off the park? Their position in the bottom of the table suggested otherwise, but you never know. Every team plays out of their skin against FC. By a strange quirk of the fixtures and as a consequence of repeated postponements we hadn't played Chadderton yet and had to play them home and away in the last four games of the season.

The FC ultras were continuing their nomadic existence as we now moved round to the Cemetery End behind the goals. The acoustics are poorer than in the MRE but it's better than the South Stand. Ten minutes into the game I was sorely fed up. It was FC's big night and all I could hear was songs we'd brought with us from Old Trafford. I felt like jumping up and shouting: "Sing FC songs". I even got pissed off with 'Ooh aah Cantona', and, given his failure to come within five miles of Gigg Lane, I started singing 'Ou est

The ties that bind

Cantona?" I mean, we're living his dream here, creating the kind of football club he should be drooling over. But no, none of the United old boys dares to step foot outside that magic circle. Anyway, I'm a curmudgeonly old sod, and impatient too. The stand was soon echoing to 'I don't care about Rio' and 'Under the Boardwalk'.

We started scrappily and struggled to create chances in open play. Fortunately for us, Chadderton had organisation at the back but no penetration up front. It took a set-piece to put us in front. That frequent game-breaker Torpey curled a left footer over the wall and under the keeper to give us the lead and calm our nerves. You could see from the frantic celebrations of the players that they knew just what was at stake tonight. A superb Swarbrick cross and a glance of Robbie Nugent's forehead made it 2-0 before the break and we were cruising to promotion. Further entertainment came from the lad on tannoy duty. Five minutes into the second half he announced that the second FC goal had been scored by Rob Nugent. That's right, the goal scored half an hour ago. What would his next announcement be? The Titanic has sunk? Germany has surrendered to the Allies? Man has landed on the moon?

The second half drifted along uneventfully until Will Ahern hit a left-footed scorcher into the top corner and Rory rounded things off with a penalty. The whistle went and the management team of Karl, Phil Power and Daz Lyons joined the ecstatic players on the pitch. To see how stupidly, deliriously happy the lads were increased my elation. I doubt the Big United players on the pitch at the Nou Camp in 1999 were happier than these lads. Our first season, our first promotion. Where do we go from here? Well, the Waterloo for a couple of pints seemed a good starting point.

FC United 4 Chadderton 0 (att 2788)
FC Scorers: Torpey, Nugent, Patterson, Ahern

I never want to watch millionaire footballers playing for FC. Not something I'll ever have to worry about, perhaps, as a fan of a team looking up the football pyramid from the subterranean depths of the North-West Counties League. Fine, the journey has barely begun, but if we don't plan the route now and put those principles out there as signposts, we'll lose our way. We have to plan for the possibility that FC will grow and grow. We have to decide now what we want to be. The challenge for FC is to develop without losing the special feeling between the players and the fans that has made this first season such an intoxicating, heart-lifting, soul-stirring adventure.

I love the fact that Rory is a paint-sprayer, that Chaddy is a white van man, that Barry George stacks shelves in Tescos and that Margy delivers fruit and veg. I love the fact that the lads who play for us on the pitch are the lads that drink with us in the pub. I love the fact that instead of awe-struck fans we have awe-struck players that tell us how honoured they are to play in front of fans who have dropped ten divisions to watch their football. Never mind

Our Club Our Rules

Becks and Rooney and Gerrard, these lads are my heroes. They are the ones that hold down full-time jobs, train twice a week and play every weekend for fifty quid a game. And why? Because they're like us: addicted to this marvellous, magical game. After a season spent watching FC, it's hitting home to us just what has been lost at the top end of the game. Yes, we've been pleasantly surprised at the quality of the football. Yes, we've loved winning the league at our first attempt. Yes, we've loved the epic days against Winsford and Blackpool. But most of all, we've buzzed off the thrill of feeling that we're in it together, of knowing that FC – officials, managers, players, fans – is family. So how do we grow without losing that feeling?

We can keep that feeling by understanding that the essence of a football club is the relationship between the fans and the club. No matter how many fans watch FC over the next few years and no matter how high we rise up the leagues, we have to put in place now traditions that maintain the sense of FC United as one big family. The principle of one member one vote and the policy of inviting members to vote on all important issues cements this relationship in a formal way. But even more important are the informal ways. These are the means by which the day-to-day spirit of the club will be expressed. If we're a family, let's do what families do, and get together as often as we can. I want to see fans and players having the craic in the FC United social club after matches – win, lose or draw, just as we do now. I want to see the FC United Xmas party become a club tradition, only in future with microphones that work so we can hear what the players are saying. I want to see a whole range of social activities that throw fans and players together: quiz nights, question and answer sessions, 5-a-side football competitions refereed by the players. In fact, exactly what's been happening this season. The club that plays together stays together. There is also the community work that the club is putting great emphasis on over the next few years. The fans and the players will each have an important role in making this a success, providing football coaching and educational courses. If everyone at the club makes a commitment to these activities, we will create a football club with a unique spirit.

I never want to see FC become the Chelski of non-league football. With our fan base and financial resources, that is a temptation that we will face. I want to see FC resist the temptation to go too far too quickly by paying more than their rivals to attract the best players. I want to see FC pay no more than the going rate for the league we're in, because I want the lads who play for us to do it for the right reasons. I want players to be attracted to FC for the same reason the current bunch of lads were attracted – because FC United is no ordinary football club. I want them to come to FC because of the special relationship between the club and its fans. I want them to come to FC because they want to play in front of the noisiest, funniest, most loyal and most passionate fans in football. I want them to come to FC because they share the FC belief that a football club should be rooted in its community, an

The ties that bind

asset to its community, and a source of pride for that community. I want them to come to FC because they share our excitement at the thought of creating the kind of football team that fans deserve. So we won't pay ridiculous money and we'll lose out on some players. Fine. More space in the team for local youngsters and home-grown talent. And the fans will have a team filled with lads who share their values, and who 'get' what FC is about.

Chadderton, A, 19/04/06

"Can we play you every week?" should have been the chant tonight, as we toddled off to Boundary Park to play Chadderton a week after the game at Gigg Lane. But the actual chant of the night turned out to be "We won the football league again, this time at Clitheroe, this time at Clitheroe". That's right, we had won the North-West Counties League Division Two title without playing. Well, without playing a competitive match. The lads were taking on Unibond side Clitheroe in a friendly, when news came through that Nelson had lost to Oldham – told you they're a good team – and that Flixton had been held to a goalless draw at Holker. The promotion party had just turned into a championship party.

So the pressure was off, and that probably explained Margy's team selection tonight. It included two young lads that I'd never heard of: Mike O'Neill in midfield and Warren Collier at full back. In came Big Leon, Daz Lyons, Billy Mac and Chris Simms, while big guns Josh Howard and Chaddy were left on the bench. And centre-forward Joz Mitten was making the transition to centre-half. Still, got to be less frustrating than waiting for a pass from Rory. In fact, Torpey and Patterson were rested - obviously with one eye on that Champions League semi against Barca next Wednesday. Inevitably the first half saw a disjointed performance as players adjusted to new positions and new personnel. The two new boys stood out, and Mike O'Neill even popped up with a simple equaliser just before half-time after Daz Lyon's superb drive came down off the bar. For a while it had seemed that Chadderton might poop the party when they scored a soft goal direct from a free-kick, but it wasn't to be.

Wrapping up the title early provided Margy with the luxury of experimenting with a view to next season. Of course, experiments can go wrong and for a while there was a real prospect of a Chadderton win. Especially when a defensive error early in the second half allowed a Chadderton forward to run on and slip the ball under Barry George. But nothing could dampen the spirits of the FC faithful at the Rochdale Road End. They had welcomed the players on to the pitch with chants of "Championes, Championes" and they ran through the whole FC repertoire as the game progressed. I was listening from the main stand and the hairs prickled on the back of my neck when the massed choir sang "I don't care about Rio". Majestic.

Our Club Our Rules

Margy might want to experiment, but he also wants to win, so with half an hour to go on came the cavalry in the shape of Howard, Chaddy and The Power. The game was still in the balance, however, and it took a penalty decision to tip the match in our favour, as Adie dispossessed a defender and drove in on goal. The defender made a despairing effort to make good his mistake but only managed to pull Adie to the ground. Double whammy for Chadderton: penalty and a sending-off. Daz Lyons calmly despatched the penalty and we sat back more comfortably in our seats in expectation of a few FC goals. Actually, I'm lying. It is not possible for anyone of normal height to sit back comfortably in the old wooden seats in the Oldham main stand. Nature's way of telling me that I should be standing behind the goals, perhaps. We had to settle for a single goal, but it was the best of the game. A beautifully crafted one-two between Adie and Phil on the edge of the box that allowed Adie to glide past the last defender and nonchalantly stroke the ball past the keeper.

Only two more parties left before the terrifying void known as the summer. Aaaargh!

Chadderton 2 FC United 3 (att 2352)
FC Scorers: O'Neill, Lyons, Orr

Economists call it 'the opportunity cost'. It's the Jim Bowen theory of economics: look what you could have won. It's measuring the cost of something in terms of all the other things you might have spent that money on. So the opportunity cost of adding ten grand to Rio's weekly pay packet might be ten community projects that will never happen or a thirty quid reduction in the price of your season ticket that never will come. It's essentially a 'lost opportunities cost'. I don't want to see FC regretting lost opportunities in the future because we became fixated on on-field success and sacrificed too much of our income on player salaries. I want our income to determine our spending. I want player salaries to be determined by ticket prices, and not vice-versa. I don't want to see the board backed into a corner where an onerous wage bill makes an annual hike in season ticket prices a necessity. I don't want to hear the board using the cynical language of coercion used by the big boys ... well, if you want success, etc. I want to hear the board telling the fans that we chose not to pursue such and such a player because he wanted too much. I want to hear the board telling the fans that our income will be this much and therefore we have set aside this percentage to cover wages. And I want that percentage to be a sensible figure. Fifty per cent? Because every penny above that sensible figure is money that can't be spent on all the things we plan to do over the next ten years. And our plans are not modest. Bury FC have been very welcoming hosts in our first season, to such an extent that we have already agreed to rent Gigg Lane for a further three years. That's the right decision for now. Soon, however, FC will need a home of its own. They don't come cheap, especially

The ties that bind

if you aspire to something more soulful than the functional boxes that have sprung up in recent years and that look like they arrived as a flat-pack from Ikea. FC United needs a social club. FC United IS a social club, but we need a building to go with it. We need a venue for all the events that will glue the FC family together over the coming years. We need money to spend on community projects: to set up a women's football team, to set up youth teams, to create sports facilities, to employ staff to implement our sporting and educational projects. Good intentions cost money, but it will be money well spent.

Success on the pitch is wonderful, but it should be a bonus, not an expectation. We can't control what happens on the pitch. So many things can stop you winning football matches: players have off days, players get injured, players make mistakes, referees make mistakes, the luck goes against you, your opponent plays better, etc. It's the marvellous uncertainty of football that keeps us hypnotised. Is football the only game ever devised in which the best team can lose? But we can control what happens off the pitch. Whether FC remains a family club with a unique bond between the fans and the team and sits proudly in the centre of its community is a matter of choice not chance. We control that. So let's not fritter all our income away on the players – as much as we love them. Let's use that money to keep ticket prices low, to build ourselves a home and to make FC respected and loved by its community.

Great Harwood Town, H, 22/04/06

This was the day that we had been dreaming of beneath the grey skies of Stafford in October and beneath the even greyer skies of Flixton on Boxing Day. This was the picture-perfect sun-kissed Saturday when all the labours of the season would culminate in FC United lifting the North-West Counties League Division Two trophy. There had been giddy speculation about the size of the crowd on the forum all week. Some people had predicted over 4,000 and the more excitable ones were talking about smashing the 5,000 barrier. Of course, kids under 18 were being allowed in for free and everyone loves a winner, so there were grounds for optimism. But I knew people were setting themselves up for a disappointment. I even felt moved to remind people that size doesn't matter – an idea that I've always found comforting – and to remind them that it's quality not quantity that counts.

This was always pencilled in as a 'let's make a day of it, sing our hearts out for the boys, get absolutely bladdered, party like it's 1999, stagger to bed in the early hours of the morning' type of celebration. And that's exactly how it turned out. Pre-match drinks in the Waterloo with Mike and Dave and Guy – all three being occasional FC watchers – and then off to Gigg Lane. It was almost kick-off time when we arrived and though there were reasonable numbers of fans milling about, there was no endless queue of people stretching back from the turn-styles. Told them they were being wildly optimistic. As I got closer, I realised that there was no queue because the main stand turn-styles had been ... closed. No point making for the Cemetery End either as those turn-styles had been closed too. Cue a sudden feeling of excitement and panic. This crowd was big. Was it so big that the unthinkable was about to happen, ie, that I , a card-carrying FC lunatic, was going to be locked out of the biggest game of the season?! How ironic if all the people who were sampling FC for the first or second time prevented the FC regulars from getting into the game. It was a groundless fear. We simply had to join a good-natured scrum at the turn-styles for the South Stand, before emerging into a Gigg Lane that was wall-to-wall FC fans. Well, apart from the closed MRE. The ground was just a swathe of noisy red and white. Mind you, the crowd always looks bigger than it is, so I refused to speculate on how many we're there.

I suppose I'd better mention the game. It was not so much Great Harwood as Grate Harwood. Well, they certainly got on my nerves. Obviously, they're not obliged to be willing extras in the FC United story and they came to stop us winning. Their spoiling game succeeded perfectly, as United's performance fell flat and the game had nil-nil written all over it. Until Harwood crafted an injury-time winner. Some teams just have no manners. But being beaten didn't really add a sour note to proceedings. No, the only sour note came when Phil Power tangled with the Harwood full back. As they separated, Phil flicked the back of the lad's hair with his fingers. The defender looked at Phil for a second, thought about it, buried his face in his hands before collapsing theatrically to the floor. Oh dear, are you Drogba in disguise? It was so shocking to see Premiership-style cheating at this level, when almost every game we've seen has been a breath of fresh air. By the time the referee looked round, all he could see was a dying swan and out came the red card for Phil. I'm not going to name and shame the full-back, because I'm sure he now regrets making a complete arse of himself on the biggest day of his football life.

We were still seething from the sending-off and still wincing from a retributive tackle on the said full-back by Steve Spencer, when the ball-boys started walking round the pitch holding up boards announcing the crowd. Is that first number a three, a four, a five? No, it's a bloody SIX. The crowd for a non-league match ten divisions below the Premiership was 6,023. No sooner had the fans in the Cemetery End seen the figure, than they unleashed their pent-up bile at the smug men in suits at Old Trafford: "Are you watching, David Gill?" Not a bad turn-out, eh, for a team that wouldn't last till Christmas.

Neither the score-line nor the sending-off could detract attention from the real business of the day. We'd lost the game, but we'd won the league, and no one left at full-time as we all waited for the presentations. Out came the team again, now wearing red t-shirts with a simple slogan on the front: Russell Delaney. Russell who had died a few weeks into the season after

The ties that bind

working so hard to get FC up and running. Let's hope he was up there and enjoying the occasion with the rest of us. First came the individual awards. Rory was the fans' player of the season, Josh was the junior supporters' player of the season and the prestigious players' player of the season was Steve Spencer. There should have been an award for every member of that squad. Never mind, they'll have to content themselves with a place in FC United folklore.

A short pause ensued and then the players walked up one by one to receive their league winner's medal. Then came that final, climactic moment when City fan and FC legend Mr. David Chadwick accepted the silver trophy from league chairman Dave Tomlinson – Ricky's brother, by the way (My arse! No, it's really true) – and hoisted it above his shoulders. Ecstatic singing rings round Gigg Lane, as we all beam like idiots and try to convince ourselves that this is real. The players do the customary lap of honour, jigging along the touchline, grinning widely, waving to people in the crowd, and, just like the fans, not wanting this moment to end. There are days so perfect that it's painful to feel the time passing. What can you do? Well, when it comes to FC, you just wait for the next one.

Post –match celebrations involved an open-top bus ride for the conquering heroes from Gigg Lane to the Swan and Cemetery pub, an evening of drinking and singing for fans and players and a late night of happy head-shaking, as you tried to make sense of the happiest football day you've ever had at the end of the happiest football season you've ever known.

FC United 0 Great Harwood Town 1 (att 6023)
FC Scorers: Had their mind on other things!

The banners say it all: "Northern Soul", "Soul food", "The light, the resurrection", "There is a light that never fades", "Breaking into heaven". They are eloquent testimony to the emotional and spiritual fervour that fans bring to supporting their club. It's not a pastime, it's not a hobby, it's not a take-it-or-leave-it trip to a pop concert, it's a lifelong commitment. Fans don't want an entertainment to pass an idle hour, they want a cause, a passion, an ideal worthy of their deepest feelings. Wives come and go, but a football team is forever. For fans this passion – for the game, for the team – is an end in itself, but for the men in suits that run the game it's only a means to an end, and the end is money. They're happy to exploit a passion they don't feel in order to make themselves rich, but even greed and cynicism can over-reach themselves. FC United is proof positive that they can over-estimate themselves and under-estimate the fans.

For the fans football is all about soul. It's an emotional connection with something outside of themselves. It's an ideal that allows them to gather together in an act of communal worship. Yet the Premiership is becoming soulless. They want to reduce this complex connection to a simple transaction. They are ignoring the fact that football fans are incurable romantics. We want a long-term relationship and they're offering us one-night stands. We're supposed to turn up every fortnight for thirty quids' worth of unsatisfying physical activity, pretend we've enjoyed it and then clear off quietly. No wonder we often find ourselves going home feeling used, short-changed and vaguely frustrated. We don't just want the physical act - we want you tell us that you love us. But all say is: just leave the money on the sideboard on your way out, love.

Manchester United is owned by an American billionaire. In America sport is part of the entertainment business. It is entertainment and it is business, and that's it. In England football is entertainment – unless you're a Villa fan – but it is more than entertainment. It is business but it is more than a business. It is a solemn ritual that obsesses, delights and frustrates. It is a cultural activity that expresses our history, our identity and our sense of community. In America it's, well, a bit of fun, a show, another place to eat hot dogs and drink beer. They're happy with that, because they've never known anything different. Their relationship to their team doesn't have the emotional, cultural and spiritual complexity that we have with ours. And this is the subtly dangerous thing about the Glazer invasion of Old Trafford. It's not illegal: he broke no laws. It's not immoral: he broke no commandments. It's simply barbaric. He wants to take a complex cultural phenomenon like football and strip it of it of all that romantic nonsense and reduce it to yet another empty and expensive form of mass entertainment. The banalisation of a rich cultural activity. The uncultured American failing to grasp the cultural significance of European social ritual and seeing it simply as an opportunity to make money, as Henry James might have said - and he knew his football. Ok, I'm succumbing to cliché. But that's the annoying thing about clichés: they tend to be true.

Goebbels is reported as saying: "When I hear the word 'culture', I reach for my gun." To which someone riposted: "When I hear the word 'gun', I reach for my culture." Perhaps I can paraphrase that by saying: "When I hear the word 'Glazer', I reach for my FC United season ticket." You didn't have to be in the Swan and Cemetery on Saturday night to understand this fundamental truth: that a football club should be about fun, family, friendship, community and passion, in a word, culture. But you did miss a bloody fantastic night!

Padiham, A, 29/04/06

It's funny how there is a pleasing symmetry to things, how our first football season came full circle in our final game. It had been Padiham at home in glorious sunshine in August and now it was Padiham away in glorious sunshine in April. In August it had been one tentative step at a time and now it was a confident stride into next season. We had gone from wondering how long it would last to speculating on how far we could go.

The ties that bind

This game was not a dead rubber. Padiham still had hopes of claiming the second promotion spot behind FC, though Flixton were starting to emerge as favourites. I'm sure a few FC fans will relish renewing our rivalry with Flixton next season. They're fast emerging as favourites to occupy that oh so important role of bitter rivals. Margy resisted the temptation to tinker and put out a strong lineup, although he experimented with his tactics. He played 3-5-2 for the first time, accommodating Josh Howard in central midfield. I've seen the future, and I think it works. Josh oozed class and composure. His technique and vision on a superb surface allowed him to pull the strings. A goal from sniffer Carden put FC in front, before a length of the field move initiated by Josh ended in a clinical finish from Steve Torpey. Just a joy to watch. It should have been the prelude to more goals but that end-of-season complacency seemed to grip the lads as they spurned other opportunities. Padiham are a good side and always threatened to punish FC's slackness. Sub Kenny Mayers chipped a lovely goal and left FC hanging on to what should have been a comfortable win.

I sat there in the second half transfixed by the lush green of the pitch, the vivid red of FC, the royal blue of Padiham and the soft green hills in the distance and wanted the game to go on forever. It was painful to think that the end of our first ever season was only a few minutes away. I know there'll be other seasons, but there'll never be another first season. Fitba, eh, bloody 'ell.

Padiham 1 FC United 2 (att 1905)
FC Scorers: Torpey, Carden

Ask a dozen FC fans about their hopes for the future and you'll get twelve different answers. Time tends to make a mockery of our predictions, and no one can really say how FC will evolve in the next ten years. The difficulty for FC is that there is no model to follow. There is no template for the kind of football club we are trying to create. People look round for examples of the FC of the future and the name of Barcelona invariably crops up. In many people's minds Barca is the acceptable face of modern football, the ultimate fans' club that stands as a contrast and a rebuke to the money-obsessed corporate monsters such as Chelsea and Manchester United. I have never really bought into this romantic view of Barca. I certainly don't think the example of Barca will prove very useful to us in shaping the future of FC. I've talked about the damaging effects of paying superstar players several million pounds a season, about the damage it does to the relationship between the fans and the team. Well, Ronaldinho doesn't turn out for Barca for a fistful of euros and all the sangria he can drink. They pay him what United pay Rooney or Madrid pay Zidane: millions of euros a season. Of course, any money you pay the wondrous Ronaldinho seems justified, because he is the spirit of football personified: the sublime skill, the daring invention, the outrageous artistry, and the ready, childlike smile that expresses his and our love of the greatest game. But for every Ronaldinho there is a Patrick Kluivert. Big money attracts big egos.

And big money builds up big debts. Like every other superclub Barca have huge debts and they are locked into the same high-powered business world as Madrid or Milan. Their directors are driven by the same commercial pressures as Florentino Perez or Silvio Berlusconi. The fact that Barca's president is the relatively young and charming Joan Laporta who is clearly as much a fan as any Barca ultra, does not change the fact that Barca are playing high-stakes poker in a billionaires' club. The pressure to keep up makes the need to generate revenue as important at the Nou Camp as it is at Old Trafford. Fans with a rose-tinted view of Barca ignore the fact that they are a member of the G14 group – a cartel of Europe's self-styled leading clubs. Along with Madrid, United, Juventus and others, they have lobbied for changes in European football that have been driven by financial considerations and that have nothing to do with and, in fact, are completely at odds with the best interests of football. It's the G14 that turned the European Cup from a simple knock-out competition into the bloated Champions League that guarantees its clubs more games and more revenue every season. By the late 90s the European cup had become so deformed by greed that there were two six-game league stages before we even reached the knock-out stage. The G14 is the group that raised the idea that they should be compensated by national associations when any of their expensive investments gets injured while playing for their country. So the impoverished Ivory Coast football association should compensate Chelsea when Didier Drogba injures himself doing a triple twist with pike after an innocuous tackle? It's the G14 group that threatened in 2006 to form their own European super league if UEFA refused their request to expand the Champions League even further. A European super league with no promotion and relegation and entrance by invitation only. A monument to greed, arrogance and stupidity that has little to do with the interests of football and everything to do with the financial needs of the individual clubs. And Barca is an integral part of G14, and I don't see Joan Laporta breaking ranks and speaking out against these plans.

So there's no model out there for FC United. Not among the top clubs. They've all sold their soul to the devil, all obsessed with money and success at all costs. My ambition is for FC United to prove by its actions that people matter more than money and that the game matters more than success. Is that lofty idealism? Perhaps, but you don't set out on a great adventure fired by cynicism. Success for FC will not be determined purely in terms of what we achieve on the football field. It will be determined by how far we succeed in creating a football club that football fans deserve. A successful FC will forge a close bond between the players and the fans. A successful FC will have fans that glow with pride when they tell others who they support. A successful FC will be accessible, welcoming and inclusive, always striving to

The ties that bind

make others share our love of the beautiful game. A successful FC will make it clear in every decision it takes that money and success at all costs are not its master. Oh yes, a successful FC will win lots of matches. And we will celebrate those triumphs in the noisy, excessive, alcoholic manner that FC fans do so well. But success must be in accordance with our principles, not at their expense. And we'll accept the defeats that will come our way too, because this club will always be about more than success on the field. There will be seasons when we don't do well, when we tread water in mid-table or struggle against relegation, because that's how football goes – someone wins, someone loses. Only spoilt brats demand an unvarying diet of success. The best people glory in the opportunities that adversity presents. The bad years could be our best years, when we redouble our support for the lads who are trying their best, when we keep singing and laughing and drinking and re-affirming our love of this extraordinary club. Defeat on the pitch won't matter as long as FC remains a community club, a people club, an extended family that stays together through the ups and downs. As Kipling wrote: "If you can meet with triumph and disaster, and treat those two impostors just the same". And he knew his football. And he baked some pretty good cakes too.

Our Club Our Rules

Summer 2006
Summer loving

It'll all end in tears, they said. I suppose it was natural to remember that as the setting sun washed over the tree-ringed bowl of the Bruno Plache Stadium and we all stood smiling broadly or simply staring at the packed mass of LOK supporters on the terraces around us. We were drinking in the flavour of an authentic European night, listening to the insistent throb of a big bass drum, staring at blue and yellow blocks of LOK fans bouncing up and down, hearing the rhythmic chant of 'L-O-K, L-O-K' and watching the smoky aftermath of flares twisting upward against the slowly darkening sky. Paul and I just looked at each other and shook our heads in dreamy disbelief. Was it just a year ago that I'd been walking round with a face like thunder, ready to erupt in anger and frustration? And now here I was in a blissful daze trying to make sense of it all, beaming stupidly like a shell-shocked lottery winner. My heart was singing, my spirit soaring and my senses reeling from an overload of sights and sounds on a magical night in FC's history. Not even the aggressive posturing of the LOK hardcore to our right could break the spell. We'd break them down eventually. Teenage machismo was no match for the chilled-out waves of happiness and good humour radiating from the 500-strong enclave of FC supporters. What a season, and what a way to end it. The cynics had got it wrong - it was all ending in cheers. And beers, of course. Non-alcoholic ones. These Germans think of everything.

We were in Leipzig for our first genuine Euro away. We thought Blackpool would be the closest we got and here we were in Germany playing one of the great names of European football: Lokomotiv Leipzig. No longer a great force on the field but still a great name. It took me back to my youth when I'd been bewitched by teams with thunderous names like Torpedo Moscow, Dynamo Dresden and Moscow Spartak. The hard, metallic names of invincible machines - unstoppable juggernauts that would grind opposing teams into the turf. In truth, the names were usually more intimidating than the teams, as sides from Eastern Europe rarely featured in the later stages of European competitions. Still, Lokomotiv Leipzig did beat Maradona's Napoli

Summer loving

on the way to a losing UEFA Cup final against Ajax as recently as 1987. Yes, the same Lokomotiv Leipzig we were playing tonight. Except it wasn't, of course. The footballing steam engine that had flourished under the old Communist regime had been shunted into the sidings of history following the fall of the Berlin Wall. Debts had spiralled in the capitalist free-for-all that had followed and the club had folded in 2004. The fact that a Lokomotiv Leipzig still existed was due to the efforts of the supporters who had refused to let the club die and had resurrected it as a fans club playing in the eleventh tier of German football. In fact, the club president Steffen Kubald used to be the leader of the Leipzig hoolies. A bit like Andy Walsh at FC! Judging by the steroid-enhanced Arnie lookalikes directing us as we came through the turn-styles, Herr Kubald hadn't cut off all links with his erstwhile mates. So Lokomotiv Leipzig was a fans club and had recognised a soul mate in FC. Hence the invitation to come over and play this friendly. It was a gesture of solidarity, a fraternal hands-across-the-water celebration of the people's game. Just a pity that no one had told the Mad Max wannabe's to our right.

And what about the game? It came a long way behind the occasion but it wasn't too bad in an end-of-season, don't-bust-a-gut, Keystone-Cops sort of way. To be honest, I was a bit worried at the prospect of FC facing a crack German outfit. They don't do friendlies, do they? They'd probably been training for two weeks at altitude. Our lads had probably been training for two weeks on cheap lager, celebrating the North-West Counties Division Two title. I had visions of a perfectly calibrated German machine grinding us into the ground as blue and yellow blurs raced past our red-shirted heroes. And they'd probably resort to all those underhand foreign tricks that British sides always struggle to deal with - you know, pin-point passing, clever movement and instant control. Gott im Himmel, lads, just keep it respectable. Anyway, the game got under way and it was twenty minutes old before it started to dawn on me that I wasn't watching a perfect example of German precision engineering, just a half-decent team, and that, if anything, we were the better side. If it hadn't been for defending that could only be characterised as over-generous, we would have been out of sight by half-time. As it was, we went in trailing 3-2. Now, I'm all for behaving like gracious guests, but this was ridiculous.

The action in the stands was as absorbing as anything taking place on the pitch. Talk about a clash of cultures. LOK fans have a different style to FC fans, and I'm not just referring to the shaved heads and combat gear. Believe me, military chic is alive and well and living in Leipzig. The first sign that LOK fan culture was a million miles away from the FC summer of love vibe came on the packed tram that ferried us out to the stadium from the centre of town. The young LOK fans spent the entire journey glaring out at the riot police, hammering on the windows and screaming "A-C-A-B". It's not even German, for God's sake. It stands for "All coppers are bastards". Blimey, and I thought some FC fans had a problem with authority. The differences didn't

Our Club Our Rules

end there. Their way of supporting their team is also different from ours. At Gigg Lane you're doing well to get the MRE singing the same words to the same song at the same time. At LOK the singing is tightly orchestrated over the PA system. A voice booms out an 'L', the crowd obediently echoes it, and the process is repeated until they've spelt out "L-O-K". But for long periods when LOK are defending – and that was quite often on the night – the crowd falls surprisingly silent. No wonder we were singing: "You only sing when you're told to". Compare the orchestrated singing at LOK to the non-stop medley of songs belted out spontaneously by the endlessly creative, bolshie buggers at Gigg Lane. National stereotypes, eh? German order versus English anarchy. But that's the thing about stereotypes, isn't it – it's never the whole truth but there's always something in it.

The second half saw a strong performance by the lads and featured a typically audacious penalty from Rory. Good to see his new haircut hadn't sapped his strength. A Simon Carden goal then put us deservedly in front … sort of four-three durch technik. One final display of outrageous generosity gifted LOK an equaliser and the game ended very diplomatically poised at 4-4. No one cared about the result. Both sets of players came over to the section of terracing housing the FC fans and we shook LOK and FC hands through the metal fencing. It was daft grins all round. Even the moody LOK lads to our right had swapped menacing gestures for smiles and handclaps. It was a love-in. I remember Dave Brown walking round in his undies after throwing his shorts into the crowd. Thank God he stopped at his shorts. I was just about to shout: "Dave, don't forget, you're an ambassador for Heywood". God knows, Heywood needs one. As it was, I just stood there with a big gormless grin on my face trying to take it all in, trying to store away every last detail. Another memory to keep me warm when I'm old. The words commentator Martin Tyler had used when Eric's wonder strike had secured the double in 96 kept coming back to me: "You just couldn't write this story". Was it really only a year since eight hundred angry people had gathered in the Central Methodist Hall in Manchester?

The night didn't end with the football. The tram back into town was a scene of happy chaos. Manc strains of "FC all over the world" tried to make themselves heard above the chants of L-O-K, L-O-K, while one Leipzig fan treated us to a booming version of "Football's coming home". Some fans didn't make it back to the centre of town. They stopped off en route at the Sportspalast, a monumental relic of the previous era, where LOK were very kindly putting on a disco for the fans and players of both teams. Maybe it was the early start, the train journey from Berlin, the padding around Leipzig's old town or an afternoon spent sipping lager in bright sunshine at pavement cafes, but the idea of five hours of German techno was not an enticing prospect. Just call me a lightweight. I checked with Paul and he felt the same. Besides, he had his eye on a day's sight-seeing in Berlin the following day.

Summer loving

Oh yes, it wasn't all beer and bratwurst. As typical FC fans, ie. people of taste and refinement, we were determined to fit in a little cultural interlude. So we were up bright and early the next day to catch a train to Berlin. As we waited at Leipzig station, we bumped into a couple of lads who stared at us blankly, when we said we were off for a day's sight-seeing. "What you doing that for?" said one, before asking us if we knew of a decent bar near the station. Some of these lads are unbelievable. How do they do it? They only stop drinking when they're asleep. So we did Berlin. We saw the sights, visited the Wall museum, got our passports stamped at Checkpoint Charlie, bought a Russian fur hat (it seemed like a good idea at the time) and didn't have a drink all day. I knew it could be done. And all captured for posterity on Paul's mobile phone. Not even three hours in the wind tunnel known as Gary's Boogie Bus back from East Midlands airport could spoil the memory. Never mind the three days off work with flu in the middle of May – very heavy, incapacitating man-flu, of course. Just two fantastic days that would remain indelibly printed on my mind. Just as well really, as Paul rang me next day to say he'd inadvertently deleted all his pictures. Never mind, mate, we'll always have Leipzig.

FC Leipzig 4 FC United 4 (att 7500)
FC scorers: Swarbrick, Nugent, Carden, Patterson

Some people are on the last page - they think it's all over. Well, it is now. Almost. Just bear with me a little longer. I suppose the overall tone of this book could be characterised as moral indignation and I know that a ranting self-righteous Old Testament prophet can outstay his welcome, but it's hard not to get angry when you see something you love being ruined by greed and stupidity. But let's get things in perspective. We're not talking Armageddon. We're not talking about a cataclysmic struggle between the forces of good and evil. We're simply talking about the future of football and stimulating a debate about what that future should be.

When we took the decision to walk away from Old Trafford and set up FC United, it was because of the Glazer takeover, yes, but it was also because we wanted our football club to be so much more than it was. We hadn't fallen out of love with the team, but we couldn't stomach what the club had become. We no longer wanted their football club: we wanted our football club. A club that was owned by its fans and run by its fans on behalf of its fans. A club that stands or falls on the commitment or indifference of its fans. A club whose future will be determined by the choices of its fans. And call us sentimental old lefties if you like, but we wanted a football club that would make us proud by engaging with its community rather than ignoring it, that put some flesh on the bones of that hoary old cliché "the people's game" by keeping prices affordable for everyone in the community, especially the kids. And, of course, we wanted a club that loved football like we do, that believed in football played with swagger and skill and honesty and where winning is wonderful but where defeat is no disaster.

That's the FC vision of football, and we think it reflects what most fans want. Of course, the apologists for the Premiership will see things differently. They will point to rising attendances and the steady increase in Sky subscriptions as tangible and undeniable proof that the fans are already getting the football they want. It's difficult to argue with that, but I think they could be confusing passive acceptance – in the absence of an alternative – with active approval. It's been said before – a football club is a monopoly. There is no alternative branch of Manchester City providing a better spectacle and better customer service at a lower price down the road. You're stuck with it. The club know they've got you. They know that you'll grumble but keep going because, well, City's your team, a team is for life and your allegiance is non-transferable. You're not going to start watching Stockport County just because it's cheaper. Maybe we've just been lucky. Maybe circumstances that seemed disastrous at the time have actually done United fans a favour. They forced us to create an alternative.

We think that FC United represents the type of football club that most fans want. Of course, we could be wrong. We might just be a bunch of deluded idealists talking to ourselves. Time will tell. Maybe the people that run the Premiership know football fans better than we know ourselves. Maybe the majority of fans are getting the football they want. Maybe they want a football where success is simply a function of wealth, where a tiny closed shop of top clubs dominate, where young men get paid a hundred grand a week to kick a ball, where fans are consumers rather than participants, where fans have no say in the running of their club or in the future of the game, where fans simply turn up to watch an expensive entertainment, where fans do what they're told. I think fans want more than that, but I could be wrong. As someone quite rightly said, it's all about opinions. It will certainly be interesting over the coming years to see which vision of football proves more persuasive. Perhaps the only thing you can say with certainty is that ultimately fans will get the football they want.

Does it matter? Does football matter? I think it does, obviously, or I wouldn't have spent so many nights slaving over a hot keyboard writing this bloody book. Football matters. Not as much as the big things, of course: family, friends, your health, your job, having food to eat and somewhere to live, international terrorism, global warming, etc. But it matters. We're lucky. Our lives are comfortable and easy and fortunate. But that's why football matters. We need it to add colour and excitement and the illusion of purpose to our pleasant but humdrum lives. We've always needed games to stop ourselves getting bored, and now we have more time to play those games than ever before. And you only have to look around you to see how important football is to people. If you measure the importance of things by

Summer loving

the amount of time and effort and money we devote to them, who could deny that football is important?

So football is important, and football is magnificent. Let's not blow it. Let's take a clear-headed look at where football is going. It's our game. We can change it, if we don't like it. That's what we did when we created FC United and re-kindled our love affair with this magical game.